STEPHEN
OLFORD

BASICS
FOR
BELIEVERS

STEPHEN
OLFORD

BASICS
FOR
BELIEVERS

Victor®

An Imprint of Cook Communications Ministries
Colorado Springs, Colorado

Victor is an imprint of

Cook Communications Ministries, Colorado Springs, Colorado 80918

Cook Communications, Paris, Ontario

Kingsway Communications, Eastbourne, England

Basics for Believers

© 2003 by Stephen Olford

Original editions copyrighted © 1992, 1993, and 1991 by Baker Book House
Company, under the titles: *Believing Our Beliefs; Living Words and Loving Deeds;*
and *Committed to Christ and His Church*

First Printing, 2003

Printed in the United States of America

1 2 3 4 5 6 7 8 9 10 Printing/Year 08 07 06 05 04 03

Editor: Craig Bubeck, Senior Editor (over revision)

Cover and Interior Design: Dana Sherrer, iDesign Etc.

Unless otherwise noted, Scripture quotations are taken from the *King James Version.*
All rights reserved. All Scripture marked NKJV are taken from the New King James
Version. Copyright © 1982 by Thomas Nelson, Inc. Used by permission. All rights
reserved

Cataloging-in-Publication Data on file with the Library of Congress

CONTENTS

SECTION 1

Believing Our Beliefs

Teachings on the Foundations and Evidence for New Life

PREFACE

Believing our beliefs presupposes a threefold basis of faith: belief in the fact of God, belief in the Son of God, and belief in the Word of God. This quintessence of truth is the key that opens up the rest of Scripture.

The Bible starts with the *fact* of God—"In the beginning God" (Gen. 1:1, KJV)—and so must we. Indeed, the writer to the Hebrews categorically states this: "Without faith it is impossible to please Him, for he who comes to God must believe that He is, and that He is a rewarder of those who diligently seek Him" (Heb. 11:6, NKJV).

Then we consider the *Son* of God. Only in him is God revealed to men. John affirms that "no one has seen God at any time. The only begotten Son, who is in the bosom of the Father, He has declared Him" (John 1:18, NKJV). And Jesus declared, "He who has seen Me has seen the Father" (John 14:9, NKJV).

This brings us to the *Word* of God. The incarnate Word, in the good providence of God, has become the inscribed Word. The high and holy one has chosen to disclose his person and purpose in human language so that through "the holy scriptures [we are made] . . . wise unto salvation through faith . . . in Christ Jesus" (2 Tim. 3:15, KJV).

The second part of this resource book deals with the subject of *life*. In a sense, this is the message of the Bible —especially the New Testament. Count the number of times the word "life" occurs in the gospel of John! The evangelist begins with that glorious announcement: "In him was life; and the life was the light of men" (1:4, KJV).

Halfway through his twenty-one chapters he quotes one of the greatest statements our Savior ever made: "I have come that [men and women might] have life, and that they [might] have it more abundantly" (10:10, NKJV). John concludes his account with words that define the stated purpose of the Gospel: "These are written that you may believe that Jesus is the Christ, the Son of God, and that believing you may have life in His name" (20:31, NKJV). There we have it. Life and life more abundant is our message to sinners and saints alike. For sinners, because they are "dead in trespasses and sins" (Eph. 2:1, NKJV) and they need life; for saints, because there is no limit to fullness of life in Christ!

The pages that follow are rich with substance and suggestions to share with those who are ready to believe our beliefs and to live the new life in Christ.

Stephen F. Olford

Part 1
CHRISTIAN EVIDENCE

1

Why I Believe in the Fact of God

Genesis 1:1; John 1:1-4; 1 John 1:1-3

"In the beginning God" (Gen. 1:1).

Introduction

Dr. W. H. Fitchett in his book, *The Beliefs of Unbelief,* says that "God cannot be packed into a syllogism, or 'proved' in terms of logic." Then he adds: "But neither can anyone prove, in terms of logic, that the world exists, or that we ourselves exist! The three final postulates of thought are God, the world, and ourselves; and they are all incapable of absolute metaphysical proof. [The man] who limits his belief to that which can be demonstrated, in terms of formal logic, must deny them all; and all, as a matter of fact have been denied."

In the light of such a statement as this, our demand for logical proof that "God . . . is, and that He is a rewarder of those who diligently seek Him" (Heb. 11:6, NKJV) is absurd. And yet, because men are what they are, there will always be an insistence for evidence of what the Christian believes. Perhaps this is why Peter charged the scattered and persecuted Hebrew Christians to "sanctify the Lord God in [their] hearts, and always be ready to give a defense to everyone" for the hope that was in them (1 Pet. 3:15, NKJV). Similarly, if we are asked why we believe in the fact of God, we must be ready to give an answer also.

There is a threefold reason for belief in the fact of God:

I. The Recognized Arguments of Natural Reasoning

Among the many arguments that could be advanced, there are three that are simple and straightforward:

A. *The Cosmological Argument*

Otherwise known as the deductive argument, it is the argument of cause and effect.

Kosmos, which is the Greek word for "world," denotes order, arrangement, ornament, and adornment. We cannot stand back, then, and observe this order and arrangement without postulating some great initial cause. There must have been a beginning to the phenomena that we see before us, for science teaches us that the present universe has not existed from all eternity. When we turn to the Bible, the explanation is stated quite clearly and categorically. The writer to the Hebrews says: "By faith we understand that the worlds were framed by the word of God, so that the things which are seen were not made of things which are visible" (Heb. 11:3, NKJV). Here is a statement which suggests that there is nothing haphazard or accidental in the coming into being of the cosmic order.

B. *The Teleological Argument*

This is Paley's well-known argument from design. Experience has taught us that whatever is composed of parts requires a designer, and who can that designer be but God?

To quote Dr. Fitchett again: "The absolute proof of God's existence is found in the relations in which the mindless elements of the universe are set with each other, producing an order of which they are not only incapable, but unconscious."

No one can study this supernatural design and the beauty

in the universe around us without thinking of the apostle's words in Romans 1:20: "For since the creation of the world His invisible attributes are clearly seen, being understood by the things that are made, even His eternal power and Godhead." The majesty, power, and divinity of God are stamped on the creation around us in design and beauty.

Beauty in animals and birds in a measure may be explained, but how shall we account for the beauty of inorganic nature—the sky, the sea, and the flaming sunset? Surely, beauty is the very signature of God. No wonder the psalmist exclaims, "The heavens declare the glory of God; And the firmament shows His handiwork" (Ps. 19:1, NKJV). And Jesus said, "Consider the lilies of the field, how they grow: they neither toil nor spin; and yet I say to you that even Solomon in all his glory was not arrayed like one of these" (Matt. 6:28-29, NKJV). Indeed, the one who paints the sunset, who suspends the rainbow in the sky, and colors and scents the petals of the rose, is the God of creation.

C. The Anthropological Argument

This is the moral argument that infers the moral nature of God from the moral nature of man. *Anthropos* is the Greek word for man. The question is, Where did our moral nature come from? Surely our possession of it argues for the existence of a moral governor to whom man is responsible. This argument has been universally admitted by people of all lands.

Among the oldest nations known—the Sumerians and the Egyptians—the evidence, such as it is, shows that monotheism was the earliest faith. Indeed, there is proof that even the paleolithic man was a worshiping creature, though there are no means of knowing what he worshiped. He certainly believed in a future life, as shown by the articles interred with the dead.

The Scriptures make it plain that man, wherever he is found, has an inner monitor that compels belief in God apart from reasoning. Paul tells us that "when Gentiles, who do not have the law, by nature do the things in the law, these, although not having the law, are a law to themselves, who show the work of the law written in their hearts, their conscience also bearing witness, and between themselves their thoughts accusing or else excusing them" (Rom. 2:14-15, NKJV). The sense of right and wrong, and moral responsibility, suggest the intuitive recognition of a moral ruler in the universe.

Illustration

All of this calls to mind the question of God's nature. G. S. Studdert-Kennedy, a British World War I chaplain, tells of visiting a captain who was recovering from what had seemed certain death. He said, "Chaplain, tell me what God is like. Whenever I've been transferred from one regiment to another, my first question has always been, 'What's the colonel like?' because I've discovered that conditions in the regiment will be what the colonel makes them. Before the war, when taking a position with a new firm, I'd always ask, 'What's the boss like?' Now I'm told that I'll recover and live, and I must know what God is like." When we understand the nature of God as being that of complete trustworthiness, all other questions are kept in proper perspective.[1]

II. The Verified Assumptions of Biblical Revelation

The Bible adopts the scientific approach in starting with a hypothesis or assumption. It does not argue for God, but assumes that God exists, he creates, and he redeems. To believe and act upon these assumptions is to prove that "God . . . is, and that He is a rewarder of those who diligently seek Him" (Heb. 11:6, NKJV).

A. God Eternally Exists

"In the beginning was the Word, and the Word was with God, and the Word was God. He was in the beginning with God" (John 1:1-2, NKJV). Here is the clearest statement in the Bible concerning the eternity of God. The phrase, "in the beginning," goes back into the mists and mysteries of an eternity past. If this be assumed and accepted, then God is above and beyond the universe he has created. He has no need of the world, or of us. He is rich in himself. He is fullness of life. All glory, beauty, goodness, and holiness reside in him. He is sufficient unto himself. He is God. It might be asked, "To what end did he create the world?" The answer is, that it might be the theater of his glory; and man, the witness to that glory. (See Rev. 4:11.)

B. God Exclusively Creates

"In the beginning God created the heavens and the earth" (Gen. 1:1, NKJV). Dr. D. E. Hart points out that in the first chapter of Genesis the word *bārā*, which means "created," occurs only three times. The first for matter— "In the beginning God created the heavens and the earth" (Gen. 1:1); the second for animal life—"God created great sea creatures and every living thing that moves" (Gen. 1:21); the third for man— "God created man in His own image" (Gen. 1:27). Man repeats what has already been created by God; only God exclusively creates. John reminds us that "All things were made through Him, and without Him nothing was made that was made" (John 1:3, NKJV). The universe is not self-produced. Biological analysis has failed to show that a single particle of matter can transmute itself into vitality of movement. To create is a personal act, and the divine order and activity manifested in creation postulates an absolute being as the first cause of all things. The universe reveals a personal God.

C. God Effectively Redeems

"That which was from the beginning, which we have heard, which we have seen with our eyes, which we have looked upon, and our hands have handled, concerning the Word of life—the life was manifested, and we have seen, and bear witness, and declare to you that eternal life which was with the Father and was manifested to us" (1 John 1:1-2, NKJV). Here we have the revelation, once again, of the preexistent God who manifested himself in history through his incarnation for the redemption of mankind. Although facts can be collated outside of biblical revelation to prove that God visited this earth in human form, yet the purpose and effectiveness of this advent are limited entirely to the revelation given us in the Bible.

So biblical revelation assumes a God who eternally exists, exclusively creates, and effectively redeems. If we start with these hypotheses and build up the related facts of history, we find the picture is complete. The God of biblical revelation is the God of creation and the God of redemption.

Illustration

If we really accept the concept of God as Creator and Redeemer, then we should have no misgivings about allowing him to do with us what pleases him. Some years ago a South American company purchased a printing press from a company based in the States. After the machine reached its destination and had been assembled, workers could not get it to operate properly. Experts tried to remedy the situation, but to no avail. Finally the company wired a message to the manufacturer, asking for a representative of theirs to come to South America and adjust the equipment. Sensing the urgency of the request, the United States firm chose the person who had designed the press. When he arrived, the South American officials were skeptical because he was so young, so they cabled the manufacturer to send a more experienced person. The reply came back, "He made the machine. Let him fix it!"[2] God made the world and all that is in it. We can do no better than to let him fix it.

III. The Personalized Affirmations of Spiritual Relationship

"Because you are sons, God has sent forth the Spirit of His Son into your hearts, crying out, 'Abba, Father!'" (Gal. 4:6, NKJV). The most amazing thing about this God in whom we believe is that he has condescended in grace to make it possible for men and women to be related to him by the miracle of the new birth. Sons of Adam's race can be possessors of the divine nature and look up into God's face, saying, "Father."

Jesus declared this great fact to one of the leading theologians of his day. The Master expressed surprise that Nicodemus was unaware of this fact, since it was implicit and explicit in the Old Testament Scriptures. The Lord said through the prophet Ezekiel: "I will give you a new heart and put a new spirit within you; I will take the heart of stone out of your flesh and give you a heart of flesh" (Ezek. 36:26, NKJV). And Jesus said to Nicodemus: "Do not marvel that I said to you, 'You must be born again'" (John 3:7, NKJV). This life from above creates a relationship with God which is:

A. Indissoluble

Speaking through his Son, God says concerning his sheep: "I give them eternal life, and they shall never perish; neither shall anyone snatch them out of My hand" (John 10:28, NKJV). And Paul was persuaded that "neither death nor life, nor angels nor principalities nor powers, nor things present nor things to come, nor height nor depth, nor any other created thing, [can] separate us from the love of God which is in Christ Jesus our Lord" (Rom. 8:38-39, NKJV).

B. Incomparable

There is no relationship on earth to be compared with the one that exists between God and his people. David said: "When my father and my mother forsake me, Then the LORD will take care of me" (Ps. 27:10, NKJV). And Isaiah asked, "Can a woman forget her nursing child, And not have compassion on the son of her womb? Surely they may forget, Yet I will not forget you" (Isa. 49:15, NKJV). What a comforting thought!

C. Ineffable

So sweet and wonderful is this relationship that Old Testament saints, New Testament Christians, and men and women throughout the ages have shared in the joy of calling

God their very own. Listen to the satisfied affirmations that spring from a spiritual relationship with God. Job calls God "my Redeemer" (see Job 19:25), David calls God "my shepherd" (see Ps. 23:1), Solomon calls God "My beloved" (Song 2:16, NKJV), Thomas calls him "My Lord and my God!" (John 20:28, NKJV), and Paul sums up these expressions of relationship by saying, "My God shall supply all your need" (Phil. 4:19, NKJV). Such verses as these strengthen our belief in the fact of God.

Illustration

It is one thing to be presented with the facts and quite another to receive them. The story is told of a Burmese prince who had a conversation with a visitor from Europe. The visitor told the prince that in Europe there are rivers that get so hard a person can walk across them in the wintertime. The prince had never seen ice or snow and had never even experienced a cold day. So he could not be persuaded that the visitor was telling the truth. He said, Though the whole world tell me it is so, I will not believe that a river can get so hard that a person can walk across it." The facts had been presented to him, but he refused to believe.

Conclusion

We have seen that from the recognized arguments of natural reasoning, the verified assumptions of biblical revelation, and the personalized affirmations of spiritual relationship that there is every ground for a personal faith in a personal God. Do you believe in the fact of God?

2

Why I Believe in the Son of God

John 1:1-14; Colossians 2:8-12; Hebrews 1:1-2;

1 Timothy 3:16

"God was manifested in the flesh" (1 Tim. 3:16).

Introduction

It is believed that the original Christian confession consisted of three words: "Jesus Christ—Lord." We cannot approach the subject of Christianity without believing in the Lord Jesus Christ as the Son of God. His person, claims, and work are central to biblical literature and theology and to all Christian experience. There are three reasons for believing in Christ as the Son of God:

I. His Appearance in History

"God was manifested in the flesh" (1 Tim. 3:16). Professor Carnegie Simpson has said: "If the being of God is beyond your ken, the fact of Christ is not. He is a fact of history, cognizable as any other phenomenon." In other words, Christ has appeared in history, as is evidenced by:

A. *Recorded Historical Events*

There is secular and scriptural testimony to the fact that Jesus of Nazareth lived over 2000 years ago in the small country of Israel.

1. THE SECULAR TESTIMONY

Sir J. G. Fraser, who will not be suspected of any bias toward Christianity, once said: "My theory assumes the historical reality of Jesus of Nazareth as the great religious and moral teacher who founded Christianity and was crucified at Jerusalem, under the governorship of Pontius Pilate. The testimony of the gospels, confirmed by the hostile evidence of Tacitus and younger Pliny, appears amply sufficient to establish these facts to the satisfaction of all unprejudiced inquirers."

2. THE SCRIPTURAL TESTIMONY

There is ample New Testament material to satisfy the keenest of ancient and modern critics, but we shall limit ourselves to two verses from I Corinthians, a book that no historical critic can doubt. Here Paul sums up the appearance of Christ in history as follows: "Christ died for our sins according to the Scriptures, ... He was buried, and . . . He rose again the third day according to the Scriptures" (1 Cor. 15:3-4, NKJV). In that statement Paul presupposes and includes the birth, life, death, resurrection, and ascension of Jesus Christ.

From the secular and scriptural testimonies, therefore, there is sufficient evidence to lead us to believe in the fact of the incarnation, which is the foundation of Christianity; and the fact of the resurrection, which is the completion of the incarnation and the keystone of the arch of Christianity. Here we have Christ appearing in history as an indisputable fact— one that demands a reasonable belief.

B. Resultant Historical Events

Among them are four:

1. THE CHRISTIAN CHURCH

The church has been here for nearly two millennia. Its origin can be traced historically to the period when Christ appeared in Israel.

2. THE CHRISTIAN ORDINANCES

Baptism and the breaking of bread have been observed since the life and death of a man called Jesus of Nazareth.

3. THE CHRISTIAN SUNDAY

This is not the same as the Jewish Sabbath. That was the seventh day of the week. Sunday is the first day of the week, and Christians observe that day in honor of our Lord's resurrection.

4. THE CHRISTIAN EASTER

This yearly festival, kept in five continents, can be associated with the same historical time and circumstances: Friday, to commemorate the crucifixion; and Sunday, the resurrection.

Such resultant historical events presuppose and substantiate the appearance of the Lord Jesus Christ in history, and satisfy any honest inquirer who is prepared to believe.

Illustration
Ralph Waldo Emerson has said, "The name of Jesus is not so much written as plowed into the history of the world." And men never tire of reading about him.[1]

II. His Aloneness in History

To quote Professor Simpson again: "Jesus Christ is beyond all reasonable question the greatest man who ever lived." Instinctively, therefore, we do not class him with others. Jesus is not one of the group of the world's great ones. We can talk about Alexander the Great, Charles the Great, and Napoleon the Great, but Jesus is greater. He is not Jesus the Great, but Jesus the Only! He stands out in his aloneness and uniqueness from other men, yet he was a real man.

Charles Lamb once said: "If Shakespeare were to come into this room we should all rise up to meet him. But if Christ were to come into it, we should all fall down and try to kiss the hem of his garment."

Observe Christ's claim to:

A. *Absolute Deity*

We cannot read the gospels without encountering his claim to deity in:

1. THE WORDS HE ACCENTED

Think of three instances in John's gospel alone concerning the claim he made to objective personal existence prior to the foundation of the world: "Before Abraham was, I AM" (John 8:58, NKJV). Then in his great high-priestly prayer he said, "Father, glorify Me. .. with the glory which I had with You before the world was" (John 17:5). Since it might be said he could have existed with God before the foundation of the world as a created being, we quote another utterance where he claimed co-equality and co-eternity with the Father—"I and My Father are one" (John 10:30).

2. THE WORKS HE ACCOMPLISHED

Here we are not focusing on the miracles performed in the days of his flesh (similar miracles were done by Old Testament saints and later by the apostles), but rather on those works of creation, preservation, and redemption. John 1:3 tells us: "All things were made through Him, and without Him nothing was made that was made" (see also Col. 1:16). The eternal Son was the active cause of all creation.

Concerning the work of preservation, we read that, as the

Son of God, Jesus Christ was "before all things, and in Him all things consist" (Col. 1:17, NKJV; see also Heb. 1:3).

As for redemption, this is a work which transcends all others in magnitude and importance, and everywhere in Scripture it is ascribed to Christ (see Heb. 9:11-12).

3. THE WORSHIP HE ACCEPTED

The Lord Jesus, unlike his disciples, always accepted worship, proving that he was on an equality with God (cf. Acts 10:26). When a woman came and worshiped him, saying, "Lord, help me," he did not rebuke her but said, "O woman, great is your faith! Let it be to you as you desire" (Matt. 15:25-28, NKJV). Thomas, convinced of the identity of the Lord Jesus in that upper room, cried, "My Lord and my God!" (John 20:28, NKJV). Later, we read that the eleven disciples went away into Galilee, to a mountain where Jesus had appointed them, "And when they saw Him, they worshiped Him" (Matt. 28:16-17, NKJV). Speaking of his Son, God says, "Let all the angels of God worship Him" (Heb. 1:6, NKJV). Paul sums up the absolute deity of the Son of God in one of the most profound statements in all the Bible: "In Him dwells all the fullness of the Godhead bodily" (Col. 2:9, NKJV).

B. Absolute Purity

The greatness of a man is estimated by two things: first, by the purity and dignity of his character; second, by the extent of his influence among mankind. Tried by both these tests, Jesus is supreme among men. He could face friends, foes, and fiends and say, "Which of you convicts Me of sin?" (John 8:46, NKJV). No wonder a writer of great insight stated that the solitariness and splendor of Christ's character centered in his sinlessness. Paul could say, "He . . . knew no sin" (2 Cor. 5:21, NKJV). And John could write: "In Him there is no sin" (1 John 3:5, NKJV). And Peter declared that he "committed no sin" (1 Peter 2:22, NKJV). Even the unbelieving Strauss had to confess: "Jesus had a conscience unclouded by the memory of any sin." Such sinlessness was the holiness and goodness of his life which impacted people during his ministry, and does so even to the present day.

Illustration

Socrates taught for forty years, Plato for fifty, Aristotle for forty, and Jesus for only 3. Yet the influence of Christ's three-year ministry infinitely transcends the impact left by the combined 130 years of teaching from these men who were among the greatest philosophers of all antiquity. Jesus painted no pictures; yet, some of the finest paintings of Raphael, Michelangelo, and Leonardo da Vinci received their inspiration from him.

Jesus wrote no poetry; but Dante, Milton, and scores of the world's greatest poets were inspired by him. Jesus composed no music; still Haydn, Handel, Beethoven, Bach, and Mendelssohn reached their highest perfection of melody in the hymns, symphonies, and oratorios they composed in his praise. Every sphere of human greatness has been enriched by this humble carpenter of Nazareth.[2]

C. Absolute Sovereignty

The outstanding evidence of his absolute sovereignty was expressed when he said, "I lay down My life that I may take it again . . . . I have power to lay it down, and I have power to take it again" (John 10:17-18, NKJV). No one before or since Christ has been able to say that. His sovereignty stands alone and unique. In his ability to dismiss his spirit in death and assume his spirit in resurrection is included every other power that the Lord Jesus demonstrated in thought, word, and deed here upon earth.

This unique aloneness of Jesus Christ compels us to choose between the only other two alternatives—both of which are unthinkable. Jesus was either an imposter or he was demented. His sinlessness precludes the idea that he was an imposter, and his amazing influence on subsequent history makes absurd the idea that he was insane. If, therefore, he was neither a fraud nor a lunatic, he must have been what he claimed to be: God incarnate.

Illustration

The story is told of a Frenchman who came to Talleyrand and asked, "Why is it that everybody laughs at my religion?" After explaining his system of religion to Talleyrand, he claimed, "My religion is better than Christianity. What can I do to spread it through the world?" The wiser man replied, "You can live and die serving the people, then on the third day rise from the dead to confirm the hope of humanity, then the people will listen to you." Talleyrand understood that only the Christ can claim sovereignty through the resurrection.

III. His Authority in History

Ever since Christ was in the world men have never been able to rid themselves of the feeling that in him—if in anyone at all—is the quest of faith most likely to find its answer. All who have considered the reality of Jesus Christ have had to admit with Peter, "Lord, to whom shall we go? You have the words of eternal life" (John 6:68, NKJV). He is irresistibly authoritative in history. As the authoritative Son of God he has:

A. Power to Search Men and Women

"I, the LORD, search the heart, I test the mind, Even to give every man according to his ways, And according to the fruit of his doings" (Jer. 17:10, NKJV). Christ is a fact of conscience. We cannot think of him without being examined ourselves, interrogated authoritatively, reviewed even to our innermost minds, hearts, and wills. We study Aristotle and are intellectually edified; we study Jesus and are in the profoundest way spiritually disturbed. If we search to know him we soon feel his eyes, which are as a flame of fire, piercing us through and through (Rev. 1:14).

B. Power to Save Men and Women

Jesus put forth certain claims which no other man would dare to make. He claimed to have authority to forgive sins. This was made clear on the occasion when he cured the paralytic at

Capernaum. His words were: "The Son of Man has power on earth to forgive sins" (Matt. 9:6, NKJV). No one has turned in genuine repentance to the Son of God for forgiveness and found him to fail. He alone, as the God-man, has the word that is both authoritative and saving. No one who has ever heard that word spoken to his soul can fail to believe in Jesus Christ as the Son of God.

C. Power to Satisfy Men and Women

Nature is benign and beautiful, but it gives no answer to your faith. History is but a disappointing and dubious murmur of voices. Look within yourself and you will only find contradiction and confusion. But turn to Jesus Christ and faith always meets its answer. Only Christ can authoritatively say to weary and restless mankind: "Come to Me, all you who labor and are heavy laden, and I will give you rest" (Matt. 11:28, NKJV).

It was a German author of deep insight who said of Christ that "He knew no more sacred task than to point men and women to His own person." This matchless Savior and Son of God is still doing that today! The hymnwriter put it perfectly when he said:

All Things in Jesus

Friends all around me are trying to find/What the heart yearns for, by sin undermined;/I have the secret, I know where 'tis found:/Only true pleasures in Jesus abound. All that I want is in Jesus;/He satisfies, joy He supplies;/Life would be worthless without Him,/All things in Jesus I find.[3]

—Harry Dixon Loes

Conclusion

Criticism may attempt to banish—and the church to bury—his authority, but he always emerges as the authoritative Christ to search, save, and satisfy men and women. That is why countless people believe in Christ as the Son of God; indeed, it is impossible to do otherwise in the light of his appearance in history, his aloneness in history, and his authority in history. In this threefold way Christ appeals to the whole of man's personality. His appearance in history challenges the mind, his aloneness challenges the heart, and his authority challenges the will, and belief is born. Hallelujah, what a Savior!

3

Why I Believe in the Word of God

2 Timothy 3:14-17; 1 Peter 1:22-25; 2 Peter 1:19-21

"But the word of the Lord endureth for ever. And this is the
word which by the gospel is preached unto you"
(1 Pet. 1:25).

Introduction

Someone once said that even though heaven, earth, the visible church, and man himself, crumbled into nonentity, he would, through grace, hold on to the Word of God as the unbreakable link between his soul and God. That man believed the Bible—and so must we, in a day of human speculation and hopeless uncertainty.

Our text teaches that the Bible claims for itself (1) infallibility, for it is "the word of the Lord"; (2) indestructibility, for it "abides for ever"; and (3) indispensability, for it is "by the gospel" that good news is preached unto men. Let us consider this threefold basis for belief in the Bible:

I. The Infallibility of the Bible

"The word of the Lord . . ." (1 Pet. 1:25, KJV). By infallibility we are not implying that all the actions recorded in the Bible have divine approval, nor that the words reported have divine authority. In other words, we do not defend Jacob's deception of his father, nor David's sins of immorality and murder. Nor do we mean that the present-day translations and renderings of the original autographs are faultless, for anyone familiar with translations will admit that there have been discrepancies in the medium of expression. At the same time, it is important to note that over 1,150 Old Testament manuscripts exist in the original language that have been examined by Hebrew scholars and proved to be in agreement with each other on all essential points. The number is even higher for New Testament manuscripts.

With that backdrop we can positively state that "the word of the Lord"—the Bible—is:

A. God's Infallible Record to Men

"The word of the Lord" (1 Pet. 1:25, KJV). Note the Bible's claims for itself. It is a record that is:

1. DIVINELY INSPIRED

"All Scripture is given by inspiration of God" (2 Tim. 3:16, NKJV). Inspiration has been defined as "the supernatural activity of God on the human mind by which the apostles, prophets, and sacred writers were qualified to set forth divine truth without any mixture of error."

The validity of this definition can be illustrated by *the miracle of the Bible's unity*. The Bible was written over a period of 1,500 years by nearly forty authors of different backgrounds. It was penned in three distinct languages—Hebrew, Aramaic, and Greek—in countries far apart; yet the entire book is a harmonious whole. Dr. R. A. Torrey says that "the Bible is not a superficial unity, but a profound unity." Such unity in diversity can only be accounted for by the fact that the Bible has one author—the Holy Spirit.

Then there is *the miracle of the Bible's accuracy*.

Take one instance alone. There are 333 prophecies concerning Christ that have been fulfilled to the letter. By the law
of probability, there is only one chance in eighty-three billion
that 333 prophecies could be fulfilled in one person. How do
we account for the accuracy and dependability of the Old
Testament prophecies concerning Christ? The answer is the
Holy Spirit (see Acts 1:16).

2. DIVINELY INDITED

"Holy men of God spoke as they were moved by the Holy
Spirit" (2 Pet. 1:21, NKJV). Such men were so impelled by the
power of the Holy Spirit, above and beyond their times, that
they were able to see, hear, and record things quite outside
the realm of human imagination. Under such control, fallible
men became infallible and faultless in the act of speaking or
writing—sometimes even unconsciously, as in the case of
Caiaphas when he prophesied of the death of Christ (see John
11:49-52); or Balaam, when he blessed the children of Israel,
instead of cursing them (see Num. 23-24).

3. DIVINELY IMPRINTED

"Beginning at Moses and all the Prophets, He expounded to
them in all the Scriptures the things concerning Himself"
(Luke 24:27, NKJV). The Bible was not only inspired by God
the Father, indited by God the Holy Spirit, but also imprinted
by God the Son. He put his stamp of authority not only on the
Old Testament Scriptures, but also on the New Testament
record that was yet to be written. St. Augustine once said:
"Jesus is latent in the Old Testament, and patent in the New."
Christ set his imprint on every page (see John 9:39; 14:26;
16:13).

Therefore, we cannot accept less of that which he inspires,
indites, and imprints.

B. God's Infallible Rule for Men

"The word of the Lord " (1 Pet. 1:25, KJV). Many think the

Bible should be an authority on every subject, but this is essentially wrong. The Bible was never intended to teach knowledge which men, by patient labor, may obtain for themselves. For example, the Bible was never intended to be an authority on science. It was Sir Charles Marston who categorically asserted that "there are no contradictions between facts stated in the Scriptures and facts that have been ascertained and brought to light in any department of literary and scientific research." The Bible was never intended to be an authority on philosophy, though this wonderful book contains sound philosophy. Moreover, the Bible was never intended to be an authority on history though no other book gives such an accurate record of human history and the true character of the heart of man. In the last analysis, the Bible was intended to be an infallible record to men and an infallible rule for men in all matters of faith and practice. For this reason, the church has acknowledged the supreme authority of the Bible as God's written Word; as the deposit of the message of salvation; as the "only rule of faith and obedience, teaching what man is to believe concerning God, and what duty God requires of man." Paul sums this up in his great statement in 2 Timothy 3:16-17: "All Scripture is given by inspiration of God, and is profitable for doctrine, for reproof, for correction, for instruction in righteousness, that the man of God may be complete, thoroughly equipped for every good work." In light of this, we may state confidently that the Bible is infallible: it is "the word of the Lord" (1 Pet. 1:25, KJV).

Illustration

Dr. Robert D. Wilson, former professor of Semitic philology at Princeton Theological Seminary, said, "After . . . years of scholarly research in biblical textual studies and in language study, I have come now to the conviction that no man knows enough to assail the truthfulness of the Old Testament. Where there is sufficient documentary evidence to make an investigation, the statements of the Bible, in the original text, have stood the test."[1]

II. The Indestructibility of the Bible

"But the word of the Lord endureth for ever" (1 Pet. 1:25, KJV). The Bible is indestructible in that it outlives its foes. Jesus said, "Heaven and earth will pass away, but My words will by no means pass away" (Matt. 24:35, NKJV); and again: "The Scripture cannot be broken" (John 10:35, NKJV). To believe in the indestructibility of the Bible we need to consider something of the story of:

A. *Its Preservation*

The Bible contains the oldest books in the world. The first portions were written over 3,000 years ago—nearly a thousand years earlier than any other history we have. Herodotus, one of the oldest historians whose writings are with us today, was contemporary with Ezra and Nehemiah, the last of the historians of the Old Testament. Between these men and Moses there was an interval of nearly a thousand years. Throughout its long history, the Bible has been burned, hidden, criticized, ridiculed, and neglected; yet God has preserved it.

Illustration

Infidels have been at work for centuries firing away at the Bible and making as much impression as you would shooting boiled peas at the Rock of Gibraltar! Voltaire, toward the end of his life, declared that his writings would displace the Bible, and that in 100 years the Word of God would be forgotten. In twenty-five years, the publishing house that propagated Voltaire's works became the center for the Geneva Bible Society, and the ninety beautifully-bound volumes written against the Bible were sold for pennies apiece. About the same time, one very old copy of an Old Testament manuscript was sold for thousands of dollars. Truly, "the word of the Lord endureth for ever!"

B. *Its Publication*

The Bible is never off the printing press. At least one book of the Bible has been translated into 1,431 languages, the complete Bible into more than 240 languages, and the complete New Testament into more than 320 languages. For years past, Bibles and New Testaments have sold at the rate of thirty million copies a year; that is, fifty every minute. It is by far the world's best seller. As missionary literature, the Bible has reached more nations, tribes, and people than any other book in the world. Missionaries have gone to people with no written language, have caught the significance of words, built an alphabet and grammar, and put the Bible into that language. This has been done over 300 times. These statistics are constantly changing because of the miracle of publication. God has promised to prosper his Word (see Isa. 55:11).

Illustration

Robert J. Thomas, a Welshman working with the Scottish Bible Society, yearned to take Bibles to Korea. His knowledge of the language taught him that Korean is based on Chinese, and that the educated Koreans could read it. He boarded an American ship, but a battle broke out between the ship's officers and the Korean Coast Guard. The ship was destroyed and all passengers lost. Before his death, Thomas managed to stagger out of the water carrying Bibles for Koreans, who clubbed him to death. Today, Korea has a larger Christian population than any other Far Eastern country.

III. The Indispensability of the Bible

"And this is the word which by the gospel is preached unto you" (1 Pet. 1:25, KJV). We can do without many books, but we cannot dispense with the Bible. It contains the only word of the gospel—the good news for men and women. Within its covers we have an authoritative statement concerning:

A. The Revelation of God

"God, who at various times and in different ways spoke in time past to the fathers by the prophets" (Heb. 1:1, NKJV). While Christ is the final and authoritative revelation of God, the

Bible is the final and authoritative revelation of Christ. John brings these two thoughts together in the first and twentieth chapters of his gospel. Speaking of Christ as the revelation of God, he says, "No one has seen God at any time. The only begotten Son, who is in the bosom of the Father, He has declared [or expounded] Him" (John 1:18, NKJV); and again: "These [signs] are written that you may believe that Jesus is the Christ, the Son of God, and that believing you may have life in His name" (John 20:31, NKJV). Christ is central to the book. Every page of Holy Scripture focuses on him. To encounter Christ is to look into the very face of God, for in the Lord Jesus we have "the brightness of His glory and the express image of His person" (Heb. 1:3, NKJV). Yes, we can observe the majesty, divinity, and authority of God in creation, but we know nothing of his personal love, mercy, and grace until we meet Jesus Christ.

B. *The Redemption of Man*

"And this is the word which by the gospel is preached unto you" (1 Pet. 1:25, KJV). Man needs redeeming, but where does one find the plan of redemption? Search the philosophies of men, and the religions of the world, but you search in vain. The Bible says, "Nor is there salvation in any other, for there is no other name under heaven given among men by which we must be saved" (Acts 4:12, NKJV).

John Wesley once wrote: "I am a creature of a day, passing through life as an arrow through the air. I am a spirit, coming from God, and returning to God; . . . I want to know one thing—the way to heaven . . . . God Himself has condescended to teach the way. He hath written it down in a book. O give me that book! At any price, give me the book of God!"

In the sweep of redemption, the Bible is indispensable to:

1. PERSONAL SALVATION

Writing to young Timothy, Paul reminds him that from child-hood he had known the Holy Scriptures. This is the only book able to make a person wise unto salvation through faith in Christ Jesus (see 2 Tim. 3:15). No wonder the Chinese man who had read through the Bible several times admitted, "Whoever made this book made me."

2. SOCIAL INTEGRATION

Writing to husbands and wives, parents and children, masters and servants, Paul says: "Let the word of Christ dwell in you richly in all wisdom" (Col. 3:16, NKJV). Only then would husbands love their wives, wives submit to their husbands, children obey their parents, parents provoke not their children to wrath, servants obey their masters, and do all things heartily as to the Lord. The sanctity of married life, the security of family life, and the stability of social life are linked to the moral and ethical codes taught in Old and New Testaments.

3. NATIONAL REFORMATION

"Righteousness exalts a nation, But sin is a reproach to any people" (Prov. 14:34, NKJV). The Bible is the only authority on the kind of righteousness that exalts a nation. No other book has to its credit such a record of lives redeemed, moral outcasts regenerated, distressed and anxious souls cheered, and individuals and nations remade. Never has the world known a higher code of ethics. Nor has any other book ever so influenced for good literature, language, art, music, and education. Personal, social, and national prosperity can only come through the preaching of the Word of God.

Illustration

Bruce Buursma, religion editor of the Chicago Tribune Press Service, did a write-up entitled "Bible Cure for U.S.: Meese" which appeared in the March 4, 1982 issue of the paper. In it he said: "Presidential Counselor Edwin Meese, a layman in the Lutheran Church-Missouri Synod, told a gathering of conservative Christians here [San Diego] . . . that the Bible holds the answers to the nation's problems. Speaking at the start of a four-day Congress on the Bible, Meese said: 'Nothing is more important in this nation today than this conference on the Bible—not unemployment, not rebuilding our defense capabilities. What is important is rebuilding our relationship to God and a right view of the Bible.' He said: 'There is in our nation a general poverty of the soul. Too many of our people have taken too many wrong roads. We need a reliable road map, and that road map is the Bible.' Meese said President Reagan applauds the involvement of 'Bible-believing Christians' in public policy debates."[2]

Conclusion

If we accept our text then we must believe the Bible is infallible and *learn* it; we must believe the Bible is indestructible and *love* it; we must believe the Bible is indispensable and *live* it.

Part 2
NEW LIFE FOR YOU

4

The Seed of the New Life

1 Peter 1:13-2:3

"Being born again, not of corruptible seed, but of incorruptible, by the word of God, which liveth and abideth for ever" (1 Pet. 1:23, KJV).

Introduction

Our theme for this series of studies is *New Life for You.*

There is no more exciting truth in all the range of biblical revelation than that of new life in Christ. It is the essence of the gospel. This is why Christ identified himself with life when he said, "I am . . . the life" (John 14:6, NKJV). The purpose for which he came into the world was to bring life to those "who were dead in trespasses and sins" (Eph. 2:1, NKJV). Just as *human* life starts with the seed necessary for physical birth and growth, so divine life starts with the seed which brings about spiritual birth and growth. So Peter speaks of "being born again, not of corruptible seed, but of incorruptible, by the word of God, which liveth and abideth for ever" (1 Pet. 1:23).

This seed is described as the living and abiding Word of God. Let us examine this a little more closely:

I. The Seed of New Life Is the Distinctive Word of God

"The word of God, which liveth and abideth for ever" (1 Pet. 1:23, KJV). The message of new life is not the subject of human speculation, but the substance of divine revelation; it is the Word of God. When we think of the new life we are confronted with four aspects of the Word of God:

A. It Is the Word of Inerrancy

"The word of God, which liveth and abideth for ever" (1 Pet. 1:23, KJV). Since the Bible reflects the nature and character of an infallible God, we must accept the fact that this Book is divine truth without any admixture of error. Its unity, prophecy, and history prove its inerrancy.

Illustration

In his booklet, *Does Inerrancy Matter?*, Dr. James Montgomery Boice tells of two members of the International Council on Biblical Inerrancy who were speaking on a seminary campus at the invitation of a conservative student group. They presented the case for inerrancy as a necessary element for the authority of Scripture, but many of the students objected by denying the need for authority in general. Later, a student wrote to one of the participants in the following manner:

I have never held to the doctrine of inerrancy, and yet I found myself siding with you as today's discussion proceeded. Is it not true that behind most of the questions you received was a crypto-cultural Christianity; that is, a secret capitulation to the "try it, you'll like it" mentality of our civilization? That is how it seemed to me. Most questioners did not seem to be engaged in a point-for-point argument of any substantial theological issue. Rather, most seemed to think that to preach the gospel in this day and age one does not need a place to stand. All that one has to do is stand in the pulpit and say, not "Thus saith the Lord," but "Try it, you'll like it."

I am surprised that I found myself feeling that you two were right and all of us were wrong, at least insofar as this very basic point [is concerned]—why we stand where we stand makes all the difference in the world![1]

That quote is extremely revealing and will help you to make your point on inerrancy.

B. It Is the Word of Authority

"The word of God, which liveth and abideth for ever" (1 Pet. 1:23, KJV). St. Augustine says, "When the Scriptures speak, God speaks," and this is the only way in which we can view the Bible. So as we listen to Scripture we must remember that we are listening to God. We have no right to debate or question what he says. The Bible is the word of authority.

Amplification

Show that in a day of relativism and compromise there is only one way in which we can be sure of what is right and wrong, and that is by listening to the only voice of divine authority, the Word of God.

C. It Is the Word of Eternity

"The word of God, which liveth and abideth for ever" (1 Pet. 1:23, KJV). Peter reminds us of the words of Isaiah where he says, "All flesh is as grass . . . . The grass withereth, and the flower thereof falleth away: But the word of the Lord endureth for ever" (vv. 24-25). Jesus declared, "Heaven and earth shall pass away: but my words shall not pass away" (Mark 13:31, KJV). The words of men may fail, but the Word of God stands firm forever. We can depend on what God says. This is why Paul insists that, faced with a choice between man's word versus God's Word, our position must always be: "Let God be true, but every man a liar" (Rom. 3:4, NKJV).

D. It Is the Word of Vitality

"The word of God, which liveth and abideth for ever" (1 Pet. 1:23, KJV). As we shall see, it is the instrument that the Holy Spirit uses to bring about the miracle of new life in Christ. We can read the words of man and be interested and informed, but something supernatural happens to us when we hear the Word of God. Jesus said, "The words that I speak unto you, they are spirit, and they are life" (John 6:63, KJV).

The seed of the new life is the distinctive Word of God. There is something unique and supernatural about this Book we call the Holy Bible.

II. The Seed of the New Life Is the Dynamic Word of God

"Being born again, not of corruptible seed, but of incorruptible, by the word of God" (1 Pet.1:23). Inherent in the Word of God is a dynamic power, and from this passage we find that:

A. The Word of God Has a Revealing Power in Jesus Christ

Peter states, "This is the word which by the gospel is preached unto you" (1 Pet. 1:25, KJV). Outside of the Bible we have no gospel, no message for a sin-sick world; but as we read Holy Scripture we see revealed the only hope of mankind in Jesus Christ. No other book in all the world contains the Gospel of Jesus Christ. This is why the Bible is indispensable.

Illustration

I will never forget watching the face of a blind, paramount chief in Angola, Africa as my missionary father read to him some verses from John's prologue. Father had just completed the translation of this portion of Scripture into the A-Chokwe dialect and was trying it out on a man who was totally ignorant of the Gospel. As he came to those words, "in him [the Lord Jesus] was life; and the life was the *light of men*" (John 1:4), the chief interjected with a plea—"Say that again, say that again. I am in darkness and I need a light." His face was aglow and his sightless eyes were filled with tears as the simple message of life and light in Christ penetrated his darkness, through the illuminating power of the Holy Spirit. This is what Peter means when he says, "This is the word which by the gospel is preached unto you" (1 Peter 1:25).

B. The Word of God Has a Redeeming Power in Jesus Christ

"Forasmuch as ye know that ye were not redeemed with corruptible things, as silver and gold, from your vain conversation received by tradition from your fathers; But with the precious blood of Christ, as of a lamb without blemish and without spot" (1 Pet. 1:18-19).

As we read the Word of God we discover that men and women are slaves to sin. You and I know that this is true; and the central fact of the Gospel is that the Lord Jesus came to redeem us at the cost of his own blood by paying the price on Calvary's cross. He made possible our salvation from sin, self, and Satan, as recorded in the Scriptures. So there is a redeeming power in this seed of the Word.

Illustration

Illustrate the redeeming power of the Gospel in your own life, or in some other conversion story.

C. The Word of God Has a Renewing Power in Jesus Christ

"Being born again, not of corruptible seed, but of incorruptible, by the word of God, which liveth and abideth for ever" (1 Pet. 1:23). As the gospel is read or preached, the Spirit of God uses the truth to bring about the miracle known as the new birth. As natural seed falls into the ground, germinates, and brings forth life, so the seed of the Word falls into the human heart and spiritual life begins.

Nourished by this same Word, new life grows and matures. Peter puts it simply and clearly when he writes: "As newborn babes, desire the sincere milk of the word, that ye may grow thereby" (1 Pet. 2:2).

Amplification

Amplify this by applying the thrust of this truth. Ask your congregation such questions as: Have you been born again? Do you know this new life in Christ? Point out that this miracle can take place even as they listen to the message.

III. The Seed of the New Life Is the Directive Word of God

"Seeing ye have purified your souls in obeying the truth. . . love one another with a pure heart fervently" (1 Pet. 1:22). No one can listen to the Word of God and stay neutral. The Bible demands obedience. Failure to obey is disobedience, and disobedience is sin (1 Sam. 15:22-23) judged by God with eternal punishment (2 Thess. 1:8-10). So we must be quick to obey what the Bible teaches. The Bible directs us into three areas of obedience:

A. *The Word of God Demands the Obedience of Faith*

Peter writes here of "faith . . . in God" (1 Pet. 1:21). The Bible never directs us to place our faith in men, in works, or institutions, but rather in God. This calls for repentance, or a change of mind. The reason for this is that our natural tendency is to depend on ourselves or on human resources—and God calls this sin. Repentance is a change of mind that leads to a change of direction and destiny. Faith in God means commitment or surrender to Jesus Christ, because no man can come to God except through Jesus Christ. So we read that "faith cometh by hearing, and hearing by the word of God" (Rom. 10:17, KJV).

B. *The Word of God Demands the Obedience of Hope*

Peter also speaks of "hope. . . in God" (1 Pet. 1:21, KJV). Outside of the Christian Gospel man is utterly hopeless. This is becoming more and more apparent to thoughtful people in the secularized world in which we live. There is no hope in human inventions and institutions. All around us are failure and frustration. We understand why the existentialist describes life as "a long, dark tunnel without an end." Life, he tells us, is an absurdity, a meaningless nightmare. This is the doctrine of despair.

What a relief, therefore, to turn to the Gospel of our Lord Jesus Christ and find hope! The Son of God died and rose again to give us hope, and because he lives we can know this living hope in a personal, powerful way.

Amplification

Extend this thought of hope beyond this life to the eschatological outlook for the true believer.

C. The Word of God Demands the Obedience of Love

In "obeying the truth" we are told to "love one another with a pure heart fervently" (1 Pet. 1:22, KJV). The world knows little about true love. This is why there is so much failure in human relationships in the home, in business, and in society. But the Bible gives us the secret of true love. What we can't do, the Holy Spirit can perform in our hearts through this new life in Christ, creating in us active, fervent love to both God and man. The human heart was made for love and will never be satisfied without it. This is why life is meaningless until we come to know new life in Christ.

Illustration

Show how *agape* love transforms human relationships.

Conclusion

We have seen that this new life in Christ starts with a seed— the Word of God. It is a distinctive Word, trustworthy and authoritative. It is a dynamic Word that has power to reveal, redeem, and renew. It is a directive Word that demands obedience. To listen to this Word calls for a verdict. To accept its message is to come into blessing; to reject its message is to remain in bondage. In the final analysis, when we refer to the Word we speak not only of the written Word but also of the Living Word, our Lord Jesus Christ. He is God's seed who longs to be planted and nourished in our hearts. Are we prepared to accept or reject him? This is the crucial issue.

5

The Source of the New Life

John 10:1-11

"The thief cometh not, but for to steal, and to kill, and to destroy: I am come that they might have life, and that they might have it more abundantly" (John 10:10, KJV).

Introduction

Forty-four times or more the word "life" occurs in the gospel of John. In fact, it is the key word of this book, and we cannot read through its pages without seeing quite clearly that the purpose for which Christ came into this world was to bring life, and life more abundant.

"More abundant than what?" we ask. Before we go any further, we must define what we mean by this new life in Christ. If we were to walk through a forest and pick a flower we would be touching *vegetable life.* As we proceeded on our walk, our attention might be attracted by a beautiful dog, and we would be looking at *animal life.* Later on, we might meet a hunter, coming our way with a gun over his shoulder, and as we greeted him we would encounter *human life.* Then as we continued we might be fortunate enough to see a young woman relaxing under a shady tree, reading her Bible, and after questioning her we would discover that she possessed *spiritual life,* a life qualitatively different than vegetable, animal, or human life. This is what Jesus was talking about when he said, "I am come that they might have life, and that they might have it more abundantly." When he gave expression to this tremendous statement he was declaring himself to be the source of a new kind of life. In him, and in him alone, can we know this abundant life. In presenting this potential of life to men and women, Jesus spoke of three important matters that demand our close attention:

I. The Enemies of This New Life in Christ

"The thief cometh not, but for to steal, and to kill, and to destroy: I am come that they might have life, and that they might have it more abundantly" (John 10:10). The enemies, of course, refer to the thieves, robbers, strangers, and hirelings mentioned in this opening paragraph. Unfortunately, in many of our churches and pulpits today are men who are nothing more than thieves and robbers, holding back that "more abundant" life from hungry and thirsty people. Satan is out to rob the church of this gift of abundant life. If he cannot deprive us of the gift of life, he proceeds to deceive us about the glory of that life. And so the Master warned us against the enemies of this new life. He pointed out that:

A. The Enemies Are Deceptive in Their Methods

"Verily, verily, I say unto you, He that entereth not by the door into the sheepfold, but climbeth up some other way, the same is a thief and a robber" (John 10:1). Not only in Christ's day, but in our time, there are enemies of the Gospel who insist that there is more than one door into the sheepfold of God's salvation. But this is a lie, and we must not be deceived. Jesus said, "I am the door: by me if any man enter in, he shall be saved" (10:9). He also declared, "I am the way . . . no man cometh unto the Father, but by me" (14:6).

Illustration

Tell the story of Simon the sorcerer (Acts 8:5-25).

B. The Enemies Are Defective in Their Message

"A stranger will they not follow, but will flee from him: for they know not the voice of strangers" (John 10:5).

The voice verbalizes and articulates the identity, reality, and authority of the message that is preached.

Illustration

Explain how the modern and post-modern voices (including liberalism, humanism, relativism and others) fail in their message to redeem man from sin.

C. The Enemies Are Destructive in Their Motives

"The thief cometh not, but for to steal, and to kill, and to destroy" (John 10:10). Enemies of the Gospel don't give; they take. They don't quicken; they deaden. They don't bless; they damn. In other words, they kill, they steal, and they destroy. That last word is strong in the original Greek. It means "to utterly destroy."

Illustration

Explain the various methods that the enemies of the cross use for "climbing up some other way." A good biblical example is the story of Balak (meaning "devastator"). Balak was king of Moab when Israel emerged from the wilderness to enter Canaan. Having seen what the Hebrews had done to the Amorites, he attempted to prevent Israel's advance by hiring Balaam to curse them (see Num. 22:1-6). He built altars at three different sites for the purpose, but each attempt failed. He is remembered throughout biblical history as an example of the folly of attempting to thwart Jehovah's will (see Josh. 24:9; Judg. 11:25).

II. The Certainties of This New Life in Christ

Jesus said, "I am come that they might have life, and that they might have it more abundantly" (John 10:10). This victorious and continuous life in Christ is not just a philosophy or a theology, it is a person, the Lord Jesus Christ, concerning whom there are certainties that we cannot ignore or escape.

A. This New Life in Christ Is Historically Observable

Jesus said, "I am come that they might have life" (John 10:10).

Amplification
Show how this life in Christ was manifested by his incarnation, demonstrated by his crucifixion, and vindicated by his resurrection.

B. This New Life in Christ Is Dynamically Obtainable

"I am come that they might have life, and that they might have it more abundantly" (John 10:10). He also declared: "I give unto them eternal life; and they shall never perish" (10:28). John picks up this great theme in his epistle and says: "And this is the record, that God hath given to us eternal life, and this life is in his Son. He that hath the Son hath life; and he that hath not the Son of God hath not life" (1 John 5:11-12).

Illustration
Illustrate by using three envelopes of different sizes. Label the smallest size *life*, the next size *Christ*, and the largest size *me* or *you*. Put the *life* envelope into the *Christ* envelope, and then insert the *Christ* envelope into the *me/you* envelope. As *you* do this, quote slowly and emphatically, "And this *life* is in his Son. He that hath the Son hath life."

III. The Qualities of This New Life in Christ

"I am come that they might have life, and that they might have it more abundantly" (John 10:10). And again: "The good shepherd giveth his life for the sheep" (John 10:11). As we examine these tremendous words, notice three things about this new life in Christ; and as we consider each one, challenge your own heart as to whether or not you have personally experienced this quality of life.

A. *It Is a New Life Which Is Appealing*

"I am come that they might have life" (John 10:10).

Exegesis

Explain the meaning of "the good shepherd," and use Galatians 5:22-23, and other Scriptures, to describe our Lord's beauty and glory.

B. *It Is a New Life Which Is Abounding*

"I am come that they might have life, and that they might have it more abundantly" (John 10:10); or, as the New English Bible has it, "I have come that men may have life, and may have it in all its fullness." This is a wonderful thing about the new life in Christ. As the Word of God deepens our capacity, so the Son of God fills that capacity with all his fullness. In him is all the fullness of the Godhead bodily, and we are complete in him (Col. 2:9).

Illustration

The story is told of A. B. Simpson who heard of D. L. Moody's encounter with the Holy Spirit, when, in a moment of time, he seemed to be filled with the very glory of heaven. So he traveled to Chicago to hear the great evangelist preach. Sitting at the back of the auditorium he waited for Moody to come on to the platform. In the meantime, the songleader introduced a hymn with the words, "Isn't it wonderful to know that 'everything is in Jesus, and Jesus is everything'?" For A. B. Simpson, that was all he needed to hear. Picking up his briefcase, he left the tabernacle and never heard Moody preach on that occasion. Later he made those words the motto of his ministry: "Everything is in Jesus, and Jesus is everything; tell the world as fast as you can!"

C. It Is a New Life Which Is Abiding

"I am come that they might have life, and that they might have it more abundantly" (John 10:10). And if we ask the question, "What kind of life?" the answer is clear and conclusive: it is eternal life. Jesus said, "This is life eternal, that they might know thee the only true God, and Jesus Christ, whom thou hast sent" (17:3). This abiding life does not die when we die physically. Indeed, physical death is only an open door into a fuller life in Jesus Christ. This abiding life is eternal because it begins on earth and continues in heaven. What a glorious gift for those who are prepared to receive it! And we have learned that the source of this life is Christ himself, who said: "I am come that they might have life, and that they might have it more abundantly" (10:10).

Illustration
Illustrate the endlessness or permanence of this life in Christ, both personally and eschatologically.

Conclusion

Remember the enemies of this new life, the certainties of this new life, and the qualities of this new life. With these truths in mind I invite you to receive this new life in Christ. He is God's "unspeakable gift." To reject him is to reject life, and to reject life is to perish eternally. Won't you say, "Thanks be unto God for his unspeakable gift" (2 Cor. 9:15) then open the hand and heart of your faith and say "thank you"?

6

The Start of the New Life

John 3:1-16; 7:50; 19:39

"Except a man be born again, he cannot see the kingdom of
God . . . . Except a man be born of water and of the Spirit,
he cannot enter into the kingdom of God" (John 3:3, 5, KJV).

Introduction

The greatest message on new life ever delivered by the Lord
Jesus Christ was addressed to a deeply religious man named
Nicodemus. What is so significant is that this ruler of the Jews,
with all his religion, was a very dissatisfied man. Something
vital was missing in his life. So we find him coming to one in
whom he had recognized a quality of life which transcended
the religious formalism of his day. It is evident that Nicodemus
longed for this new life in Christ, for he came to find out how
he might possess it. In the dialogue that followed, Jesus indicated three conditions for the start of this new life:

I. There Must Be the Sense of Need

Nicodemus said, "Rabbi, we know that thou art a teacher

come from God: for no man can do these miracles [these signs of new life] that thou doest, except God be with him" (John 3:2). In these words Nicodemus was admitting a three-fold, basic need that could only be met in Jesus Christ:

A. Man Is Blind in Sin and Therefore Needs New Life

"Except a man be born again, he cannot see the kingdom of God" (John 3:3). This means that without divine life no one can see or understand the things that pertain to the spiritual realm.

Illustration

Illustrate the solemn truth of 1 Corinthians 2:14 and 2 Corinthians 4:4. Until the eyes of the heart are open, by the revealing power of the Holy Spirit, the natural man can only say, "I don't believe it," or, "I cannot see it," or "it is utter nonsense."

B. Man Is Bound in Sin and Therefore Needs New Life

"Except a man be born of water and of the Spirit, he cannot enter into the kingdom of God" (John 3:5). In other words, sin has so bound man in mind, heart, and will to his good works, self-righteousness, religious opinions, and fear of man, that without life from God he cannot break free to enter the kingdom of God.

Illustration

Illustrate how religionism, traditionalism, and even denominationalism can bind men and women in their sin.

C. Man Is Born in Sin and Therefore Needs New Life

"That which is born of the flesh is flesh; and that which is born of the Spirit is spirit" (John 3:6). And Paul tells us that "flesh and blood cannot inherit the kingdom of God" (1 Cor. 15:50).

You see, "that which is begotten carries within it the nature of that which begat it" (author paraphrase) is an irrevocable law of life.

Illustration

Henry Moorhouse tells of a father and son who were walking down the streets of New York City when they came to a sign which read, "Come inside and see the performing pig." "Oh, Daddy, let's go in," begged the boy. "We haven't time," replied the father—but you can guess who won the argument! When they were seated inside and sufficient people had gathered, the proprietor opened a little door and out came the cleanest looking pig—complete with trousers, waistcoat, and bow tie. When there was silence, the proprietor announced that he was going to ask the pig to form a sentence with some wooden letters on the floor. The pig nosed the letters around until they spelled, "I'm a good pig." By this time the little boy's eyes were like saucers, and looking at the pig, and then at his father, he blurted out, "B-but, it's still a pig, isn't it?" The answer, of course, was "Yes, it's still a pig," with all its cleanness, clothes, and cleverness.

And so Nicodemus, like every son of Adam, was born in sin—in spite of all his education and religious refinements. In consequence, he could not inherit the kingdom of God. Is it any wonder that Jesus exclaimed, "Marvel not that I said unto thee, Ye must be born again" (John 3:7).

II. There Must Be the Step of Faith

Addressing this religious leader, Jesus declared, "God so loved the world, that he gave his only begotten Son, that whosoever believeth in him should not perish, but have everlasting life" (John 3:16). With those glorious words that contain the core of the Gospel, Jesus emphasized that this new life is not merited or inherited by human means: rather, it is the gift of God to be received by faith. For this to happen:

A. *The Spirit Must Produce This New Life*

"The wind bloweth where it listeth, and thou hearest the sound thereof, but canst not tell whence it cometh, and whither it goeth: so is every one that is born of the Spirit" (John 3:8). Humans can no more control life from above than they can govern the light breezes in the treetops. It is the sovereign power and prerogative of the Holy Spirit alone to produce this new life in those who are sensitive to his prompting. This is why it is so serious to resist him when he strives with us. To refuse his offer may mean the damning of our souls. God warns, "My spirit shall not always strive with man" (Gen. 6:3).

Amplification
Amplify the seriousness of resisting the Spirit of God (see Acts 7:51).

B. *The Savior Must Provide This New Life*

"As Moses lifted up the serpent in the wilderness, even so must the Son of man be lifted up: That whosoever believeth in him should not perish, but have eternal life" (John 3:14-15). By this reference to the Old Testament story, Jesus implies that just as Moses lifted up the serpent in the wilderness to show God's answer of life to the sting of death for the snake-bitten Israelites, so, by the lifting up of the Son of Man (on the cross and in resurrection), God declared, once and forever, his answer of life to the sentence of death, which is upon all who have sinned and come short of his glory.

Amplification
Amplify the story of Moses and the bronze serpent in the wilderness (Num. 21).

C. *The Sinner Must Possess This New Life*

"Whosoever believeth in him should not perish, but have eternal life" (John 3:15) The one who believes in Christ possesses

God's life, for "he that hath the Son hath life" (1 John 5:12). The moment Christ is received by faith, the miracle of the new birth takes place. At once the sinner enjoys a new sight, a new liberty, and a new nature in Christ. This is the result of a step of faith.

Illustration

Illustrate this step of faith by relating a clear-cut story of conversion.

III. There Must Be the Sign of Life

Jesus said, "We speak that we do know, and testify that we have seen" (John 3:11). Jesus was undoubtedly referring to his disciples who had already received this new life in Christ. But, even more important, he was underscoring the necessity of *expressing* this new life in Christ. It is significant that the next two references to Nicodemus in this gospel describe his confession of Christ before others. In examining the relevant passages, observe two characteristics of this sign of new life in Christ.

A. *The Confession of Christ Must Be Fearless*

"Nicodemus saith unto them [the religious leaders], (he that came to Jesus by night, . . .) Doth our law judge any man, before it hear him, and know what he doeth?" (John 7:50-51). The context here reveals that the religious leaders had sent officers to apprehend the Savior, but these soldiers had returned without Jesus, saying, "Never man spake like this man" (7:46). The Pharisees were furious at this reaction and expressed themselves accordingly. But in that atmosphere of hostility Nicodemus challenged the whole Sanhedrin as to the fairness of judging anyone before seeing him and hearing him. Here was a clear-cut example of a fearless stand for Christ.

Illustration

Cite instances of fearless confession that you have witnessed.

B. The Confession of Christ Must Be Faithful

"And there came also Nicodemus, which at the first came to Jesus by night, and brought a mixture of myrrh and aloes, about an hundred pound weight. [And] . . . took . . . the body of Jesus, and wound it in linen clothes with the spices, as the manner of the Jews is to bury" (John 19:39, 40). After Christ had been crucified, two people were concerned that the body should have an honorable burial. One was Joseph of Arimathea, and the other was Nicodemus. So they asked Pilate for permission to perform the burial rites. It was Nicodemus, however, who brought along a hundred pounds of myrrh and aloes to embalm the body, identifying himself forever with the Christ of the cross. We can never think of Calvary without thinking of Nicodemus. By embalming that precious body, Nicodemus publicly symbolized his identification with the death, burial, and resurrection of the Savior. The apostle Paul later described this identification as being "dead and risen with Christ" (Rom. 6). What a splendid testimony Nicodemus gave to this new life in Christ, and how carefully we should remember this when thinking of the man who came to Jesus by night.

This is God's threefold condition for new life in Christ: there must be the sense of need, the step of faith, and the sign of life in Christ.

Conclusion

Do you want to start a new life in Christ? Then emulate Nicodemus. Come as he did, and you will leave as he did.

7

The Seal of the New Life

Ephesians 1:3-14; 4:29-32; 5:15-21

"In whom ye also trusted, after that ye heard the word of truth, the gospel of your salvation: in whom also after that ye believed, ye were sealed with that holy Spirit of promise"
(Eph. 1:13, KJV)

Introduction

We all know that no official document is of any value unless it has been notarized. To be valid it must have the stamp or seal of authority. What is true in the commercial world is equally true in the spiritual realm. To be an authentic Christian, a person must have the seal of the Holy Spirit—and this is what Paul is talking about in the passages before us. He was writing to Christians who were familiar with the use of the seal. Ephesus was a seaport that shipped, among other things, large quantities of lumber. When buyers came to purchase this commodity they stamped each beam with their seal so that it could be claimed without question when it reached its destination. The seal was the symbol of ownership and security.

So, writing to the believers, Paul says, "[You] were sealed with . . . [the] holy Spirit of promise" (Eph. 1:13), and later on he warns them not to grieve the Spirit of God, "whereby [they were] . . . sealed unto the day of redemption" (4:30). Then he concludes his letter by saying, "Be filled with the Spirit" (5:18). From these statements we learn:

I. The Seal of the New Life Is the Possession of the Holy Spirit in Personal Experience

"In whom ye also trusted, after that ye heard the word of truth, the gospel of your salvation: in whom also after that ye believed, ye were sealed with that holy Spirit of promise" (Eph. 1:13). For this miracle to take place in personal experience:

A. A Person Must Hear the Word of the Gospel

"In whom ye also trusted, after that ye heard the word of truth, the gospel of your salvation" (Eph 1:13). God has ordained that the gospel message should be preached throughout the world to every creature. This explains why every Christian should be a witness, why evangelistic missions and outreaches are held, and why local churches are established. Elsewhere Paul tells us that the Gospel is the Good News of God's love to men and women who are dead in trespasses and sins. It is the story of how Christ "died for our sins according to the scriptures; And that he was buried, and that he rose again the third day according to the scriptures" (1 Cor. 15:3-4).

Amplification
Show the need for preaching the Gospel in every age to all nations (see Matt. 28; Rom. 10:13-14).

B. A Person Must Heed the Lord of the Gospel

"In whom . . . after that ye believed, ye were sealed with that holy Spirit of promise" (Eph. 1:13). The implication here is quite clear. It is not sufficient to hear the word of the Gospel, we must heed, or obey, the Lord of the Gospel. Jesus waits to enter our lives, by the power and presence of the Holy Spirit, but we must first obey him in repentance and faith. This means confessing and forsaking our sins, and then placing our trust in the Lord Jesus who died to put away our sins, and rose again to make us right with God. The Bible teaches that when we truly hear the word of the Gospel and then heed the Lord of the Gospel, a miracle takes place. The Holy Spirit of promise enters our lives, and we are sealed forever. God puts his stamp of ownership and security upon us, and no angel in heaven, no man on earth, no demon in hell, can ever break that seal.

Exegesis

Exegete the word "seal" in this context and elsewhere, for example, Matthew 27:66; John 3:33; Romans 15:28; 2 Corinthians 1:22; Revelation 7:3-5; 10:4; 20:3. (William Barclay has some helpful comments in his *Letters to the Ephesians* rev. ed. [Westminster Press, 1975].)

II. The Seal of the New Life Is the Position of the Holy Spirit in Personal Experience

"Grieve not the holy Spirit of God, whereby ye are sealed unto the day of redemption" (Eph. 4:30). It is quite obvious from this verse that the Holy Spirit is a person who can be grieved and hurt. This happens when we fail to give him his rightful place in our lives as the *Holy* Spirit who has sealed us unto the day of redemption. The purpose of God, through the ministry of the Holy Spirit, is to purify our lives until we become more and more like our Lord Jesus. This progressive work of the Holy Spirit will not be completed until the day of redemption. In the meantime, however, we must avoid grieving him. In the context of this passage, the apostle shows:

A. What It Means to Give Place to the Devil

"Neither give place to the devil" (Eph. 4:27). We give place to the devil when we tell untruths (4:25), when we lose our tempers (4:26), when we rob our neighbors (4:28), when we use bad language (4:29), and when we show bitterness of spirit (4:31). In simple terms, we give place to (or accommodate) the devil when we grieve the Holy Spirit by unholy thoughts, words, and deeds. God has called us to holy living, and that is why he has given us the Holy Spirit. Therefore, anything contrary to the nature of a holy God grieves the Spirit.

Illustration

Illustrate with stories of living situations where the devil has had his way in a believer's life.

B. What It Means to Give Place to the Spirit

"Speak every man truth with his neighbour: for we are members one of another" (Eph. 4:25). We are to be honest with our neighbors (4:25), we are to work hard in our jobs (4:28), we are to show grace in our speech (4:29), and we are to be kind and forgiving to all (4:32). Once again, this simply means accommodating the Holy Spirit, giving him his rightful position in every department of our lives. This is the seal of the new life in Christ—not only in the possession of the Holy Spirit, but the position of the Holy Spirit. It should be evident to all that our lives are controlled by the Spirit of God.

Amplification

Explain what it means to be filled with the Spirit (Eph. 5:18).

III. The Seal of the New Life Is the Provision of the Holy Spirit in Personal Experience

"Be not drunk with wine, wherein is excess; but be filled with the Spirit" (Eph. 5:18). If God's Spirit is both acknowledged and obeyed in our lives, certain things follow which are described to us in this wonderful passage.

A. A New Melody Comes into Our Lives

"Singing and making melody in your heart to the Lord" (Eph. 5:19). Instead of singing the songs of drunkenness and sordidness we are caught up in the psalms, hymns, and spiritual songs of the church, giving thanks to God for all things (Eph. 5:19-20).

Illustration
Illustrate from stories of revival how spirit-filled men and women become a singing community.

B. A New Harmony Comes into Our Lives

"Submitting yourselves one to another in the fear of God" (Eph. 5:21). There will be a harmony in the church between pastor and people, and the whole congregation will love and be loved among its members. There will be a harmony in the home between husbands and wives, parents and children, and the whole family will love and be loved among its members. There will be a harmony in the business between employer and employee because each will love the other. This does not mean that everything will be perfect this side of heaven, but there is no question that relationships grow sweeter and stronger when the Holy Spirit is in control.

Amplification
Amplify the meaning of reciprocal love in the relationships of life.

C. A New Victory Comes into Our Lives

"Be strong in the Lord, and in the power of his might" (Eph. 6:10). We discover that in spite of the principalities, powers, and rulers of the darkness of this world, in spite of spiritual wickedness in high places arrayed against us, we have an offensive and defensive armor in Jesus Christ that guarantees victory every day of our lives.

Amplification
Amplify by detailing the pieces of armor, both for defensive and offensive spiritual warfare.

D. *A New Liberty Comes into Our Lives*

"That . . . I may speak boldly, as I ought to speak" (Eph. 6:20). With Paul the apostle we can testify that through the prayers of God's people and the power of the Holy Spirit we can open our mouths anywhere, at any time, to share the message of the Gospel.

Illustration

Show from the book of the Acts what it means to be bold in Christian witness.

Conclusion

Remember that the seal is a person, the Holy Spirit. We must therefore know by experience his possession, his position, and his provision in our lives. Only then can we call ourselves true Christians. Have you received the Holy Spirit? If not, will you repent, believe in the Lord Jesus Christ as your Savior, and then, as an act of faith, ask the person of the Holy Spirit into your life right now?

8

The Song of the New Life

Psalm 40:1-4

"He hath put a new song in my mouth, even praise unto our God" (Ps. 40:3, KJV).

Introduction

We have been created to sing. This explains why a nation has its national anthem, why the armed forces march to the strains of martial music, why a college has its alma mater, and why each of us has a favorite song.

When we come to the Bible, we find that the God of creation and redemption is the God of song. When the universe was brought into existence "the morning stars sang together, and all the sons of God shouted for joy" (Job 38:7, KJV). And when God brought his people out of the bondage of Egypt the children of Israel sang the song of Moses (Exod. 15). One day, when God's purposes of redemption are consummated, we are all going to sing the song of the Lamb.

So we see that our singing is an evidence of our life. And no one helps us to understand this better than the psalmist

David. He could testify: "He hath put a new song in my mouth, even praise unto our God" (Ps. 40:3).

I. This New Song Speaks of a Life of Deliverance

"He brought me up also out of an horrible pit, out of the miry clay" (Ps. 40:2). Here David is describing in graphic terms what it means to be delivered from the guilt and grip of sin. Whatever historical events occasioned the writing of this psalm are incidental to the basic principle that he is enunciating. This shepherd-king could sing because he knew a twofold deliverance:

A. Deliverance from the Guilt of Sin

"He brought me up also out of an horrible pit" (Ps. 40:2).The Hebrew reads: "He brought me up out of a pit of noise"—and this is most suggestive. David has in mind the pits that were often dug to capture wolves, bears, or lions, but occasionally thieves and robbers were also trapped this way. The pit was so shaped that every cry for help would echo and reverberate. A trap of this kind was truly a "pit of noise."

How graphically this illustrates the guilt of sin. Until we know the deliverance of God, we are forever haunted by the accusations of the devil, as well as by the voice of our self-condemnation.

Illustration
Illustrate in terms of your personal experience.

B. Deliverance from the Grip of Sin

"He brought me up . . . out of the miry clay" (Ps. 40:2). We are told that the bottom of these pits was often covered with a miry clay, or sticky sediment, which impeded attempts to escape. Indeed, the more the victim struggled to get free, the deeper he sank into the miry clay.

Illustration
I can never think of this psalm without recalling an experience

I once had in Angola, West Africa. I arose one morning to hunt a wild goose for our Christmas dinner. As I waited at the rice fields a flock of these birds flew in, and I took aim and fired, killing one and wounding another. But as I chased the wounded bird I found myself caught in a bog; the more I fought to free myself, the deeper I sank, and the horror of a ghastly death overwhelmed me. At this point there was nothing I could do but cry for help—and to my utter relief I saw, emerging from the bushes, one of the faithful men who served on our mission compound. Although he was wearing a beautiful native print cloth, he stripped it from his body and threw one end to me. I grasped it with the strength of desperation, and little by little my deliverer drew me safely out of the bog. My struggle was over. A saving hand had been stretched out at the sacrifice of something that was very valuable to my African friend. I could sing a new song. I was alive!

This is the Gospel in a nutshell. Our Lord and Savior Jesus Christ laid aside the glory of heaven in order to save us not only from the guilt of sin, but also from the grip of sin. By his death we were reconciled to God, but by his life we are constantly being delivered from the power of the indwelling sin nature. To struggle in our own strength is to sink deeper and deeper into trouble, but to trust the saving life of Christ is to know deliverance day by day.

II. This New Song Speaks of a Life of Direction

"He brought me up also out of an horrible pit, out of the miry clay, and set my feet upon a rock, and established my goings" (40:2). The godless are always described in Scripture as lost. They don't know where they have come from, where they are, or where they are going; but it is quite different for the Christian. He knows where he stands, and he also knows where he is going. Direction implies:

A. The Christian's Position in Christ
"He [hath] . . . set my feet upon a rock" (Ps. 40:2). In this

particular context we are told the Christian is standing securely on the rock.

Amplification

Amplify the thought of being on the rock as the place of security (Exod. 33:22), the place of sufficiency (Isa. 32:3; 1 Cor. 10:4), and the place of serenity (Isa. 26:3-4, marginal rendering).

B. The Christian's Progression in Christ

"He . . . established my goings" (Ps. 40:2). Long before the foundations of the world were laid, the God of foreknowledge planned our lives. One of the most exciting things about the Christian experience is to find, follow, and finish that plan as we walk the pathway of obedience.

Amplification

Expound the meaning of Ephesians 2:10.

III. This New Song Speaks of a Life of Devotion

"He hath put a new song in my mouth, even praise unto our God: many shall see it, and fear, and shall trust in the Lord" (Ps. 40:3). This is the climactic thought in the whole progression of ideas that David shares with us. Deliverance leads to direction, but direction to devotion. When we know our salvation in Christ, as well as our standing in Christ, then and only then can we fully express our song in Christ. God made us to love him, and this response finds expression in:

A. The Devotion of Worship

"He hath put a new song in my mouth, even praise unto our God" (Ps. 40:3). "Man's chief end is to glorify God, and to enjoy him forever" states the Westminster Shorter Catechism; therefore, his greatest activity is that of worship. More is said in the Bible about worship than about service.

Illustration

Show from example of Scripture that God desires our worship before he desires our service.

B. *The Devotion of Witness*

"Many shall see it, and fear, and shall trust in the Lord" (Ps. 40:3). Where there is worship there is also witness. No one can live in the presence of God without reflecting the glory of God. This is what made the early apostles so distinctive and effective in that first-century church.

Illustration

Illustrate from the life and witness of the early apostles, for example, Acts 4:13.

Conclusion

The question arises how this song can begin. David gives the answer. He said: "I waited patiently for the LORD; and he inclined unto me, and heard my cry" (Ps. 40:1). Literally, the Hebrew idiom is "Waiting I waited for the Lord; and he inclined unto me, and heard my cry." First, there must be *submission*—"I waited." Until we stop struggling and start trusting, God will never hear our cry. As long as we think that we can save ourselves from the guilt and grip of sin we are doomed to defeat and destruction. So waiting on the Lord suggests utter submission to his saviorhood and sovereignty.

Then, second, there must be *petition*—"He . . . heard my cry." We are assured that "whosoever shall call upon the name of the Lord shall be saved [or delivered]" (Rom. 10:13, KJV). When Peter began to sink beneath the boisterous waves he cried, "Lord, save me" (Matt. 14:30, KJV), and instantly the Master was there to deliver him and to restore his faith.

Will you cry right now and know this song of deliverance, this song of direction, and this song of devotion? This is the song of the new life.

9

The Sense of the New Life

John 10:14-18, 26-30

"My sheep hear my voice, and I know them, and they follow me: And I give unto them eternal life; and they shall never perish, neither shall any man pluck them out of my hand. My Father, which gave them me, is greater than all; and no man is able to pluck them out of my Father's hand" (John 10:27-29, KJV).

Introduction

Psychologists tell us that one of the strongest instincts in man is that of self-preservation. Wherever people are found on the face of the earth they are afraid of insecurity. Talk to any reasonable person and he will share with you his concern for personal, social, and even for national security. Indeed, much of our time is spent on insuring ourselves against poverty, sickness, and death.

There is another dimension of security to which many people give very little attention. It is that of eternal, or spiritual, security. The Bible speaks of this again and again throughout its progressive revelation. Paul could say, "I know whom I have believed, and am persuaded that he is able to keep that which I have committed unto him against that day" (2 Tim. 1:12, KJV). But the greatest statement on the subject came from our Lord when he declared:

"My sheep hear my voice, and I know them, and they follow me: And I give unto them eternal life; and they shall never perish, neither shall any man pluck them out of my hand. My Father, which gave them me, is greater than all; and no man is able to pluck them out of my Father's hand" (John 10:27-29).

Here he taught that:

I. The Sense of New Life Is a Divine Relationship

Jesus said, "I give unto [my sheep] . . . eternal life" (John 10:28). When the Savior specifically underscored the words, "my sheep" and "eternal life," he was presupposing a divine relationship. It is described in this passage as:

A. A Personal Relationship

"I give unto [my sheep] . . . eternal life" (John 10:28). The Gospel of Jesus Christ is the gospel of eternal life. It is for this very purpose that the Savior came into the world. As we read, in this very context, he could look into the faces of men and women and say, "I am come that they might have life, and that they might have it more abundantly" (10:10). And John, in his epistle, reminds us that "this is the record, that God hath given to us eternal life, and this life is in his Son. He that hath the Son hath life; and he that hath not the Son of God hath not life" (1 John 5:11-12). And so we see that this divine relationship involves a living union with Jesus Christ.

Amplification
Amplify how this relationship takes place, by using such verses as John 1:12-13 and Revelation 3:20.

B. A Permanent Relationship

"I give unto [my sheep] . . . eternal life; and they shall never perish" (10:28). There are two vital truths in this statement. The first concerns the word "eternal." The term denotes not only a quality of life, but also a quantity of life. In quality, this eternal life is part of the very nature of God. By receiving eternal life we become "partakers of the divine nature" (2 Pet. 1:4). But this life is also enduring and endless. Indeed, the mind begins to reel when we try to think of the lastingness of the life that Jesus gives.

Illustration

I remember talking to my son, Jonathan, after he had received Christ into his life. I asked him if he was sure that he had received eternal life, and he answered "Yes." Then I asked him how long this life would last, and he replied "forever." But I insisted further, "How long is forever?" to which he had no answer. In an effort to illustrate how we might conceive of the length of eternal life, I said, "Think of all the leaves on all the trees in the world. Count them all up and multiply them by a billion. Then number all the grains of sand on all the beaches of the oceans and multiply that total by a billion. Next, calculate how many drops of water there are in all the rivers and oceans and multiply that by a billion. Add your figures together and that would only be the beginning of eternal life." Jonathan's only remark was, "That's a *long* time."

This permanent relationship is also strengthened by the second thought, which is expressed in the words, "I give unto [my sheep] . . . eternal life; and they shall never perish" (10:28). In the Greek, that is expressed by a double negative, which is the strongest positive you can find in Scripture. The word "perish" is a solemn word that carries the idea of ruination and purposelessness. A person who perishes not only deteriorates, but fails to fulfill the purpose for which he was created. This can happen in time, but through a living relationship to Jesus Christ we cease to perish, and enter into the fullness of eternal life.

Amplification
Amplify the conditions that determine eternal security.

II. The Sense of New Life Is a Divine Reliability

"My sheep hear my voice, and I know them, and they follow me" (John 10:27). Jesus teaches us in these words that the reliability of eternal security is contingent upon:

A. *The Authority of His Word*

"My sheep hear my voice" (John 10:27). Whenever the Savior opened his mouth the scribes and Pharisees, and all men and women were astonished at his doctrine because he spoke as one having authority (Mark 1:22). We can rely on what he has to say about our eternal security. He declared: "Heaven and earth shall pass away, but my words shall not pass away" (Matt. 24:35, KJV). And again: "The Scripture cannot be broken" (John 10:35, NKJV). And his message to your heart and mine is simply this: "My sheep hear my voice, and I know them, and they follow me: And I give unto them eternal life; and they shall never perish" (John 10:27-28). What greater reliability can we have than the authority of his Word?

Illustration
Illustrate how this sense of reliability comes through resting upon the Word of God.

B. *The Finality of His Work*

"My sheep hear my voice, and I know them, and they follow me" (John 10:27). In that phrase, "I know them," is gathered up the redemptive act by which he has made possible the salvation of every believing man or woman.

Exegesis
Explain verses 14-18 to show what it cost God to secure our salvation.

III. The Sense of New Life Is a Divine Reassurance

"I give unto [my sheep] . . . eternal life; and they shall never perish, neither shall any man pluck them out of my hand. My Father, which gave them me, is greater than all; and no man is able to pluck them out of my Father's hand" (John 10:28-29). Two hands are referred to in these verses. The one is the Savior's hand, and the other is the Father's hand. How completely reassuring it is to know that once we become related to the Son of God we are held not only by the hand of our wonderful Shepherd, but also by the hand of our heavenly Father. Notice the significance of these hands:

A. *The Savior's Hand of Saving Grace*

"I give unto [my sheep] . . . eternal life; and they shall never perish, neither shall any man pluck them out of my hand" (John 10:28). This is the pierced hand that has been stretched out to lay hold of us in saving grace.

Illustration

Holman Hunt has beautifully depicted this aspect of the saving grace of Jesus. He has painted the Good Shepherd bending over a precipitous rock in order to lift the lost and wounded sheep from imminent danger and death. As you examine the picture, you can see the marks on his hands and feet from the thorns and briars. Love and tenderness are written all over his face. But the supreme message of the painting is that of the firm grip of the Shepherd's saving hand. Here is true security!

B. *The Father's Hand of Sovereign Choice*

"My Father, which gave them me, is greater than all; and no man is able to pluck them out of my Father's hand. I and my Father are one" (John 10:29-30, KJV). Here is a glorious fact. Long before the worlds were thrown into orbit and the universe was established by an act of the divine will, God, in sovereign grace, chose everyone who would respond to the call of the Shepherd's voice. Paul puts it succinctly when he says,

> Blessed be the God and Father of our Lord Jesus Christ, who hath blessed us with all spiritual blessings in heavenly places in Christ: According as he hath chosen us in him before the foundation of the world, that we should be holy and without blame before him in love (Eph. 1:3-4, KJV).

If God in his foreknowledge has laid his hand upon me, can I have any doubt whatsoever about eternal security?

Illustration

Evangelist Tom Rees tells of an occasion when he led a dear lad from the slums of London to a saving experience of Jesus Christ. The time came for the boy to return to his difficult home and surroundings. To give the boy some reassurance, the evangelist read the verses we have been considering and explained something of the meaning of that safe hand of Jesus Christ. "But," remarked the boy, with typical wit, "supposing I slip through his fingers?" "Ah, but that's impossible!" said Tom Rees, "for when the Savior laid hold of you, you *became* one of His fingers!"

Conclusion

Here, then, is the offer of eternal security. Will you receive Christ and enter into the joy of this living and lasting relationship? Then you can sing:

> His for ever, only His:/Who the Lord and me shall part?/Ah, with what a rest of bliss/Christ can fill the loving heart./ Heaven and earth may fade and flee,/First-born light in gloom decline;/But, while God and I shall be,/I am His, and He is mine.
> W. Robinson

10

The Signs of the New Life

1 John 2:29; 3:9; 4:7; 5:1, 4, 18

"If ye know that he is righteous, ye know that every one
that doeth righteousness is born of him ....Beloved, let us
love one another: for love is of God; and every one that
loveth is born of God, and knoweth God ....Whosoever
believeth that Jesus is the Christ is born of God: and
every one that loveth him that begat loveth him also that
is begotten of him" (1 John 2:29; 4:7; 5:1, KJV).

Introduction

Scientists tell us that "life is correspondence to environment."
This is true of all forms of life. Where there is no correspondence (that is, no outward expression of life) there is death.
The New Testament has a lot to say about the signs of this new
life. The apostle John in his first epistle helps us to understand
three important evidences of being born again:

I. A New Certainty in Christ

"Whosoever believeth that Jesus is the Christ is born of God"

(1 John 5:1). Believing means more than just an intellectual assent to the facts concerning the Messiahship of Jesus. The apostle James tells us that "the [demons] also believe, and tremble" (James 2:19, KJV). In other words, there are no unbelievers in hell. The essential difference is that their intellectual belief never became a saving faith in Jesus Christ. When a person truly believes, in the gospel sense, Christian certainty follows, and our text says, "Whosoever believeth that Jesus is the Christ is born of God" (1 John 5:1).

The title "Christ" is important here. It means "Messiah" or "Anointed One." It is a term which applied to prophets (Ps. 105:15), priests (Lev. 4:3), and kings (Ps. 2:2) in Old Testament times. When applied to the Lord Jesus, the title encompasses all these offices in one complete and infinite sense, for as Prophet, Priest, and King, Christ transcends the prophets, priests, and kings of all the ages.

Amplification

Amplify these three offices to show the certainty of the revelation of Christ as prophet, the mediation of Christ as priest, and the supervision of Christ as king.

II. A New Loyalty to Christ

"Every one that loveth is born of God" (1 John 4:7). And the apostle John leaves us in no doubt as to how such love expresses itself. To be born of God means:

A. A Loyalty of Love to the Son of God

"We love him, because he first loved us" (1 John 4:19). To know experientially what it means to be born again is to fall in love with the Son of God. Love has been defined as the desire for and delight in the person and interests of the one loved. When applied to Jesus Christ, this means a desire for, and a delight in, the person and purposes of the Son of God.

Illustration

A missionary was once visiting the Yorkshire moors in

England. While there, he was told of a godly old shepherd who had been minding the sheep on those moors. The missionary wanted to meet the old man and started to look for him. He soon found him among his sheep, and walking up to him said, "Brother, may I shake hands with you? I hear you love the Lord Jesus." "Yes, sir," replied the shepherd, "I love the Lord Jesus, and me and him's very thick." Could you say that? Are you on such intimate terms with the Lord Jesus?

B. A Loyalty of Love to the Word of God

"Whoso keepeth his word, in him verily is the love of God perfected" (1 John 2:5). Love for God must always be measured by obedience to his Word. The Savior summed this up when he said, "If ye love me, keep my commandments" (John 14:15, KJV). King David's profound regard for the Word of God is beautifully expressed in the longest Psalm he ever wrote. He says, "O how love I thy law! It is my meditation all the day"; and again: "I love thy commandments above gold; yea, above fine gold" (119:97, 127, KJV).

Amplification

Amplify by developing such questions as, Do you value the Word of God? Do you read it, obey it, live it, and preach it?

C. A Loyalty of Love to the Church of God

"Every one that loveth him that begat loveth him also that is begotten of him" (1 John 5:1). This means that if we are truly born again we cannot help loving those who share our common life in Christ. Jesus said, "By this shall all men know that ye are my disciples, if ye have love one to another" (John 13:35, KJV). Such love must not be confused with sentimentality or infatuation. On the contrary, it is a very sacrificial (1 John 3:16) and practical (1 John 3:17) thing.

Illustration

In an engine room it is impossible to look into the great

boiler and see how much water it contains. But attached to the boiler is a tiny glass tube that serves as a gauge. As the water stands in the little tube, so it stands in the great boiler. When the tube is half full, the boiler is half full; when the tube is empty, the boiler is empty. If you want to know how much you love God, look at the gauge. Your love for your brother is the measure of your love for God.

III. A New Victory in Christ

"Every one that *doeth* righteousness is born of him" (1 John 2:29). By nature, we are incapable of doing righteousness. The Bible says, "There is none righteous, no, not one . . . there is none that doeth good" (Rom. 3:10, 12, KJV). But when the miracle of the new birth takes place all that is changed; we become "partakers of the divine nature" (2 Pet. 1:4, KJV), and instead of living defeated lives we begin to live victorious lives. We enjoy:

A. Victory over Sin

"Whosoever is born of God doth not commit sin" (1 John 3:9). The better reading here is "Whosoever is born of God does not practice sin." In other words, a born-again person does not continue willfully in sin because he is possessed of a divine nature that abhors sin. Therefore, as he feeds the new nature and counts upon it for victory, he finds it to be the liberating power of God over his old sinful nature. Thereafter, failure only occurs when the old nature is allowed to dominate; otherwise, it is victory all along the way!

Illustration
Illustrate how to starve the old nature and how to feed the new.

B. Victory over Self

"[Whosoever] is born of God overcometh the world" (1 John 5:4). In this epistle John teaches that the world, for the believer, is the lust of the flesh, the lust of the eyes, and the pride of life (1 John 2:16). In a word, this is self—that subtle, assertive ego within us that mars the home, splits the church, and ruins the world. So a very evident sign of the new life is the indwelling power which conquers the self-life. This involves more than overcoming sin. Sin is the outcome of conceived lust. So, to conquer and control the inner self-life is to forestall sin in its outworking. This victory which overcomes the self-life is the faith which hands over the lust and pride of our self-centeredness to the control of the indwelling Christ.

C. Victory over Satan

"Whosoever is born of God sinneth not; but he that is begotten of God keepeth himself, and that wicked one toucheth him not" (1 John 5:18). Here is the supreme mark of the new life. Very simply, it is overcoming the evil one. Satan may and does assault, but he need never hold us down. We can defeat him through faith in the indwelling Son of God who was manifested "that he might destroy the works of the devil" (3:8). Every truly born-again person can say with confidence, "Greater is he that is in. . . [me], than he that is in the world" (4:4).

Conclusion

Here, then, are the vital signs of new life in Christ: first, a certainty in Christ; second, a loyalty to Christ; and third, a victory in Christ. Are these signs evident in your life or are you living a lie? If so, quit shamming and trust Christ as your prophet, priest, and king. Open the door of your heart and let him in, and trust him to reproduce in you the signs of his new life.

11

The Steps of the New Life

Romans 6:1-14

"Therefore we are buried with him by baptism into death: that like as Christ was raised up from the dead by the glory of the Father, even so we also should walk in newness of life" (Romans 6:4, KJV).

Introduction

Many figures of speech are used to describe the Christian life. Sometimes it is called a fight, and we think of the soldier in his armor with a sword in his hand. Or the Christian is depicted as an athlete—boxing or running. But perhaps the most frequent picture is that of a walker. Seven times over in the Epistle to the Ephesians the believer is told how to *walk* in Christ. The walk suggests action, direction, and destination. The important thing about a walk, however, is that it is the extension of a step. Every journey starts with the first step, and we must never forget that. Paul reminds us that "as [we] . . . have . . . received Christ Jesus the Lord, so [we are to] walk in him" and again, we are to: "walk in newness of life" (Col. 2:6, KJV; Rom. 6:4). From Romans 6 we learn about:

I. The Steps in the New Life of Liberation

"He that is dead is freed from sin" (Rom. 6:7). This chapter opens with a question, "Shall we continue in sin, that grace may abound?" (v. 1). In other words, is the grace of God an excuse for sinning? Now this is an important issue that we must face if we are to understand the new life in Christ. There are those who believe that as long as they confess their sins to a priest, or a pastor, they can live as they please. Paul condemns this outright. He exclaims, "God forbid. How shall we, that are dead to sin, live any longer therein?" (v. 2). In other words, the pathway of liberation is not to continue in sin, but rather to live in victory. And so he declares, "He that is dead is freed from sin" (v. 7).

A. The Death of Christ Brings Liberty from the Penalty of Sin

"Know ye not, that so many of us as were baptized into Jesus Christ were baptized into his death?" (Rom. 6:3).

To be united to Jesus Christ through simple faith is to be free from the penalty of sin. Christ died for our sins in order that we might not die. He took the punishment we deserved in order that we might not be punished. To understand this is to be liberated from the wages of sin.

Illustration

Behind the platform of Faneuil Hall, Boston, stands a large painting of Webster's debate with Hayne inscribed "Union and Liberty, one and inseparable, now and forever." Preaching in this hall, General William Booth of the Salvation Army concluded his sermon with a dramatic peroration. Turning to the painting, he cried: "'Union and liberty'—unity with Christ and liberty from sin— 'one and inseparable, now and forever!'" The one standard against sin's thralldom is union with the living Christ. There is no spiritual liberty apart from this union.

B. The Death of Christ Brings Liberty from the Cruelty of Sin

"Therefore we are buried with him by baptism into death"

(Rom. 6:4). The Lord Jesus was not only put to death, he was also buried. This is why Paul spells out the Gospel by saying, "Christ died for our sins according to the scriptures; And that he was buried, and that he rose again the third day according to the scriptures" (1 Cor. 15:3-4, KJV). This matter of Christ's burial is often overlooked in our preaching, but in Paul's mind there was clearly a divine purpose in the burial of Christ. Not only did it certify his death, and therefore enhance the full significance of his resurrection, but it robbed sin of its cruelty. The grave is a cruel place. Solomon says that "jealousy is cruel as the grave" (Song 8:6, KJV), but since the burial of Christ we can say with Paul, "O death, where is thy sting? O grave, where is thy victory?" (1 Cor. 15:55, KJV). To be united with Christ by faith in his burial is to be liberated from the cruelty of sin.

C. The Death of Christ Brings Liberty from the Slavery of Sin
"Like as Christ was raised up from the dead by the glory of the Father, even so we also should walk in newness of life . . . . Knowing this, that our old man is crucified with him, that the body of sin might be destroyed, that henceforth we should not serve sin" (Rom. 6:4, 6). The secret of victory over sin in all of its subtle and multiple forms is that we can be united by faith to a Christ who rose from the dead to become our indwelling Savior and deliverer. This is what Paul means when he says, "I am crucified with Christ: nevertheless I live; yet not I, but Christ liveth in me" (Gal. 2:20, KJV). By his indwelling power Christ can save us, moment by moment, from the slavery of sin.

Illustration
Madam Guyon wrote prolifically in prison in France for her Savior's sake. This cultured, refined, educated, and (until smitten with smallpox) exceedingly beautiful woman spent ten years of her life in various French prisons between 1695-1705. Here are some of her words:

My cage confines me round;/Abroad I cannot fly;/But though my wing is closely bound,/My heart's at liberty./My prison walls cannot control/The flight, the freedom of the soul./Oh, it's good to soar/These

*bolts and bars above,/To Him whose purpose I adore,/Whose provi-
dence I love;/And in Thy mighty will to find/The joy, the freedom of
the mind.*

II. The Steps in the New Life of Dedication

"Yield yourselves unto God, as those that are alive from the
dead, and your members as instruments of righteousness unto
God" (Rom. 6:13). Paul is here using language that would be
well understood by his readers in Rome, a city filled with
wickedness, corruption, and sin. He makes clear that the steps
of the new life of dedication must involve two things:

A. *The Dethronement of Sin*

"Let not sin therefore reign in your mortal body, that ye
should obey it in the lusts thereof" (Rom. 6:12). Personifying
sin as a king, the apostle says, "Don't let sin reign in your mortal body." In other words, set your mind, heart, and will against
the attempt of sin to occupy the throne of your heart. This
does not mean that we lose our sinful nature while here upon
earth. That will happen only when we get to heaven; but it
does teach that sin must no longer have dominion over us
(v.14). Sin may be dormant but it need not be dominant; sin
may be the slave in our lives without being the master. But we
must resolutely determine that sin will not rule and reign in
our hearts and lives.

Illustration

A father and his small son were walking one evening in the
quiet village. Suddenly the boy's voice piped, "Daddy, don't
look, just come closer to me, 'cause there's something dirty
on the sidewalk." Isn't that a lesson for us Christians as we
walk through this defiled world! We know things are there—
vain things, unclean things, filthy things. God tells us they are
in the world—but we don't have to look at them. Just as that
boy refused to be contaminated with the filth of the sidewalk,
so we must dethrone sin in our lives.

B. *The Enthronement of God*

"Yield yourselves unto God" (Rom. 6:13). This is both an initial act and a continual attitude. It is the handing over of our total personalities to the sovereignty and authority of God in our lives.

Illustration

I remember so clearly when this happened in my own life. I had been a Christian for some time, but had never understood the meaning of full surrender until God showed me the utter wastefulness and uselessness of a life lived for self. Jesus Christ is Lord, whether we like to admit it or not, and he will see to it that we submit to that Lordship, even if it means chastening us, in order to make us what he wants us to be. Only when God is enthroned in the person of his Son, Jesus Christ, can we know true deliverance and victory. Let me ask you: Is every part of your life yielded—your spirit, soul, and body? The verse says, "Yield yourselves unto God . . . and your members as instruments of righteousness unto God" (Rom. 6:13). That means your eyes, your ears, your lips, your hands, your feet, your all.

These are the important steps in the life of dedication—the dethronement of self and the enthronement of God.

III. The Steps in the New Life of Occupation

"But now being made free from sin, and become servants to God, ye have your fruit unto holiness, and the end everlasting life" (Rom. 6:22). Having declared that the Christian is a liberated and dedicated person, Paul proceeds to show that the Christian is someone who occupies his time in the service of the kingdom. So he points out further steps in the new life of occupation:

A. *A Loyal Servant Must Own His Master*

"Know ye not, that to whom ye yield yourselves servants to obey, his servants ye are to whom ye obey; whether of sin unto death, or of obedience unto righteousness?" (Rom. 6:16). Quite clearly, two masters are personified in the words "sin" and "obedience." As servants, we must choose our master and then serve him. If we choose Christ, then we must serve him and no other. Jesus laid down this principle when he declared, "No man can serve two masters" (Matt. 6:24, KJV). The tragedy is that so many Christians have this double loyalty. Instead of accepting their union with Christ in death, burial, and resurrection, and therefore rejoicing in their liberty in Christ for service and fruitfulness, they become spurners of the grace of God and shirkers in the church of God. The true servant of Jesus Christ is the person who has declared, before witnesses, that he is committed to his Master forever.

Illustration

Illustrate the master/servant relationship as recorded in Exodus 21:1-6.

B. A Loyal Servant Must Obey His Master

"But God be thanked, that ye were the servants of sin, but ye have obeyed from the heart that form of doctrine which was delivered [unto] you" (Rom. 6:17). In the Greek New Testament there are six words that are translated "servant," and it is significant that the one Paul selects to describe the believer in this passage is the term translated "slave" or "bond-slave." Without doubt, Paul had in mind the thousands of slaves who were in the city of Rome. To such, the very word would stir up a sense of horror if used without some qualification. But in these verses Paul takes up this word and associates it with the Lord Jesus Christ. The Savior called himself the bondslave of God. So the apostle loved to call himself a bond-slave of Jesus Christ. In this sense, Paul not only retrieved the word, but redeemed it. He took all the bitterness out of it, not only for the slaves of Rome, but for every Christian throughout succeeding centuries. When he speaks of obedience to the Master he means an obedience of love.

Amplification

Show that obedience must be rendered in terms of doctrine
(Rom. 6:17) and duty (v. 22).

Conclusion

So we see what it means to walk in newness of life. It involves
steps in the life of liberation, dedication, and occupation.
Have you started this walk? Remember, it begins with the first
step—stepping out of yourself into Christ. This means repentance, faith, and obedience—turning from yourself, trusting
in Christ, and then taking this new life of Christian liberation,
dedication, and occupation. Will you take this step right now?
If you will, new life will truly begin.

12

The Strength of the New Life

Philippians 4:1-13

"I can do all things through Christ which
strengtheneth me" (Phil. 4:13, KJV).

Introduction

This is one of the most exciting verses in all the Bible. Paul is
in prison, chained to soldiers, and awaiting trial and impend-
ing death. In spite of these circumstances, however, he could
write one of his happiest letters and conclude with the words
that we have chosen for our text. He says:

I have learned, in whatsoever state I am, therewith to be content. I know both how to be abased, and I know how to abound:
every where and in all things I am instructed both to be full and
to be hungry, both to abound and to suffer need. *I can do all
things through Christ which strengtheneth me* (see Phil. 4:11-13).

Paul had discovered the strength of new life in Christ. In
every situation and circumstance he had proved Christ to be
more than adequate; indeed, he claimed he could do all
things through Christ who strengthened him.

Here is a secret we cannot afford to overlook or ignore. Let us examine Paul's statement and find out what was, in fact, the supernatural secret that he discovered in Christ.

I. The Strength of a Satisfied Life in Christ

"I have learned, in whatsoever state I am, therewith to be content" (Phil. 4:11). Contentment in Christ was the reward of spiritual discipline. No matter what state Paul was in, he was content because he knew how to apply the laws of spiritual discipline. He accepted adversity with cheerful resignation, he respected prosperity with careful moderation; in both states he was content because his ultimate satisfaction was centered in Christ. His attitude toward life is beautifully summed up in the words we find in the Hebrew epistle: "Be content with such things as ye have: for he hath said, I will never leave thee, nor forsake thee" (13:5, KJV). His contentment was not an insensible stoicism, but rather a disciplined adjustment to life, by the power of the indwelling Christ.

Illustration
The story is told of a child of wealthy parents who was brought to a wonderful old Christian who lived in abject poverty. For a few moments he looked at the little girl. Then gently stroking her lovely blonde curls he said, "My child, may God make this world as beautiful to you as it has been to me." Like Paul, this dear old saint knew the secret and strength of satisfaction in Christ.

A. *Physical Satisfaction in Christ*

"I have learned, in whatsoever state I am, therewith to be content" (Phil. 4:11). Let us remember that Paul carried to his death an affliction which he described as "a thorn in the flesh" (2 Cor. 12:7, KJV), and yet he triumphed.

Amplification
Expound on 2 Corinthians 12:7-9.

B. *Spiritual Satisfaction in Christ*

"I have learned, in whatsoever state I am, therewith to be content" (Phil. 4:11). Earlier in this same letter he could say, "For me to live is Christ" (1:21), or more literally, "For me, living itself is Christ." He knew the difference between living and existing.

Illustration

A bishop was contented and cheerful through a long period of trial and was asked the secret of his contentment. He said, "I will tell you. I made right use of my eyes." "Please explain." "Most willingly," was the answer.

"First I look up to heaven and remember that my principal business is to get there. Then I look down upon the earth and think how small a place I shall occupy when I am dead and buried. Then I look around and see the many who are in all respects much worse off than I am. Then I remember where true happiness lies, where all our cares end, and how little reason I have to complain."

The bishop had learned in whatsoever state he was, therewith to be content.

II. The Strength of an Edified Life in Christ

Paul says: "I know both how to be abased, and I know how to abound: everywhere and in all things *I am instructed* both to be full and to be hungry, both to abound and to suffer need" (Phil. 4:12). Literally, that sentence reads: "I have been taught the secret." As someone has put it, Paul, the slave of Christ, was led to a mastery over circumstances, which made him a king. He could face adversity, but, more importantly, he could face prosperity.

A. *Maturity in Times of Adversity*

"I know . . . how to be abased" (Phil. 4:12). We live in a world where nothing is stable. Overnight we may lose everything we possess. Tragedy may strike because of a tornado, a burglary, a revolution, terrorism, and so on. The question is, are we able to face disasters of this kind with quiet maturity? Have we been edified "both to be full and to be hungry, both to abound and to suffer need" (Phil. 4:12)? Only as we sit at the feet of Jesus can we learn this secret.

Illustration
Illustrate by using the example of Job (Job 13:15).

B. Humility in Times of Prosperity

"I know how to abound" (Phil. 4:12). Though Paul dictated this letter in a Roman dungeon, he also knew what it was to live in wealthy homes. Many times he had enjoyed the luxury and hospitality of generous hosts. In certain circles he was one of the most respected men of his day, and yet the extraordinary thing was that he never lost his head. He was so edified in Christ that he knew Christ's humility. Earlier in this epistle he deals with this in great depth and richness. He says: "Let this mind be in you, which was also in Christ Jesus: Who, being in the form of God, thought it not robbery to be equal with God: But made himself of no reputation, and took upon him the form of a servant, and was made in the likeness of men: And being found in fashion as a man, he humbled himself, and became obedient unto death, even the death of the cross" (2:5-8).

Illustration
Cite examples from your own experience of those who have been exalted and yet remained humble.

III. The Strength of a Fortified Life in Christ

"I can do all things through Christ which strengtheneth me" (Phil. 4:13). Another version has it: "I am strong for all things in the One who constantly infuses strength in me" (Kenneth S. Wuest, *The New Testament: An Expanded Translation.* Grand Rapids: Eerdmans, 1961. Reprinted 1994). To be able to say and mean "I can do all things through Christ which strengtheneth me" is to know the very essence of Christian living.

Although the context here indicates that Paul meant that he was able to cope with any given situation, the principle implicit in this great utterance may be extended to include God's enabling for any and all Christian responsibilities. To know the conscious and continual power of the indwelling Christ guarantees:

A. Strength to Live Faithfully

"Therefore, my brethren . . . stand fast in the Lord" (Phil. 4:1).

B. Strength to Live Joyfully

"Rejoice in the Lord always: and again I say, Rejoice" (v. 4).

C. Strength to Live Helpfully

"Let your moderation be known unto all men. The Lord is at hand" (v. 5). Etymologically, moderation means "that yielding-ness which urges not its own rights to the uttermost."

D. Strength to Live Prayerfully

"Be careful for nothing; but in every thing by prayer and supplication with thanksgiving let your requests be made known unto God" (v. 6).

E. Strength to Live Thankfully

"With thanksgiving let your requests be made known unto God" (v. 6).

F. Strength to Live Peacefully

"And the peace of God, which passeth all understanding, shall keep your hearts and minds through Christ Jesus" (v. 7).

G. Strength to Live Thoughtfully

"Finally, brethren, whatsoever things are true, whatsoever things are honest, whatsoever things are just, whatsoever things are pure, whatsoever things are lovely, whatsoever things are of good report; if there be any virtue, and if there be any praise, think on these things" (v. 8).

Amplification
Amplify these seven points to round off the sermon and illustrate, where necessary.

Conclusion

So the challenge of this message confronts us with the only one in the universe who can satisfy, edify, and fortify our lives with supernatural strength. If you don't know him already in your life, this wonderful Christ stands before you and says, "Behold, I stand at the door, and knock" (Rev. 3:20, KJV). If you let him in he will become the very strength of your life—the strength which satisfies, edifies, and fortifies for any situation or circumstance of life. Don't reject him. Rather, accept him and obey him as Savior and Lord of your life.

13

The Scope of the New Life

2 Peter 3:1-14

"Nevertheless we, according to his promise, look for
new heavens and a new earth, wherein dwelleth
righteousness" (2 Pet. 3:13, KJV).

Introduction

Millions of people in every land are anxiously looking into the future and wondering what it holds in store for them. Parents are concerned about their children, and young people want to know what awaits them in a world that is confused and desperate. The blind optimism of former days is gone, and thinking people are beginning to see the utter emptiness of any form of human utopianism. Someone recently put it, "A survey of the world leaves one with the uncomfortable feeling that, in spite of the efforts of many well-intentioned men in every country, civilization is sliding downhill." That, in a few sentences, is the story of our modern world. And a hopeless story it is, were it not for the Christian message, for it is into this very context that Peter's words fit with profound significance. "We," says he, "according to . . . [Christ's] promise, look for new heavens and a new earth, wherein dwelleth righteousness" (2 Pet. 3:13). God's answer to world chaos is the coming new world. This is the scope of the new life.

I. The Promise of the Coming New World

"We, according to his promise, look for new heavens and a new earth" (2 Pet. 3:13). Earlier in this chapter Peter says, "I stir up your pure minds by way of remembrance: That ye may be mindful of the words which were spoken before by the holy prophets, and of the commandment of us the apostles of the Lord and Saviour" (vv. 1-2). The apostle here reminds his readers that the subject of the coming again of Jesus Christ was no new truth. In general terms, the prophets of old had already foretold it, and it had been described in more specific terms by the apostles who followed. In other words, the promise of the coming new world was both foretold and foreshadowed in Holy Scripture.

A. The Promise Foretold

"The words which were spoken before by the holy prophets (2 Pet. 3:2). From Genesis to Malachi there are no less than 333 direct prophecies concerning our Lord's first coming, and scholars tell us that there are at least double that number relating to his second coming.

Amplification
Draw on Old Testament prophecies to support the second advent.

B. The Promise Foreshadowed

"We, according to his promise, look for new heavens and a new earth" (2 Pet. 3:13). Peter answers the scoffers who say, "Where is the promise of his coming? For since the fathers fell asleep, all things continue as they were from the beginning of creation" (v. 4). The point that Peter makes three times over is that God is absolutely precise in all his timing.

Amplification

Amplify a) the timing of God's act of creation (2 Pet. 3:5); b) the timing of God's act of destruction (v. 6); and c) the timing of God's act of redemption (v. 9).

II. The Purpose of the Coming New World

"We . . . look for new heavens and a new earth, wherein dwelleth righteousness" (2 Pet. 3:13). In what is known as the prophetic present, Peter uses language in this paragraph to anticipate the fulfillment of God's prophetic program. In God's purpose for the coming new world Peter sees a three-fold design:

A. A Personal Design

"We, according to his promise, look" (2 Pet. 3:13). Here we glimpse Christ's personal design to fulfill the expectations of his own people, who look for the new world.

Illustration

At night, as Dr. Horatius Bonar retired to rest, his last action before he lay down to sleep was to draw aside the curtain and look into the starry sky and say, "Perhaps tonight, Lord?" In the morning, as he arose, his first movement was to raise the blinds, look out upon the gray dawn and remark, "Perhaps today, Lord?"

B. A Punitive Design

"New heavens and a new earth" (2 Pet. 3:13). This presupposes the dissolving of the old heavens and earth. Until recently, those who talked about the end of the world were termed "cranks" and "religious fanatics." Today, the scoffing has ended. Men have covered their mouths. Indeed, the philosophers, politicians, and scientists themselves have become the prophets of doom.

Illustration

In September, 1946, Sir Winston Churchill (then Mr.

Churchill) shook the world with this statement: "It may well be that, in a few years, the atom bomb will not only ring an end to all that we can call civilization, but may disintegrate the globe itself." Update this prediction with the facts as we know them today.

C. A Permanent Design

"New heavens and a new earth, wherein dwelleth righteousness" (2 Pet. 3:13). Christ's permanent design, in the new world, is a lasting habitation of righteousness. "Behold, I make all things new" (Rev. 21:5, KJV), he says, and he will surely fulfill his Word.

Illustration
Illustrate how Lot fled to a city of refuge after Sodom and Gomorrah were destroyed by the fires of wrath.

III. The People of the Coming New World

"Seeing then that all these things shall be dissolved, what manner of persons ought ye to be in all holy conversation and godliness, Looking for and hasting unto the coming of the day of God" (2 Pet. 3:11-12). When Peter says, "What manner of men ought ye to be?" he is describing the people of the new world. The construction of the sentence implies that the state in which such people are to be found is one that has continued for some time before the day arrives.

A. They Must Be Holy

"What manner of persons ought ye to be in all holy conversation [or life]" (2 Pet. 3:11). Holiness is both a gift and a process. It is a good gift from God in Christ; it is also a process to be worked out in daily life.

Amplification
Expound on such verses as 1 Corinthians 1:30, Hebrews 12:14, and 1 Peter 1:14, 15.

B. They Must Be Godly

"What manner of persons ought ye to be in . . . godliness" (2 Pet.3:11). Godliness is the realization of God's abiding presence, resulting in God-likeness.

Amplification
Amplify by using such verses as Psalm 4:3, 2 Timothy 3:12, Titus 2:12, and Hebrews 12:28.

C. They Must Be Busy

"What manner of persons ought ye to be . . . Looking for and hasting unto the coming of the day of God" (2 Pet. 3:11-12). There is no "unto" in the original. The sense of the verse is rather "hastening the coming" (NKJV) by winning souls to Christ through the spread of the Gospel.

Amplification
Amplify the ways and means by which we could speed the work of the Gospel.

Conclusion

The world stands on the brink of total destruction. With the passing of the Cold War, new threats of mass destruction loom. Despit efforts to avoid destruction, one thing is painfully clear:

> The world is very evil,/The times are waxing late;/Be sober, then, and watchful—/The Judge is at the gate! (*The World Is Very Evil*, by Bernard of Morias [12th c.]; translated by Robert J. Pearsall, 1863)

Are you going to be judged and destroyed with the old world, or are you going to be saved and included in the new world? Oh, that your response might be:

> Make me holy by Thy blood,/Make me godly, Lamb of God;/Keep me busy in the fray,/ Make me ready for "that day."

Stephen F. Olford

ENDNOTES

Chapter 1

1. Adapted and reprinted from *The Word for Every Day* by Alvin N. Rogness, copyright © 1981 Augsburg Publishing House, p. 156. Used by permission of Augsburg Fortress.

2. Paul R. Van Gorder, *Our Daily Bread* (Grand Rapids: Radio Bible Class), adapted.

Chapter 2

1. Ralph Waldo Emerson, quoted in Paul Lee Tan, *Encyclopedia of 7,700 Illustrations* (Dallas: Bible Communications, 1979), p. 647.

2. Henry G. Bosch, quoted in ibid.

3. Copyright 1915. Renewal 1943 by Hope Publishing Company, Carol Stream, Illinois. All rights reserved. Used by permission. (See www.cyberhymnal.org.)

Chapter 3

1. Tan, p. 186.

2. Copyrighted, March 4, 1982 Chicago Tribune Company, all rights reserved, used with permission.

Chapter 4

1. James Montgomery Boice, *Does Inerrancy Matter?* Published by the International Council on Biblical Inerrancy, and used by permission of Evangelical Ministries, Inc., 1716 Spruce Street, Philadelphia, PA 19103.

FOR FURTHER READING

Part 1: Christian Evidence

Anderson, James Norman Dalrymple. *Jesus Christ: The Witness of History*. Downers Grove, Ill.: InterVarsity Press, 1984.

Anderson, Robert. *The Lord from Heaven*. Grand Rapids: Kregel Publications, 1978.

Bavinck, Herman. *The Doctrine of God*. Trans. William Hendriksen. Edinburgh: Banner of Truth Trust, 1977.

Baxter, James Sidlow. *Majesty: The God You Should Know*. San Bernardino, Calif.: Here's Life Publishers, 1984.

Blailock, E. M. *Jesus Christ, Man or Myth?* Nashville: Thomas Nelson Publishers, 1984.

Boice, James Montgomery. *The Sovereign God*. Vol. 1. Foundations of the Christian Faith. Downers Grove, Ill.: InterVarsity Press, 1978.

——————. *Standing on the Rock*. Wheaton, Ill.: Tyndale House Publishers, 1984.

Bruce, F. F. *Jesus and Christian Origins Outside the New Testament*. Grand Rapids: Wm. B. Eerdmans Publishing Co., 1974.

Carroll, Benajah Harvey. *Inspiration of the Bible*. Nashville: Thomas Nelson Publishers, 1980.

Clark, Gordon Haddon. *God's Hammer: The Bible and Its Critics*. Jefferson, Md.: Trinity Foundation, 1982.

——————. *The Trinity*. Jefferson, Md.: Trinity Foundation, 1985.

France, R. T. *The Living God*. Downers Grove, Ill.: InterVarsity Press, 1973.

Haldane, Robert. *The Authenticity and Inspiration of the Holy Scriptures*. Minneapolis: Klock and Klock Christian Publishers, 1985.

Hogan, Ronald F. *The God of Glory*. Neptune, N.J.: Loizeaux Brothers, Inc., 1984.

Law, Peter W. *A Portrait of My Father: The Wonder of Knowing God*. Portland, Ore.: Multnomah Press, 1985.

Lawlor, George. *When God Became Man.* Chicago: Moody Press, 1978.

Liddon, Henry Parry. *The Divinity of Our Lord and Saviour Jesus Christ.* Minneapolis: Klock and Klock Christian Publishers, 1978.

Lightner, Robert Paul. *The First Fundamental: God.* Nashville: Thomas Nelson Publishers, 1973.

——————. *The God of the Bible: An Introduction to the Doctrine of God.* Grand Rapids: Baker Book House, 1978.

Lindsell, Harold. *The Battle for the Bible.* Grand Rapids: Zondervan Publishing House, 1976.

MacArthur, John F., Jr. *Why Believe the Bible?* Ventura, Calif.: Regal Books, 1980.

M'Intosh, Hugh. *Is Christ Infallible and the Bible True?* Minneapolis: Klock and Klock Christian Publishers, 1981.

Morris, Henry M. *The Genesis Record: A Scientific and Devotional Commentary on the Book of Beginnings.* Grand Rapids: Baker Book House, 1976.

Packer, James I. *Knowing God.* Downers Grove, Ill.: InterVarsity Press, 1973.

Radmacher, Earl D., ed. *Can We Trust the Bible?* Wheaton, Ill.: Tyndale House Publishers, 1979.

Robertson, A. T. *The Divinity of Christ in the Gospel of John.* 1916. Reprint. 1 vol. Grand Rapids: Zondervan Publishing House, 1975.

Sanders, J. Oswald. *The Incomparable Christ.* Chicago: Moody Press, 1971.

Saphir, Adolph. *Divine Unity of Scripture.* Grand Rapids: Kregel Publications, 1984.

Smail, Thomas Allan. *The Forgotten Father.* Grand Rapids: Wm. B. Eerdmans Publishing Co., 1981.

Stott, John R. W. *The Authentic Jesus: The Centrality of Christ in a Skeptical World.* Downers Grove, Ill.: InterVarsity Press, 1985.

Tenney, Merrill C. *John: The Gospel of Belief.* Grand Rapids: Wm. B. Eerdmans Publishing Co., 1969.

Toon, Peter. *God Here and Now: The Christian View of God.* Wheaton, Ill.: Tyndale House Publishers, 1979.

Toon, Peter, and James D. Spiceland, eds. *One God in Trinity.* Westchester, Ill.: Cornerstone Books, 1980.

Vine, W. E. *The Divine Sonship of Christ.* 2 vols. in 1. Minneapolis: Klock and Klock Christian Publishers, 1984.

Part 2: New Life for You

Anderson, Robert. *Redemption Truths.* Grand Rapids: Kregel Publications, 1980.

Barker, Harold. *Secure Forever.* Neptune, N.J.: Loizeaux Brothers, Inc., 1974.

Baxter, James Sidlow. *God So Loved.* Grand Rapids: Zondervan Publishing House, 1960.

—————. *His Part and Ours.* Grand Rapids: Zondervan Publishing House, 1964.

Boice, James Montgomery. *Awakening to God.* Vol. 3. Foundations of the Christian Life. Downers Grove, Ill.: InterVarsity Press, 1979.

Chafer, Lewis Sperry. *Grace.* Grand Rapids: Zondervan Publishing House, 1965.

—————. *Salvation.* Grand Rapids: Zondervan Publishing House, 1965.

Clark, Gordon Haddon. *Faith and Saving Faith.* Jefferson, Md.: Trinity Foundation, 1983.

Denney, James. *The Biblical Doctrine of Reconciliation.* Minneapolis: Klock and Klock Christian Publishers, 1985.

Erickson, Millard John, ed. *Salvation: God's Amazing Plan.* Wheaton, Ill.: Victor Books, 1978.

Graham, William Franklin. *Peace with God.* Waco, Texas: Word Books, 1984.

Gromacki, Robert Glenn. *Salvation Is Forever.* Chicago: Moody Press, 1974.

Holliday, John Francis. *Life From Above: The Need for Emphasis on Biblical Regeneration.* London: Marshall, Morgan & Scott, 1957.

Horne, Charles M. *Salvation*. Chicago: Moody Press, 1971.

Hoyt, Herman Arthur. *Expository Messages on the New Birth.* Grand Rapids: Baker Book House, 1961.

Kevan, Ernest Frederick. *Salvation*. Grand Rapids: Baker Book House, 1963.

SECTION 2

Living Words and Loving Deeds

Teachings on Christ's Claims and Miracles in the Gospel of John

PREFACE

As you teach or preach these expository sermons, I want to emphasize the need for the *application* of truth to your hearers. No one has put this more succinctly and ably than Rev. John R. W. Stott. He writes:

> Exposition is not a synonym for exegesis. True biblical preaching goes beyond the elucidation of the text to its application. Indeed, the discipline of discovering a text's original meaning is of little profit if we do not go on to discern its contemporary message. We have to ask of every Scripture not only "what did it mean?" but "what does it say?" Perhaps it is the failure to ask both these questions, and to persevere with the asking until the answers come, which is the greatest tragedy of current preaching. We evangelicals enjoy studying the text with a view to opening it up, but we are often weak in applying it to the realities of modern life. Our liberal colleagues, however, tend to make the opposite mistake. Their great concern is to relate to the modern world, but their message is less than fully biblical. Thus almost nobody is building bridges between the biblical world and the modern world, across the wide chasm of 2,000 years of changing culture. Yet preaching is essentially a bridge-building exercise. It is the exacting task of relating God's Word to our world with an equal degree of faithfulness and relevance.

> If we are to build bridges for the Word of God to penetrate the real world, we have to take seriously both the biblical text and the contemporary scene, and study both. We cannot afford to remain on either side of the cultural divide. To withdraw from the world into the Bible (which is escapism) or from the Bible into the world (which is conformity), will be fatal to our preaching ministry. Either mistake makes bridge building impossible and noncommunication inevitable. On the one hand, we preachers need to be as familiar with the Bible "as the housewife with her needle, the merchant with

his ledger, the mariner with his ship" (Spurgeon). On the other, we have to grapple with the much more difficult—and usually less congenial—task of studying the modern world. We have to look and listen and read and watch television. We have to go to the theater and the movies (though selectively), because nothing mirrors contemporary society more faithfully than the stage and the screen.

It has been a great help to me to have the stimulus of a reading group. Its members are intelligent young graduates (doctors, lawyers, teachers, architects, and others). We meet monthly when I am in London, having previously agreed to read the same book or see the same play or movie. Then we spend a whole evening together, share our reactions, and seek to develop a Christian response.

As the nineteenth-century German theologian Tholuck said, "a sermon ought to have heaven for its father and the earth for its mother." But if such sermons are to be born, heaven and earth have to meet in the preacher.[1]

With the foregoing in mind, I enthusiastically commend to you the outlines in this section of *Basics for Believers*. The studies in John's gospel are under the general subject of *God Alive*. Seven sermons will be on God Alive in Living Discourses and another seven on God Alive in Living Miracles. In these two series of sevens we have the two aspects of John's portrait of the Son of God. In the seven "I am's" we have a revelation of his *person;* in the seven "signs" we have the revelation of his *power.* What a Christ we have to preach! Is it any wonder that Paul, in his ministry, determined to "preach Christ crucified, to the Jews a stumbling block and to the Greeks foolishness, but to those who are called, both Jews and Greeks, Christ the power of God and the wisdom of God" (1 Cor. 1:23-24, NKJV).

May I remind you that these are not "canned sermons," but rather resource materials for adaptation and application to your own style of expository preaching. So I exhort you, "Preach the word . . . . Do the work of an evangelist, fulfill your ministry" (2 Tim. 4:2, 5, NKJV).

Part 1
GOD ALIVE IN DISCOURSES FROM THE GOSPEL OF JOHN

1

The Bread of Life

John 6:29-36, 47-58

"I am the bread of life" (John 6:35, KJV).

Introduction

In the East, bread was the staple of life, or the principal food of the people. All other dishes were considered accessories. Therefore, bread had a sacredness all its own. Even today, if you go to the East you will find that Jews or Arabs never tread a piece of bread under foot. However soiled or contaminated it might be, they never despise nor disregard it. An Arab walking down a village street and seeing a piece of bread on the ground would be careful to pick it up and put it in a niche in the wall, ready for some hungry beggar or dog.

This view of the importance and sanctity of bread is expressed over and over again in the Bible, so that the words of our Savior carry an even greater significance when interpreted by the rest of Scripture. Needless to say, the bread of which our Lord was speaking, in the passage before us, was not the material bread which satisfies physical hunger, but the heavenly bread which satisfies the spiritual hunger of man. And just as the material bread is fundamental to man's physical life, so the heavenly bread is essential to man's spiritual life.

I. Heavenly Bread Supplies Spiritual Life

"I am the living bread which came down from heaven: if any man eat of this bread, he shall live for ever" (John 6:51). In order to become the Bread of Life to men and women who were spiritually dead:

A. *Christ Was Bruised for Us*

He was the "bread corn . . . bruised" (Isa. 28:28, KJV). Before bread can be made, corn has to be crushed under the grindstone, and then mixed in the kneading trough. This is a truly vivid picture of the suffering through which our Lord had to go, before he could provide spiritual nutrition for you and me. Isaiah tells us that "he was wounded for our transgressions, he was bruised for our iniquities" (Isa. 53:5, KJV).

Illustration

An unbelieving fireman once rescued a little boy from a burning cottage. To do so he had to climb a hot piping, and his hands were badly scarred. The woman who cared for the boy perished in the fire. The question arose as to who would take the boy. A couple came forward, saying, "We should like to have him; we have plenty of money and no children of our own; we would give him a good education and a good start in life." Others offered the boy a home. Then the fireman spoke up: "I should like to have him," and he showed his scarred hands. All agreed that he had the greatest claim to the child. Some objected, knowing the man was an unbeliever. However, the boy was adopted by the fireman who proved a good father to him and loved him as his own child. One day he took him to an art gallery. The boy caught sight of a painting of Christ on the cross and asked the man, "Who was that, Daddy?" The man tried to silence the boy, and quickly drew him away from the picture, which so impressed the child he gave him no peace till he had heard the gospel story. As the man was saying that Jesus let them put Him on the cross for our sins, the truth shone into his heart, and he believed and yielded himself to the One who has the greatest claim on each one of us.[1]

B. Christ Was Baked for Us

He was the "grain offering baked in the oven" (Lev. 2:4, NKJV). What transpired in the darkness of that oven of God's holy wrath will never be understood by finite minds. All we know is that it was in the heat of that indescribable experience that the Son of God cried out, "My God, my God, why hast thou forsaken me?"

Illustration

Yet once Immanuel's orphaned cry the universe hath shaken:
It went up single, echoless, "My God, I am forsaken!"
It went up from His holy lips amid His lost creation
That no one else need ever cry that cry of desolation.[2]

Amplification

Amplify the symbolic meaning of the meat offering: "(1) Fine flour speaks of the evenness and balance of the character of Christ, of that perfection in which no quality was in excess, none lacking; (2) fire, of his testing by suffering, even unto death; (3) frankincense, of the fragrance of His life before God (see Exod. 30:34, note); (4) absence of leaven, of His character as 'the Truth' (John 14:6, cf. Exod. 12:8, marg.); (5) absence of honey—His was not that mere natural sweetness which may exist quite apart from grace; (6) oil mingled, of Christ as born of the Holy Spirit (Matt. 1:18-23); (7) oil upon, of Christ as baptized with the Spirit (John 1:32; 6:27); (8) the oven, of the unseen, sufferings of Christ—His inner agonies (Matt. 27:45-46; Heb. 2:18); (9) the pan, of His more evident sufferings (e.g., Matt. 27:27-31); and (10) salt, of the pungency of the truth of God—that which arrests the action of leaven." [3]

C. Christ Was Broken for Us

Speaking of his death, he could say, through Paul, "This is my body, which is broken for you" (1 Cor. 11:24, KJV).

By being bruised, baked, and broken for us, the Lord Jesus became the Bread of Life. He could say, "If any man eat of this bread, he shall live for ever" (John 6:51). Will you look up into his face right now and say, "Lord Jesus, I thank you for being bruised, baked, and broken for me. I now receive you as the Bread of Life."

Illustration

During a fearful famine in India some years ago a missionary visiting around the villages met a boy who was nothing but skin and bones. He ordered him to go at once to the mission compound and ask for food. The boy pleaded that he would not be admitted to the compound unless he had some authorization. So the missionary, taking a slip of paper, addressed a note to the storekeeper and handed it to the boy, saying, "That is my promise of food for you." Several days later the poor boy was found lying dead with the piece of paper perforated and tied around his neck. He had never acted upon the promise, nor appropriated what would have been the means of life for him!

How many people are dying around us today, because they will not act upon God's promise and come and take the Bread of Life as it is in the Lord Jesus!

II. Heavenly Bread Sustains Spiritual Life

Jesus said, "As the living Father hath sent me, and I live by the Father; so he that eateth me, even he shall live by me" (John 6:57). Now while the supply of life is communicated the moment the sinner appropriates Christ as the Bread of Life, this new life grows and develops only as the believer continues to feed upon Christ. It is interesting to notice that the Lord Jesus intends us to feed on him, even as he fed on the Father. Listen to these words again: "As the living Father hath sent me, and I live by the Father; so he that eateth me, even he shall live by me" (v. 57). How did the Lord Jesus live by the Father?

A. By Feeding on the Word of God

When the Lord Jesus answered Satan's attack in the wilderness he revealed the method by which he sustained his spiritual life. Recall his words for a moment: "Man shall not live by bread alone, but by every word that proceedeth out of the mouth of God" (Matt. 4:4, KJV). In other words, Jesus was teaching that material bread is not sufficient. One must feed constantly on the Bread that comes from God, if his spiritual life is to be sustained.

Jeremiah must have known something of this in his experience when he said, "Thy words were found, and I did eat them; and thy word was unto me the joy and rejoicing of mine heart" (Jer. 15:16, KJV).

Illustration

In France, there once lived a poor blind girl who obtained the gospel of Mark in raised letters and learned to read it by the tips of her fingers. By constant reading, these became callous, and her sense of touch diminished until she could not distinguish the characters. One day, she cut the skin from the ends of her fingers to increase their sensitivity, only to destroy it. She felt that she must now give up her beloved book, and weeping, pressed it to her lips, saying "Farewell, farewell, sweet word of my heavenly Father!" To her surprise, her lips, more delicate than her fingers, discerned the form of the letters. All night she perused with her lips the Word of God and overflowed with joy at this new acquisition.[4]

B. By Feeding on the Will of God

He could say, "My meat is to do the will of him that sent me" (John 4:34). As he fulfilled the divine will, so his soul was fed by his heavenly Father. Similarly for us, to fulfill God's will in everything is to prove the sustained and sustaining quality of the Bread of Life.

Amplification
Study carefully the words of John 4:34 in context, and explain how Jesus, dealing with the woman of Samaria, was in fact feeding on the will of God.

Illustration
"I had rather be in the heart of Africa in the will of God, than on the throne of England out of the will of God."[5]

C. By Feeding on the Work of God

Once again, his words were, "My meat is . . . to finish his work" (John 4:34). The Lord Jesus worked to an hourly program. He was never ahead of his time and never behind it. Each day's work was carefully planned and thoroughly done. In fact, on one occasion when his respected mother suggested he perform a miracle before the appointed moment he said, "Mine hour is not yet come" (John 2:4). And as he did each day's work, so he found the very doing of his task for God food for his soul.

Eating of Christ day by day, as the Bread of Life, involves meditation on his Word, dedication to his will, and consecration to his work.

Illustration
Our life's work is a complete whole, yet it is made up of little things, good works. "We are God's workmanship": and the word Paul uses is the Greek word from which we derive the English word "poem." In her book *Odd Patterns in the Weaving*—Mrs. Sonia E. Howe in her narration mentions something seen when she was still in her teens. A famous Russian academician was working at a mosaic, a copy of an old oil painting that had been in a famous cathedral. He was putting in tiny pieces of marble, one by one, to carry out the

beautiful design. Sonia Howe approached him and said, "Is not this fearfully dull, uninteresting work?" "No, not at all," the artist replied, "for, you see, it is work for eternity."[6]

III. Heavenly Bread Satisfies Spiritual Life

"Jesus said unto them, I am the bread of life: he that cometh to me shall never hunger; and he that believeth on me shall never thirst" (John 6:35). Every person's deepest hunger is spiritual. Whether or not he knows it, he hungers for God, he hungers for truth, and he hungers for life. Whatever else he has in the world he will never be satisfied until he finds the answer to this threefold spiritual hunger. Material things can never fill the soul of a person—whether things to eat, things to see, things to wear, or things to do. Neither can the human soul be filled with another human soul, for one empty vessel cannot fill another empty vessel. No wonder St. Augustine expressed it, "Thou hast made us for Thyself, and our restless souls can find no rest until they find their rest in Thee." But the glory of the Gospel is this, that in Jesus Christ all spiritual hunger can be satisfied. As the Bread from heaven, he satisfies our hunger for God, our hunger for truth, and our hunger for life.

A. The Hunger for God

"The bread of God is he which cometh down from heaven, and giveth life unto the world" (John 6:33). The quest for God is universal. Even the worship of pagan idols witnesses to the fact that the human soul hungers for God. That is true both in the so-called depths of heathenism, or at the heart of civilization. Man has a vast capacity for God, and therefore a vast emptiness without him. But Jesus Christ answers that hunger with these remarkable words: "The bread of God is he which cometh down from heaven, and giveth life unto the world" (v. 33).

B. The Hunger for Truth

"My Father giveth you the *true* bread from heaven" (v. 32). From childhood to adulthood, people have an insatiable hunger for truth. The tragedy is that instead of being satisfied with the true Bread from heaven, thousands upon thousands feed upon the false bread supplied by the devil himself. Instead of feeding at the Father's table, they attempt to fill themselves with "the husks that the swine [do] . . . eat," like the prodigal son, and so ultimately "perish with hunger." Only a small minority of people come to their senses and remember the "bread enough and to spare" (Luke 15:17, KJV), which is to be found in Jesus Christ in the home of the Father. True Bread feeds the mind with knowledge, the heart with happiness, and the will with liberty.

Illustration

At the battle of Bothwell Brig the ammunition of the Covenanters ran out. They were waiting for a barrel of bullets, but instead, a barrel of raisins was sent to them. So they sat down in defeat. Today, as then, the soldiers of Jesus Christ must have less confectionery and more of the truth of God. [7]

C. The Hunger for Life

He said, "I am the bread of life" (John 6:35). Man is hungry for life. He cannot laugh, labor, or love unless he has life. He fights for life in war, he defends life in peacetime, he works for life in daily employment, he dreams of life in sleep, he eats for life at mealtimes. His hunger is for life. And yet so many try to be satisfied with a mere existence, whereas Jesus offers the Bread of *life!*

If you are searching for life among the world's treasures and pleasures, lift your eyes to the one who holds the secret of life in all its fullness. Listen to his words: "I am the living bread which came down from heaven: if any man eat of this bread, he shall live for ever" (v. 51).

Illustration

Sadhu Sundar Singh was distributing gospels in the Central Province of India. He came to some non-Christians on the train and offered a man a copy of John's gospel. The man took it, tore it into pieces in anger and threw the pieces out of the window. That seemed the end. But it so happened, in the providence of God, there was a man anxiously seeking for truth walking along the line that very day, and he picked up, as he walked along, a little bit of paper and looked at it, and the words on it in his own language were "The Bread of Life." He did not know what it meant; but he inquired among his friends and one of them said, "I can tell you; it is out of the Christian book. You must not read it or you will be defiled." The man thought for a moment and then said, "I want to read the book that contains that beautiful phrase!" and he bought a copy of the New Testament. He was shown where the sentence occurred—our Lord's words "I am the Bread of Life"; and as he studied the Gospel, the light flooded into his heart. He came to the knowledge of Jesus Christ, and he became a preacher of the gospel. That little bit of paper through God's Spirit was indeed the Bread of Life to him, satisfying his deepest need. [8]

Conclusion

We have seen that as the Bread of Life, Christ supplies spiritual life, sustains spiritual life, and satisfies spiritual life. Now it remains for you to come to him and believe on him as the Bread of Life. Jesus said, "He that cometh to me shall never hunger; and he that believeth on me shall never thirst" (John 6:35). By coming, you trust in Christ; by believing, you taste of Christ. Will you trust him now, and then "taste and see that the LORD is good" (Ps. 34:8, KJV)? Trust him, then taste him, and you will go on eating and proving that Jesus Christ completely satisfies.

2

The Light of Life

1:1-9; 3:18-21; 8:12; 9:5

"I am the light of the world" (John 8:12, KJV)

Introduction

Our Lord had just attended the Jews' Feast of Tabernacles (John 7:2). This feast was celebrated to remind God's ancient people of their pilgrim journey through the wilderness to the Promised Land. You will remember that during their wanderings the children of Israel were supernaturally provided with manna to eat, water from the rock to drink, and the pillar of cloud and fire to shield and guide them by day and night.

In his teaching, as recorded in the gospel of John, our Lord Jesus Christ had spoken of himself, in chapter 6, as the Bread of Life; in chapter 7, as the Water of Life; and in chapter 8, as the Light of Life.

I. The Source of Divine Light

"I am the light of the world" (John 8:12). This is one of the most meaningful utterances ever voiced by the Savior. This will become evident as we proceed with our study. Consider, first of all:

A. *The Identity of That Source*

"I am the light of the world" (John 8:12). In these simple yet majestic words Jesus reveals himself to be the uncreated light of deity clothed with humanity. Think again of that pillar of cloud by which the children of Israel were led in the wilderness. In appearance it was probably "like some aerial snow mountain, which is to the heavens what the iceberg is to the seas" (F. B. Meyer). At its center was the Shekinah fire of God's presence burning unceasingly. At night, the glory of this fire was diffused through the cloud to light the entire camp of Israel.

How wonderfully this illustrates the identity of our Lord Jesus Christ! Here he is shown to be truly God and truly man. In the Shekinah glory we see his deity. In the white cumulus cloud we see his perfect humanity. During his life on earth, the vision of discerning men and women sometimes pierced that cloud and saw the glory of God. John says: "The Word was made flesh, and dwelt among us, (and we beheld his glory, the glory as of the only begotten of the Father,) full of grace and truth" (John 1:14).

Illustration

If we pick up the prism of analysis and hold it before Jesus' life, we are confronted at once with the perfections of his person. Light may be broken down into a spectrum of seven colors derived from a trinity of primary colors—red, yellow, and green. And in this unique personality, who stands before us as the light of the world, we identify the anointed Prophet, Priest, and King.

B. *The Proximity of That Source*

Jesus declared, "As long as I am in the world, I am the light of the world" (John 9:5). If we were to discuss the source of the physical light that wakes us up in the early hours of the morning and then brightens our lives throughout the course of the day, we would conclude that it was that luminous celestial body we call the sun, which is 92,900,000 miles away. Meteorologists tell us that the sun's light reaches us at a speed of 186,300 miles per second. Our minds reel as we try to comprehend the significance of such distances and speed. But when we turn to the source of the spiritual light, our hearts are comforted by the nearness, the proximity, the immediacy, of God's light of life. "Through the tender mercy of our God; whereby the dayspring from on high hath visited us, To give light to them that sit in darkness and in the shadow of death, to guide our feet into the way of peace" (Luke 1:78-79, KJV).

Illustration

Dr. John Baillie made it a practice to open his course on the doctrine of God at Edinburgh University with these words: "Gentlemen, we must remember that in discussing God we cannot talk about Him without His hearing every word we say. We may be able to talk to our fellows, as it were, behind their backs, but God is everywhere, yes, even in this classroom."[1]

II. The Course of Divine Light

"I am the light of the world: *he that followeth me* shall not walk in darkness, but shall have the light of life" (John 8:12). As the light of the world, Jesus came to guide us by a straight path into the very presence of God. The Bible has much to say on this subject of light, and we need to consider the three beams that delineate the course of light:

A. *The Light Beam of Knowledge*

"God, who commanded the light to shine out of darkness, hath shined in our hearts, to give the light of the knowledge of the glory of God in the face of Jesus Christ" (2 Cor. 4:6, KJV). If you are prepared to receive the Lord Jesus Christ as your personal Savior, you will find that the first beam of the light of the knowledge of God in Jesus Christ would penetrate your soul. As the psalmist tells us, "For with thee is the fountain of life: in thy light shall we see light" (Ps. 36:9, KJV). John assures us, "He that doeth truth cometh to the light" (John 3:21).

B. The Light Beam of Fellowship

"He that followeth me shall not walk in darkness, but shall have the light of life" (John 8:12); and again: "If we walk in the light, as he is in the light, we have fellowship one with another, and the blood of Jesus Christ his Son cleanseth us from all sin" (1 John 1:7, KJV). There is no greater experience in all the world than walking in the light with Jesus Christ. Not only are we kept clean from every sin, but the resulting fellowship with God introduces joy, power, and blessing which continue along the whole course of our Christian life.

C. The Light Beam of Holiness

"The path of the just is as the shining light, that shineth more and more unto the perfect day" (Prov. 4:18, KJV). The light of the knowledge of Christ leads us into the light of the fellowship of Christ. The light of the fellowship of Christ, in turn, leads us into the light of holiness in Christ. The writer to the Hebrews exhorts us to "follow . . . holiness, without which no man shall see the Lord" (12:14, KJV). And in his Beatitudes, Jesus says: "Blessed are the pure in heart: for they shall see God" (Matt. 5:8, KJV). The fact is that "God is light, and in him is no darkness at all" (1 John 1:, KJV5). Consequently, if we would see God we must know the light of holiness in our lives. He says, "I am the light of the world: he that followeth me shall not walk in darkness" (John 8:12).

Are you prepared to follow his light beams of knowledge, fellowship, and holiness?

Illustration

Let me recount a terrifying occasion when I was hopelessly lost just after dusk in the long grass of Central Africa. I had gone out to shoot meat for the native carriers, and, in the course of the hunt, I forgot about time and direction. Groping around in circles in the near darkness, I could make out the forms of two hunting leopards prowling around me. Visibility was too poor for me to shoot, and, in any case, there were two leopards. Only one way was open, that of prayer.

Having asked God for protection and guidance, I cupped my hands and began to call for help. My voice seemed to be strengthened by a supernatural power. Presently I had the answer to my prayers, for two headlights of our Ford truck came sweeping across the plain. Instantly, the leopards scattered, and in the straight beams of the light I was guided back to camp.

In a similar way, by means of the light beams of knowledge, fellowship, and holiness, we can be guided and helped in our walk with Jesus Christ.

III. The Force of Divine Light

"I am the light of the world: he that followeth me shall not walk in darkness, but shall have the *light of life*" (John 8:12). In the first chapter of this gospel the writer tells us that "in him [Christ] was life; and the life was the light of men" (1:4). In the physical realm, light is spoken of as a radiant force and a luminous energy. In the sphere of the spiritual, this divine light can be likened to:

A. A Searching Force

"Every one that doeth evil hateth the light, neither cometh to the light, lest his deeds should be reproved" (John 3:20). As a searching force, this divine light operates like an X-ray. It exposes life and reveals character. Someone has defined light as "the agent by which objects are made visible."

How true this is of the light of God. You may be complacent and unconcerned about your life, but the moment the divine light shines into it you will become aware of your sin and cry out, like Peter, "Depart from me; for I am a sinful man, O Lord" (Luke 5:8, KJV).

Illustration

In the context of John 8, we have the story of the adulteress caught in the very act of sin. These cruel scribes and Pharisees who accused her were confident of their position when they proposed that she be stoned according to the law of Moses. Then Jesus began to expose their lives by the searching light that emanated from his own person and Word. "He that is without sin among you, let him first cast a stone at her," he demanded. And we read: "They which heard it, being convicted by their own conscience, went out one by one, beginning at the eldest, even unto the last" (John 8:7, 9). Have you allowed God's searching light to expose your heart and life?

B. A Saving Force

Listen to the testimony of the psalmist: "The LORD is my light and my salvation . . . the LORD is the strength of my life" (Ps. 27:1, KJV). For many years it has been known that certain diseases can be successfully treated by exposure to sunlight. The general physical tone of the body can be increased by the action of ultraviolet rays. It is estimated that there is a 20 percent increase in mortality wherever direct light is not enjoyed in the home, street, or office.

Similarly, there is a saving force in God's divine light. Ponder that great word in Malachi which tells us that the Lord Jesus, as "the Sun of righteousness [shall] arise with healing in his wings" (4:2, KJV). I can never recall that verse without thinking of the dark hour of Calvary, when Jesus was "made . . . sin . . . that we might be made the righteousness of God in him" (2 Cor. 5:21, KJV). Then the third day he rose again with healing and saving power in his wings. Truly, he is the light of life to all who will personally trust him.

Illustration

Bishop Taylor Smith once queried a country minister about his sermon of the previous Sunday. "Well," the humble preacher replied, "I was preaching on 'the Lord is my light,' and I pointed out to my people that light is invisible and that God is invisible, that we only know of the existence of light by the manifestation of it through the mists and in the dust of the atmosphere. It is only thus that we realize that light exists. And then I told them how we should not know God except that He shone in the person of our Lord Jesus Christ. 'He that hath seen me hath seen the Father.'" Smith said to him, "Top marks!"[2]

Only through Christ has the eternal light become a saving force to men and women who are "dead in trespasses and sins" (Eph. 2:1, KJV).

C. A Shining Force

Jesus says, "Let your light so shine before men, that they may see your good works, and glorify your Father which is in heaven" (Matt. 5:16, KJV). If he is the light of life in your experience, then that divine life must of necessity shine out through your personality and activity. Paul reminds us: "Ye were sometimes darkness, but now are ye light in the Lord: walk as children of light" (Eph. 5:8, KJV). If you have met Jesus Christ as Light of the World, then you will inevitably be a shining light for him. If your reaction to that statement is that you are only an individual, and what good is your single small light in the dark world, then let me assure you that, just as the tiniest pin prick of light is visible in a dark cave, so, whether alone or with other Christians, the shining of your light is a reminder of the greater light that "lights the world."

Conclusion

Do you know this divine light in your life? Have you personally encountered Jesus Christ? Why not receive him as the source of light, follow him as the course of light, and experience him as the force of light?

Clear the darkened windows,
Open wide the door;
Let the blessed Sunshine in.

3

The Door of the Sheepfold

John 10:1-9

"I am the door: by me if any man enter in, he shall be saved, and shall go in and out, and find pasture" (John 10:9, KJV).

Introduction

Westerners may not understand this simile, so let us imagine that we are on holiday in the Holy Land. We visit some of those sacred and holy spots where our Lord Jesus walked, talked, and worked. Then we cross the lovely Bethlehem fields and pastures where David used to feed his sheep. Soon we come to a structure so high that we cannot scale it, and so thick that we cannot penetrate it. As we walk around it, we wonder what it can be; we see an opening, or doorway, and the hoof-marks of sheep having gone in and out, but no door. Soon a shepherd appears. A club swings from his belt, in his hand is a staff, and behind him are a hundred sheep. As he approaches we question him and to our joy find that he speaks English. When he tells us that the structure is a sheepfold, we inquire, "Do you keep your sheep here by night?" "Yes," he replies. "But how can they be safe without a door?" we ask again. With a twinkle in his eye, he stands tall and says, "*I* am the door." "Do you stay here all night?" we continue. "I do," he replies. "I build myself a shelter and sit here and keep vigil in all kinds of weather. No lion, bear, wolf, or hireling can enter my sheepfold. I am a good shepherd: I give my life for the sheep." To prove his point, he draws aside his eastern robe, and sure enough, there are scars on his arms and body. He explains that these are wounds that he has suffered as he has fought off animals while defending his sheep.

When our Lord Jesus uttered these words, he was looking beyond Calvary to resurrection life. Having suffered the wounds of battle and risen triumphantly, he stands in the doorway of God's sheepfold and says, "I am the door: by me if any man enter in, he shall be saved, and shall go in and out, and find pasture" (John 10:9). Here, then, we have:

I. The Door of Protection

"By me if any man enter in, he shall be saved" (or "safe," v. 9). Still with the pastoral picture in our minds, we learn from the historical background of this passage, as well as the context itself, that the shepherd offers protection from:

A. Severe Elements

"By me if any man enter in," he shall be safe (v. 9). Outside there may be wind, snow, rain, or fire. Many a time, when the lightning had flashed and the prairie had caught fire, the shepherd had lost his sheep as the conflagration spread over the pasture land. Outside there was danger, death, and doom; but inside the door, safety.

"What relevance has that to today?" you ask. If I am to declare to you the whole counsel of God I must remind you that this world is still under the abiding wrath of God. This sin-stained, stubborn, defiant world is moving on to its hour of judgment. God "hath appointed a day, in which he will judge the world in righteousness by that man whom he hath ordained" (Acts 17:31, KJV). And "because there is wrath, beware lest he take thee away with his stroke: then a great ransom cannot deliver thee" (Job 36:18, KJV). And again: "Our God is a consuming fire" (Heb. 12:29, KJV).

Illustration

A writer describing the settlement of the American West wrote about the prairie fire: "Until the fall rains set in, the dry scorching summer months are spent in fear and suspense. Every suggestion of haze or smoke is intensely watched. But, when once fired and swept by a breeze, its speed strikes terror to man and beast as it unmercifully consumes all in its way. Many, powerless to escape, have perished, and their farms been reduced to ashes. Others, with presence of mind, seeing their danger, have stooped and fired the long dry grass at their feet, and then, as soon as the blaze had burned off a space, taken refuge by standing where the fire had been."

"Yet more solemn and terrifying will be the coming wrath and judgment of God upon this world that has crucified, and ignored the grace of, his beloved Son. It is "reserved unto fire against the day of judgment" (2 Pet. 3:7). But thanks be unto our gracious God who has provided a place of safety where the fire has already been. On Calvary's cross Christ was, as it were, enveloped in the "fire" of God's righteous judgment to save the trembling sinner that has fled to him for refuge (Heb. 6:18)."[1]

B. Savage Enemies

"By me if any man enter in," he shall be safe (John 10:9). What if the lion, the wolf, the bear, and the hireling are all outside the sheepfold? What relevance has that to this hour? What stories we could tell today of young and old who are up against savage enemies! They intend to be pure and upright, but are constantly bruised and battered by the enemy. The Bible reminds us that "the devil, as a roaring lion, walketh about, seeking whom he may devour" (1 Pet. 5:8, KJV). And

Paul adds, "We wrestle not against flesh and blood, but against principalities, against powers, against the rulers of the darkness of this world, against spiritual wickedness in high places" (Eph. 6:12, KJV).

Illustration

The ant-lion is a little dark-looking creature that makes a hole in the sand, puts itself in the very center, and buries itself completely out of sight, except its horn which appears like a rusty needle sticking up in the sand. An observer of its tactics wrote: "A little red ant came along seeking her food in her usual busy way. So she climbed upon the rim of the sandy cup and peeped over to investigate. Presently, suspecting danger, she turned to scramble off. Alas! it was too late; the sand rolled from under her feet, and down she went to the bottom, when in an instant that little black horn opened like a pair of shears, and 'Clip,' the poor ant had lost a leg. And now the poor thing struggles to climb up, but, one leg gone, she finds it hard work. The little monster does not move or show himself. He knows what he is about. The ant has got almost to the top and liberty when the sand slips, and down she goes. 'Clip' go the shears, and another leg is gone. She struggles hard to rise, but she gets up but a little way before she slips again, and a third leg is off. She now gives up the struggle, and the lion devours her in a few minutes; and then with a flip of his tail throws the skin of the ant entirely out of the cup, and the trap is now set for another victim."

The same process is gone through with flies and other insects. No ant-lion was in sight, but the destroyer was there. The dead were pushed out of sight. "Your adversary the devil, as a roaring lion, walketh about seeking whom he may devour."[2]

C. Subtle Enticements

"By me if any man enter in," he shall be safe (John 10:9). Outside the sheepfold there are many enticements that would lead a sheep into danger, and even destruction, but for the watchful eye and loving care of the shepherd.

In a similar way, apart from our heavenly Shepherd, we are at the mercy of a cunning and cruel world. John says, "Love not the world, neither the things that are in the world. If any man love the world, the love of the Father is not in him. For all that is in the world, the lust of the flesh, and the lust of the eyes, and the pride of life, is not of the Father, but is of the world" (1 John 2:15-16, KJV). The apostle emphasizes here the attractions or enticements of a sinful life— "the lust of the eyes"; the appetites of a sinful life— "the lust of the flesh"; and the ambitions of a sinful life — "the pride of life."

Illustration

In my college days, as part of my training in evangelism, I, with another student, was assigned London's Picadilly Circus from 11 P.M. to 6 A.M. In cabarets, vice dens, and on the streets, we found former doctors, lawyers, and other people who were caught in the allurements of modern life. They never wanted to see their families or ministers again, or be known in the circle of old friends. The subtle enticements of sin had won them over to a totally new lifestyle.

II. The Door of Purpose

"He . . . *shall go in and out,* and find pasture" (John 10:9). The sheep does not fulfill the purpose of the shepherd until it has entered the sheepfold. Until we have entered the door of purpose we do not fulfill the plan for which we were created. Paul reminds us that "we are his workmanship, created in Christ Jesus unto good works, which God hath before ordained that we should walk in them" (Eph. 2:10, KJV). God has a plan for every life, and that plan is so ordered that every believer may find it, follow it, and finish it to the glory of God. The great tragedy of modern life is that many men and women are so purposeless, aimless, and thoroughly frustrated. But God promises a door of purpose to:

A. A Life of Liberty in Christ

The words "in and out" (John 10:9) suggest a liberated life—
"the glorious liberty of the children of God" (Rom. 8:21, KJV).
It is the liberty that operates only within the realm of God's
purpose. It is inseparably related to the leadership of the shepherd— "he calleth his own sheep by name, and leadeth them
out" (John 10:3, KJV).

B. A Life of Loyalty to Christ

The phrase "in and out" (John 10:9) further suggests an integrated life. Psychologists are agreed that one of the secrets of
an integrated personality is loyalty. And who can establish loyalty like the sheep-door of our chapter? He says, "I am the good
shepherd, and know my sheep"; and again: "I am the good
shepherd: the good shepherd giveth his life for the sheep" (vv.
14, 11). It is well known that the eastern shepherd *knows* his
sheep and *loves* his sheep. It has been said that such shepherds
can often be blindfolded and yet distinguish the individual
sheep by following the features of each animal with his fingers.
In addition to this, the shepherd of the East will engage in
deadly conflict in order to save them from destruction.

Illustration

The liberty in Christ and loyalty to Christ are beautifully illustrated by the following story from the early days of slavery: "A
young mulatto girl was being sold at auction one day. She was
a beautiful girl, tall and slender. The bidding was keen, and
quickly mounted higher and higher until at last only two men
were left, bidding for her ownership: the one a low, uncouth
fellow who swearingly raised his bid every time to outbid the
other, a quiet man of refinement. Finally the bidding
stopped, and to the gentleman who had bid so very earnestly
was given the papers which made him the lawful owner of the
young girl. With a shove the auctioneer presented her to her
new master. Proudly, defiantly, she stood before him, hating
him with every part of her being. Suddenly, a change came
over her face: first there was a look of pure amazement closely

followed by one of utter incredulity. Her owner was ripping up the papers of ownership, and, with a smile of kindness, said to the now trembling girl, 'My dear, you are free. I bought you that I might free you.' Too stunned for speech, the girl merely stared till finally, with a cry of happiness too deep for words, she cast herself at the man's feet, and through her tears exclaimed, 'Oh, master, I'll love you and serve you for life!' What the papers of ownership could not do, the man's kindness had won completely. The Lord Jesus has loved you and has paid such a price that he might buy you from the slavery of Satan and free you. Will you not tell him, 'Master, I'll love thee and serve thee for life?'"[3]

III. The Door of Provision

"He . . . shall go in and out, and find pasture" (John 10:9). To know Christ as the door is to enter into all the divine resources and provisions which he has prepared for them that love him. When Jesus said "pasture" or "abundant pasture" he was undoubtedly thinking of Psalm 23, for nothing could better illustrate the thought of abundant pasture than those two expressions in the opening of the psalm— "green pastures" and "still waters" (v. 2). Here is the door of provision to:

A. *Spiritual Nourishment*

"He maketh me to lie down in green pastures" or "pastures of tender grass" (Ps. 23:2, KJV). You will never find a hungry sheep lying down. The animal will wander even into danger and death in order to satisfy itself. But the pastures of the shepherd's provision are so plentiful that the sheep never has to wander. It finds its fill and nourishment within the provision of the shepherd. So true is this that he makes his sheep to lie down in green pastures.

Illustration

My own sheep hear my voice,/He said, A stranger they'll not heed./In pleasant pastures they are led,/So tenderly I feed./How can they want when near me/I lead them day by day?/How can they wander from me/When by my side they stay?

William F. Sherbert

B. Spiritual Refreshment

"He leadeth me beside the still waters" (Ps. 23:2, KJV). Those clear waters quench thirst, cleanse defilement, refresh from weariness, and calm fears. In a word, they represent the renewing work of the Holy Spirit. What a door of provision is this! All the secrets of a cleansed and settled life are to be found inside that door. No wonder the psalmist says elsewhere, "No good thing will he withhold from them that walk uprightly" (Ps. 84:11).

Now comes the question of entering this door of protection, purpose, and provision. Jesus says, "I am the door: by me if any man enter in" (John 10:9). What is "entering in"? It is a definite act of faith in which you take the Lord Jesus at his word and step into the fold. The Word of God reminds us that "all we like sheep have gone astray; we have turned every one to his own way" (Isa. 53:6, KJV). Why should you remain a wandering sheep outside the fold? It is important to realize that you are either in or out of the fold. On which side are you? As the chorus puts it:

"One door, and only one,/And yet its sides are two;/I'm on the inside,/On which side are you?

Conclusion

Tell the Lord Jesus in simple terms that you are outside the door of protection, purpose, and provision, but that you now want to enter into that eternal sheepfold, claiming him as the Door of your life.

Only a step to Jesus!/Then why not take it now?/Come, and thy sin confessing;/To Him, thy Saviour, bow./Only a step! Only a step!/Come, He waits for thee;/Come, and thy sin confessing./Thou shalt receive a blessing:/Do not reject the mercy/He freely offers thee.

Fanny J. Crosby

4

The Good Shepherd

John 10:11-18, 25-29

"I am the good shepherd: the good shepherd giveth his
life for the sheep" (John 10:11, KJV).

Introduction

The image of the Good Shepherd has caught the imagination
of men and women down through the centuries. Indeed, his
role as the Good Shepherd is referred to more often than any
of his other offices or ministries in the literature of Christian
hymns and sermons.

In the Old Testament, Israel was a predominantly pastoral
people; its religious concepts were therefore colored by the
vocabulary and vocational habits familiar to a pastoral community. So we find the image of sheep and the shepherd used
again and again. The figure of the shepherd is applied to
Yahweh (Isa. 40:11), but it is also applied to Israel's national
leaders. David is, of course, the outstanding example here
(2 Sam. 5:2 and Ps. 78:70, for example).

When we come to the New Testament, however, the

metaphor attains its highest prominence. This is particularly true as we come to the chapter now before us. In these verses the Lord Jesus explained what he meant by the Good Shepherd. He enlarged on:

I. The Attractiveness of His Character

"I am the good shepherd" (John 10:11). The literal translation is "the lovely shepherd," "the beautiful shepherd," or "the noble and genuine shepherd." How attractive is his character! Twice over this phrase "I am the good shepherd" is repeated: once in relation to his love, and the other in relation to his knowledge.

A. *The Good Shepherd Loves His Sheep Infinitely*

"I am the good shepherd: the good shepherd giveth his life for the sheep" (John 10:11). Of course, the Lord Jesus had built up a tremendous contrast before giving expression to these words. He had spoken of the marauder, or *thief,* who "[climbs] up some other way" (v. 1) and is known not so much for his violence as for his subtlety and cunning. He had spoken of the *wolf,* that fearsome beast who scatters the sheep. That is how a wolf will always attack. He scatters them first, so that they are reduced to utter helplessness and loneliness. Then he destroys and devours. The Lord Jesus is neither a thief, nor a wolf; nor is he a *hireling,* a professional shepherd who only looks after the sheep for pay and takes off when he sees any danger approaching. No, our Lord is the Good Shepherd, who gives his life for the sheep; he loves his sheep infinitely.

> **Illustration**
> In St. Paul's Cathedral, London, is a life-size, marble statue of Christ in anguish on the cross. Beneath the statue are inscribed the words: This is how God loved the world!"[1]

B. *The Good Shepherd Knows His Sheep Intimately*

"He calleth his own sheep by name, and leadeth them out" (John 10:3); and again: "I am the good shepherd, and know my sheep, and am known of mine" (v. 14). There is no one who knows you so well as does the Lord Jesus. He knows you intimately and completely. There is no strength or defect in your nature that he does not know; no thought in your mind that he does not perceive; no response in your heart of which he is not aware; no longing of your being of which he is not cognizant. He knows you better than your dearest friend.

Illustration

J. H. Jowett once wrote: "In our country we do not realize the intimacy of a shepherd with his flock as they do in Syria and in parts of Southern Europe. It was my daily delight every day for many weeks and a dozen times a day, to watch a shepherd who had this almost incredibly close communion with his flock. Many times have I accompanied him through the green pastures and by the stream. If my shepherd wished to lead his sheep from one pasture to another, he went before them, and he was usually singing. I have heard his song and his low-bird-call by the watercourse, and have seen the sheep follow his course over the rocky boulders to the still waters, where they have been refreshed. At noon he would sit down in a place of shadows, and all his flock crowded around him for rest. At night, when the darkness was falling, he gathered them into the fold. We must realize an intimacy like this if we wish to understand the shepherd imagery of the Old Book."[2]

II. The Inclusiveness of His Concern

"Other sheep I have, which are not of this fold: them also I must bring, and they shall hear my voice; and there shall be one fold, and one shepherd" (John 10:16). Here are words to stir the heart! It was these words that motivated David Livingstone to leave his home, and a promising career, to plunge into the dark, infested jungles of Central Africa in order to find the "sheep that were lost." Should you go into Westminster Abbey in London, England and see the stone that marks his resting place, you would find these words of Jesus inscribed upon it. The inclusiveness of the Good Shepherd's concern is seen as:

A. *The Shepherd Seeks the Sheep*

"Them also I must bring" (John 10:16). In that little word "bring" is the thought of the seeking Shepherd. He finds them because he has sought them, and desires to bring them into his fold. And there is no point of the compass that Jesus has not explored in seeking men and women who have been lost. At Calvary's cross, Jesus Christ measured every distance that the sinning and straying sheep could ever traverse.

Illustration
About 1842, George Clephane, a young Scottish lad, stepped ashore in Canada to try and begin a new life. Although only in his early twenties, George was an alcoholic. However, the change of country did not solve his problem. In company with the wrong kind of people, he spent his substance on riotous living. One cold morning he was picked up on the roadside in a state of complete collapse, the result of a drunken carousal and exposure to the elements. Shortly afterwards he died. The news of his death stirred great sorrow in his old home in Fife, but most of all in the heart of his youngest sister, Elizabeth Cecilia. She had never ceased to love the black sheep of the family, and never wavered in her conviction that God loved him too. The conviction that somehow in his dying hours, her brother had come to Jesus and been saved shaped itself into an immortal hymn:

> There were ninety and nine, that safely lay/In the shelter of the fold/But one was out on the hills away,/Far off from the gates of gold—/Away on the mountains, wild and bare,/Away from the tender Shepherd's care.

> "Lord, Thou hast here Thy ninety and nine,/Are they not enough for Thee?"/But the Shepherd made answer,/"This of mine Has wandered away from Me;/And although the road be rough and steep/I go to the desert to find My sheep."/But none of the ransomed ever knew/How deep were the waters crossed,/Nor how dark was the night that the Lord passed through,/Ere He

found His sheep that was lost./Out in the desert He heard its cry,/Sick and helpless, and ready to die.

"Lord, whence are those blood-drops all the way,/That mark out the mountain's track?"/"They were shed for one who had gone astray,/Ere the Shepherd could bring him back."/ "Lord, whence are Thy hands so rent and torn?"/"They are pierced tonight by many a thorn."

But all through the mountains, thunder-riven,/And up from the rocky steep,/There arose a cry to the gate of heaven,/ "Rejoice! I have found My sheep!"/And the angels echoed around the throne,/"Rejoice, for the Lord brings back His own!"

She died in 1869, her poem still unpublished, but it found its way into a Glasgow paper in 1874, while Moody and Sankey were in Scotland. Sankey bought a newspaper at a Glasgow station, and as he glanced through it hurriedly, his eye caught sight of Elizabeth Clephane's poem. He cut it out for his musical scrapbook. At the noon meeting on the second day into a mission in Edinburgh the subject was "The Good Shepherd" on which Mr. Moody preached his sermon. [Afterward] Mr. Moody asked Ira D. Sankey if he had a solo appropriate to the subject with which to close the service. Sankey, lifting up his heart in prayer to God for help, placed the little newspaper slip on the organ, and began to sing note by note the hymn to the tune to which it is still sung.[3]

B. The Shepherd Shelters the Sheep

"There shall be one . . . [flock], and one shepherd" (John 10:16). "Is there not already one flock down here?" someone asks. No, some are here, and some are in heaven. But when the Chief Shepherd shall appear, all the lost sheep he has ever saved will be welcomed into heaven itself and sheltered there forever. As Charles C. Ryrie puts it: "As the Good Shepherd, Christ gave His life for the sheep and became the Door into God's fold (v. 7); as the Great Shepherd (Heb. 13:20-21), He rose from the dead to care for His sheep; as Chief Shepherd (1 Pet. 5:4), He will come again for His sheep."[4]

Exegesis

The misleading English translation of the word "flock" should be especially noticed. If our Lord had meant to convey the idea of the rigid enclosure into which all the scattered sheep should be gathered, he would have used the word *aule*—"a sheepfold"—in this context. The word *poimne* is carefully chosen. It is used here metaphorically of all Christ's followers. The King James Version is erroneous at this point and has led to serious misinterpretation of this passage. The fact is that there may be many folds, representing different nations, ages, times, and denominations, and many variations of these; but there is only one flock under the watchful guardianship of one shepherd. This verse has an obvious bearing on the methods of seeking Christian unity (cf. Eph. 2:11-22; Ezek. 34:23). As in John 11:52, it is Christ himself who gathers "together in one the children of God who were scattered abroad."

III. The Effectiveness of His Call

"My sheep hear my voice, and I know them, and they follow me: And I give unto them eternal life; and they shall never perish, neither shall any man pluck them out of my hand" (John 10:27-28). Although there is a difference of opinion among scholars as to the sequence of verses 27-30, the main thrust of the teaching is inescapable. Christ's knowledge of his sheep answers to their obedience; his new life offered to his sheep answers to their progress, and his victory gained for his sheep answers to full salvation. In essence, this is the effectual call of our heavenly Shepherd.

A. The Call Expects a Response

"My sheep hear my voice, and . . . they follow me" (John 10:27). Unless a person resolutely turns his back on the Good Shepherd and is determined to be independent, he will respond to the divine call; for in God's good purpose he has been elected to be sought and sheltered. There are those in every country, race, and rank who have heard and responded to that call. Each one can say:

I heard Him call,/"Come, follow!"/That was all./My gold grew dim,/My soul went after Him,/I rose and followed—/That was all./Who would not follow/If they heard Him call?
Henry Wadsworth Longfellow

B. The Call Establishes a Relationship

"I give unto them eternal life; and they shall never perish, neither shall any man pluck them out of my hand" (John 10:28). Every sheep that comes to the Lord Jesus, confessing that he has sinned and strayed, is cleansed and immediately becomes related to him, sharing his very life.

Observe carefully that it is an *indestructible* relationship— "They shall never perish" (v. 28). Without any presumption (unless it be on the truth of the Word of God), each follower of Christ should be able to say, "I am as sure of heaven as though I were already there."

Notice further that the relation is *indissoluble*—"Neither shall any man pluck them out of my hand" (v. 28). There's security! Jesus said, "My Father, which gave them me, is greater than all; and no man is able to pluck them out of my Father's hand" (v. 29). There's double security! Paul puts it beautifully when he says: "Your life is hid with Christ in God" (Col. 3:3, KJV). What a relationship! What a joy! What a peace! What a salvation!

Conclusion

As we have looked at this beautiful picture of our Lord and Savior Jesus Christ we have discovered that he is the Good Shepherd who died for us, the Great Shepherd who lives for us, and the Chief Shepherd who will one day come back for us. When he addresses us as "my sheep," let us respond by calling him "our Shepherd."

5

The Resurrection and the Life

John 11:20-27

"I am the resurrection, and the life: he that believeth in me, though he were dead, yet shall he live" (John 11:25, KJV).

Introduction

All the titles of the Lord Jesus Christ are a self-disclosure of the wonder of his person and the effectiveness of his work. We come now to what is perhaps one of the most profound of his utterances— "I am the resurrection, and the life"—Christ, the quickener of our souls. The context of this utterance is tremendously important. Our Lord Jesus was speaking in the very atmosphere of death, decay and distress. Lazarus had been dead four days, and his family and friends were sorrowing. Yet with utter certainty Jesus could declare, "I am the resurrection, and the life."

I. Christ Is the Great Dispenser of Life

"I am the resurrection, and the life" (John 11:25). Resurrection presupposes death; death prepares for new life, and life predicates God. We come right back to the fact of God, for only God can both beget and dispense life, and the life he gives is active both in the physical and spiritual realms.

A. He Gives Physical Life

"He giveth to all life, and breath, and all things" (Acts 17:25, KJV), said the apostle Paul, when preaching on Mars' hill to the Athenians. All forms of physical life have come first from God. It is true that scientists already have brought together certain components that have actually begun to live; even so we can only say with Johannes Kepler, the German astronomer (1571-1630), that they are "thinking God's thoughts after Him." Ultimately life comes from God alone, and without God there is no life. He is the dispenser of physical life.

B. He Gives Spiritual Life

"I am come that [you] might have life, and that [you] might have it more abundantly" (or "above the common," John 10:10). This gospel of John is the gospel of *life.* The key-word "life" appears again and again. Looking into the faces of men and women, who were on the level of mere existence, Jesus said, "The dead shall hear the voice of the Son of God: and they that hear shall live" (John 5:25, KJV). He is the dispenser of spiritual life.

Illustration

Dr. Walter Lewis Wilson in his book, *The Romance of a Doctor's Visit,* narrates that, on one occasion, going to a funeral, he had permission to ride to the cemetery with the undertaker in the hearse. As they went along, he said to the driver, a young man of thirty, "What do you suppose the Bible means by saying, 'Let the dead bury their dead'?" He replied, "There isn't a verse like that in the Bible." The doctor assured him that there was, and he said then, "It must be a wrong translation. How could a dead person bury a dead person?" The doctor then explained the verse by pointing out to him, "You are a dead undertaker in front of the hearse driving out to bury the dead friend at the back of the hearse. That person is dead to her family, and you are dead to God." He quoted to him John 10:10 and 1 John 5:12. The conversation resulted in the conversion of the undertaker as he accepted eternal life through faith in the Lord Jesus Christ.[1]

II. Christ Is the Great Restorer of Life

"I am the resurrection" (John 11:25). The word "resurrection" comes from two Greek words that mean "to cause to stand up." The thought is of someone who was standing in life, and now is lying in death. The Lord Jesus makes them stand up again.

A. Christ Restores Spiritual Life

"You hath he quickened, who were dead in trespasses and sins" (Eph. 2:1, KJV). Outside of a living union with Jesus Christ, who is the resurrection and the life, all men and women are "dead in trespasses and sins." God told Adam that in the day he violated his will and took of the forbidden fruit he would most surely die. And Adam did die—spiritually, though his physical, emotional, and rational life continued. Man was given a probationary period, but he failed, and by disobedience forfeited the very life of God. So all the children of Adam have been born physically, emotionally, and rationally alive, but dead spiritually. "Behold, I was shapen in iniquity; and in sin did my mother conceive me" (Ps. 51:5, KJV).

You may be trained academically, you may be cultured, warm-hearted, refined, and charming, but if you are not joined in a vital union with the Lord Jesus, the resurrection, and the life, you are in a moral sepulchre—"dead in trespasses and sins" (Eph. 2:1, KJV). The wonder of the gospel message is that Christ affirms: "I am the resurrection, and the life: he that believeth in me, though he were dead, yet shall he live: And whosoever liveth and believeth in me shall never die" (John 11:25-26).

B. Christ Restores Physical Life

"As in Adam all die, even so in Christ shall all be made alive"

(1 Cor. 15:22, KJV). In that magnificent chapter (1 Cor. 15), Paul argues his way right through to a climax. Jesus Christ has proved that he is the resurrection and the life by undergoing death and emerging in the power of his own authority. He could say of his own life, "I have power [authority] to lay it down, and I have power [authority] to take it again" (John 10:18, KJV). No one in the universe has ever voluntarily dismissed his spirit, as did Jesus at Golgotha when he cried, "It is finished" and gave up the ghost (John 19:30, KJV). From resurrection ground we hear him saying, "I am he that liveth, and was dead; and behold, I am alive for evermore" (Rev. 1:18, KJV).

And so, on the basis of the resurrection of Jesus Christ, Paul argues that every man who has ever died will live again. Those who are believers will be raised in Christ, "in a moment, in the twinkling of an eye, at the last trump." Their bodies will be changed to become like his glorious body. The "corruptible [shall] put on incorruption, and [the] mortal [shall] put on immortality . . .Death [will be] swallowed up in victory" (1 Cor. 15:52-54, KJV).

Those who are not believers in Christ will rise just as surely, not at the first resurrection but rather at the resurrection of the unregenerate where small and great will stand before God's bar of judgment; and because of their rejection of Jesus Christ all such will be banished from his presence forever.

Illustration

When that great Christian and scientist, Sir Michael Faraday, was dying, some journalists questioned him as to his speculations for a life after death. "Speculations!" said he, "I know nothing about speculations. I'm resting on certainties. I know that my redeemer liveth, and because He lives, I shall live also."[2]

C. Christ Restores Cosmical Life

When Jesus Christ said, "I am the resurrection, and the life" (John 11:25), he was thinking not only of that which was spiritual and physical, but that which had cosmic proportions as well. We look around today and use the words of the old hymn,

"Change and decay in all around I see." There is the rotting tree, the chill blast of winter, the minor note in the little bird's song, and creation "red in tooth and claw." Paul speaks in Romans 8 of the whole creation being subjected to wastefulness and the bondage of corruption. But one day, by virtue of the resurrection of Jesus Christ, the whole creation, which "groaneth and travaileth in pain together until now" (Rom. 8:22, KJV) will be released. Then will the birds sing, the flowers bloom and never fade again, and the whole creation will be purified and restored to a redeemed paradise: the utopia that we all yearn for.

Illustration

Some years ago a man who kept a marine aquarium saw on the surface of the water a tiny creature, appearing to be half fish, half snake, not an inch long, writhing as if in distress. With convulsive efforts it bent its head to tail, now on this side, now on that, springing in circles with a strength amazing in a creature so small. The observer bent over to remove it lest it should sink and die and pollute the clear waters, when, in a moment, its skin split from end to end, and there sprang out a delicate fly with slender legs and pale lavender wings. Balancing itself for a moment on its discarded skin, it preened its gossamer wings and then flew out of an open window. This phenomenon made a deep and lasting impression on the one who watched. He learned once again that *nature hints at the truth of the resurrection.*

III. Christ Is the Great Preserver of Life

"I am the resurrection, and the *life*" (John 11:25). Having restored life he preserves it. That is an added benefit of redemption. Adam in innocence was on trial, and having failed, he forfeited life. But now life has been restored, and our Lord Jesus Christ has made it possible for it never to be lost again. Through grace he has become our very life, and to lose life is to lose him, and that cannot be, for every believer shares the life of Christ. As every branch is part of the vine, so we are members one of another.

A. *Christ Preserves Us by His Protective Word*

"Man shall not live by bread alone, but by every word that proceedeth out of the mouth of God" (Matt. 4:4, KJV); and again, the words of the Lord Jesus: "The words that I speak unto you, they are spirit, and they are life" (John 6:63, KJV). It is difficult to understand how anyone who calls himself a Christian does not have an insatiable appetite for the Word of God. "As newborn babes, desire the sincere milk of the word, that ye may grow thereby," says Peter in his first epistle (2:2, KJV). A little baby will cry for milk, and there is something wrong if a spiritual child does not seek his Father's provision day by day.

Creation, too, is held together by the outgoing of that same word. "Through faith we understand that the worlds were framed by the word of God" (Heb. 11:3, KJV), and he upholds "all things by the word of his power" (Heb.1:3, KJV). When men and women are raised to life from the grave, it will be by the power of that same word.

B. *Christ Preserves Us by His Redemptive Work*

Jesus said, "Except ye eat the flesh of the Son of man, and drink his blood, ye have no life in you" (John 6:53, KJV); and again: "He that eateth my flesh, and drinketh my blood, dwelleth in me, and I in him" (v. 56, KJV).

This is the redemptive work of Christ by which life is maintained. It was at the cross that life was first made available, and it is there that life is maintained.

Illustration

Herbert Lockyer in the *London Christian Herald* tells of a friend of his in Glasgow who "found himself in Barlinnie prison because of his sin. He was given to drunkenness, became a sot, and grieved the heart of his godly mother. After serving his term of imprisonment, he found his way back again to the old home, and the mother who loved him pleaded with him to sign his pledge. But, like the honest man he was, he said, 'No, Mother, I have signed enough pledges to paper the wall; I need something more than a pledge. I need a power that can make me a sober man, and change my life.' Growing desperate, his mother took a knife and opened one of her veins, and dipping a pen into her flowing blood, she said, 'Sinclair, sign it with your mother's blood, and that may help you.' I heard him say one night before a crowded audience. 'What the blood of my mother could not do, the blood of Jesus Christ accomplished,' and that man tonight is preaching the Gospel of the Redeemer."[3]

C. Christ Preserves Us by His Directive Will

"Because I live, ye shall live also" (John 14:19, KJV). What comfort these words must have brought to the disciples. There they were, on the eve of the crucifixion. Jesus had told them he was going to die. But they had to be reminded that he was also the resurrection, and the life; and that it was his will that they, too, should live. The Lord Jesus will see to it that while he lives we shall never die. He says, "Whosoever liveth and believeth in me shall never die" (11:26).

Conclusion

How may we know this life? The answer is twofold: first, there must be *an acceptance of Christ*— "He that believeth in me" (John 11:25). There must be union with a person, not a doctrine. "This is the record, that God hath given to us eternal life, and this life is in his Son" (1 John 5:11, KJV). Second, there must be *an abiding in Christ*—he that "liveth and believeth in me shall never die" (John 11:26). Abiding in him through his Word, through his cross, and through his will means life, and life "more abundant." Paul's testimony was, "I live; yet not I, but Christ liveth in me: and the life which I now live in the flesh I live by the faith of the Son of God, who loved me, and gave himself for me" (Gal. 2:20, KJV).

6

The Way, the Truth, the Life

John 13:36-14:6

"I am the way, the truth, and the life" (John 14:6, KJV).

Introduction

When Thomas looked into the face of Jesus Christ and pleaded, "Lord, . . . how can we know the way?" (John 14:5), he voiced the deepest need of the human soul. His homesickness for heaven was, in the final analysis, a longing for Christ. The hymnwriter was correct when he wrote, "Where Jesus is, 'tis heaven there." The fact is that Christ had become the answer to every need in the experience of Thomas, and he dreaded the possibility of separation from his source of help. So he cried, "Lord, . . .how can we know the way?" (v. 5). In other words, "How can we know you as an ever-present reality?" The Savior's reply was a final answer, not only for Thomas, but for all men in every age. Jesus said:

I. I Am the Way in order that Men Might Be Saved

By nature man has lost himself in the maze of sin. "All we like sheep have gone astray; we have turned every one to his own way" (Isa. 53:6). The express purpose for which the Son of Man came into the world was "to seek and to save that which was lost" (Luke 19:10). Christ, therefore, has become the "way" that men might be saved.

A. *Christ Is the Only Way to Be Saved*

"I am the way," said Christ, "no man cometh unto the Father, but by me" (John 14:6). While there are as many ways to Christ as there are feet to tread them, there is only *one* way to God; that is, Christ himself. This is not a popular doctrine, and, therefore, not generally accepted, but it remains a fact.

If liberalism had its say, it would tell us that there are many ways to the Father; for instance, the way of nature, the way of aesthetics, or the way of charity. If materialism had its say, it would tell us that the way to the Father is through the improvement of man's environment, until he attains perfection. If ecclesiasticism had its say, it would tell us that the way to the Father is through the sacraments, the rites, and good works. But all these, who undertake to climb over into the fold by "some other way," are thieves and robbers. There is only one way to the Father: it is Christ. He is the *only* way to be saved. There is only one way to get into heaven, and that is by Jesus Christ, *the only way.*

Illustration

A man, wont to trust in his own merit for salvation, dreamed one night that he was constructing a ladder that was to reach from earth to heaven. Whenever the dreamer did a good deed the ladder went up higher. So in the course of years the ladder passed out of sight of the earth, clear up into the clouds. But at last when the competent builder was about to step off the topmost round onto the floor of heaven, a voice cried, "He that climbeth up some other way is a thief and a robber!" Down came the ladder with a crash. The startled dreamer awoke. He had learned his lesson. He saw that he must get salvation from Jesus Christ, for his own self-righteousness; inadequate to fulfill the whole law of God, availed not.[1]

B. Christ Is the Open Way to Be Saved

"I am the way" (John 14:6), says Christ. A way is that which makes movement in some specific direction possible. Without the work of Christ at Calvary there would be no way to heaven. He is not only the pathfinder, but the path along which he invites us to walk. He has done all that is necessary in order that we might arrive safely.

Illustration

My missionary father was preaching in the villages of Angola, Africa. After one memorable meeting with a chief and his men, Dad asked if there were other villages that would give him the same kind of welcome and hearing. The chief said "Yes, a village right through this forest." "But," replied my father, "I don't know the way." "That is no problem," assured the chief. With that he called one of his men and instructed him to take the missionary through the forest to the adjacent village. After traveling for several hours, Dad said, "We have been traveling a long time and we haven't arrived. Do you really know the way?" The man grinned, took his ax from his shoulder, and said, "White man, do you see the marks on those trees there? I made those marks when I blazed the trail. Do you see this ax I hold in my hand? With this ax I cut the way through this forest. Do you see these marks on my body? They are wounds I suffered when I first pushed my way through the undergrowth to make the way." And then standing his full height and tapping his massive chest, the African said with ringing confidence, "I am the way; follow me."

The Lord Jesus points to the marks of his passion and says, "These are the wounds I suffered when I made the way to heaven through the dark jungle of sin. I am the way; follow me."

11. I Am the Truth in order that Men Might Be Sure

When Jesus declared "I am the truth" he gave expression to one of the most profound concepts we find in Scripture. In those words he claimed to be the expression of the absolute truth about God's nature, God's idea of humanity, the relation between moral beings and God. In essence, the Lord Jesus claimed to be:

A. *Truth Embodied in the Incarnate Word*

"I am the . . . truth" (14:6). In the last analysis, truth is a moral abstraction and can only exist in relation to a person—a person who can somehow stand as its representation and end. That person is Christ. Aristotle once said, "Mind, as it came from its Maker, is organized for truth, as the eye to perceive the light, and the ear to hear sounds." That is why the man who finds Christ knows that he has found truth. There is a reality within him which witnesses to truth.

Illustration

During World War II I met a young naval officer by the name of John whose conversion story was quite dramatic. While a vociferous atheist, he had been involved in action with his fellow sailors. The bombing raid had taken a serious toll of life, including his roommate, who was a Christian. Before that fatal day he had often debated, and even derided, his Christian friend, but failed to shake his faith or rob him of his composure and cheerfulness. As John returned to his bunk that day he saw his roommate's Bible lying open. With sorrow in his heart, and a deep longing to know the secret of the faith his Christian friend possessed, he picked up the Bible and began to read the gospel of John.

As he turned the pages, the Spirit of God worked in his heart, and before he was through the twenty-one chapters he was born again.

I asked him if he still had intellectual problems. "Oh, yes, I do," replied John, "and one by one they are being resolved

146

as I continue to read God's Word. But I have no doubt that Jesus Christ is the truth. In meeting and knowing Him, I have experienced a transforming reality I never knew before."

Amplification

Christ is the truth because he is the self-revelation of God which has been manifested (John 14:7, 9), the light that has come into the world without the appropriation of which salvation is not obtained (compare John 1:14, 8:32, 14:17; 1 John 5:6 in connection with John 14:26; Eph. 4:21). "As being the perfect revelation of God the Father: combining in himself and manifesting all divine *reality*—whether in the being, the *law*, or the *character* of God—he embodies what men ought to *know* and *believe* of God; what they should *do* as children of God, and what they should be."[2]

B. Truth Embodied in the Inspired Word

"I am the . . . truth" (John 14:6). When Jesus uttered these words he was not only thinking of the testimony of the Old Testament, but predicting the witness of the New Testament, for he could say, "Search the scriptures; for in them ye think ye have eternal life: and they are they which testify of me" (John 5:39). And then he added: "The Holy Ghost, whom the Father will send in my name, he shall teach you all things, and bring all things to your remembrance, whatsoever I have said unto you" (John 14:26). In essence the Bible is the crib that contains the Christ.

Illustration

Walter F. Burke, former general manager of Project Mercury and Gemini and vice-president of the McDonnell Douglas Corporation, teaches Sunday school in his church. In an interview he declared: "I have found nothing in science or space exploration to compel me to throw away my Bible or to reject my Savior, Jesus Christ, in whom I trust. The space age has been a factor in the deepening of my own spiritual life. I read the Bible more now. I get from the Bible what I cannot get from science—the really important things of life."[3] A testimony like this encourages us to rest upon the written Word of God with quiet assurance.

III. I Am the Life In Order That Men Might Be Strong

By this term "life" the Lord Jesus intended to convey something far more than temporal life. He was offering:

A. Abundant Life

Jesus could say, "I am come that they might have life, and that they might have it more abundantly" (John 10:10). How different is this conception of life to the one commonly attached to Christianity! Here indeed is life in its fullness, life with a capital L.

Some scientists have hazarded the speculation that the origin of life on this planet came with the falling upon it of a fragment of a meteor with a speck of organic life upon it from which all else has developed. Whether that is true or not in regard to the physical life, it is absolutely true in the case of spiritual life. This abundant life of which we are speaking has come from heaven itself, by way of the incarnation, into the clouds and depressions of our terrestrial atmosphere. It is the eternal germ that Jesus has planted in the heart of his redeemed people to spread forever. It is a quality of life that can cope with any situation, under any set of circumstances.

Illustration

Henry M. Stanley, the man who found David Livingstone in Africa and lived with him for some time, gives this testimony: "I went to Africa as prejudiced as the biggest atheist in London. But there came for me a long time for reflection. I saw this solitary old man there and asked myself, 'How on earth does he stop here—is he cracked, or what? What is it that inspires him?' For months after we met I found myself wondering at the old man carrying out all that was said in the Bible— 'Leave all things and follow Me.' But little by little his sympathy for others became contagious; my sympathy was aroused; seeing his piety, his gentleness, his zeal, his earnestness, and how he went about his business, I was converted by him, although he had not tried to do it."[4] This is an example of what Jesus meant when he said, "I am come that [ye] . . . might have life, and that [ye]. . . might have it [above the common]." This is life indeed!

B. Triumphant Life

"In him was life; and the life was the light of men. And the light shineth in darkness; and the darkness comprehended it not" (John 1:4-5). Sin and holiness can never stay together for long. If you would be truly happy you must be truly holy, and the secret is bound up with this triumphant life. Paul knew this kind of life, for he could say, "The law of the Spirit of life in Christ Jesus hath made me free from the law of sin and death" (Rom. 8:2). This spiritual life not only purifies personal life, but, like salt, has the potent quality of arresting corruption in the various aspects of social and national life.

Illustration
Lloyd George once said: "I have always found throughout my career that, when there was a big moral question to settle in England, when the chapel bells began to ring in unison, the fight was over."

Conclusion

Jesus said, "I am the way, the truth, and the life." Without the way there is no going; without the truth there is no knowing; without the life there is no living. "I am the way which you should pursue; the truth which you should believe; the life which you should hope for." (Thomas á Kempis, *The Imitation of Christ*).

7

The True Vine

John 15:1-8, 16

"I am the true vine, and my Father is the husbandman"
(John 15:1, KJV).

Introduction

Authorities are disagreed as to what may have prompted our
Lord's use of the metaphor of the vine. Some say it was the celebration of the communion feast. Others suggest that when
Jesus left the supper table and went down to the brook Kidron
he had to pass the temple, and on the gate of that glorious
building was sculptured the golden vine. He might have
stopped there and given this wonderful discourse. But it is
more likely that as our Lord walked down the slopes of the hill
of Zion to the Garden of Gethsemane, he would have noticed
the surrounding vineyards. Just about that time those vines
would have been pruned, and the dead wood would be burning all over the valley. Looking out upon those vines and the
dead or barren branches that were being burned, Jesus

uttered these words, "I am the true vine, and my Father is the husbandman. Every branch in me that beareth not fruit he taketh away: and every branch that beareth fruit, he purgeth it, that it may bring forth more fruit" (John 15:1-2). The Lord Jesus invites us to consider:

I. The Identity of the Vine

"I am the true vine" (v. 1). As he spoke these words his listeners would recall the utter failure of God's ancient people, the Jews. They had never reached the fulfillment of God's purpose; but here was one who was calling himself "the true vine." As we examine the word "true," we discover that it occurs something like twenty-nine times in the New Testament, twenty-one of these being in the gospel of John. It means "perfect," "ideal," "noble," and is the root of the adverb "verily." The old Puritans often used the word "very"; when a man was true, trusted, and worthy of favor he was called "the very man." This is the source of the phrase in the Nicene Creed: "very God of very God; very man of very man." Here, then, is the true vine. Notice:

A. His Perfect Formation

"I am the true vine" (v. 1). What is the first thing a vinedresser looks for? He looks at a vine's branches. Are they characterized by pliancy? Do they move and grow thickly and symmetrically over the trellises and supports? Perhaps there is no really perfect plant on earth, in the last analysis, but Jesus says here: "You will identify the perfect vine by its formation. I am that vine."

As we confront our Lord Jesus Christ, we find that his character is the most balanced of anyone who ever lived, or will live upon this earth. When John looked upon him, with his colleagues, he was compelled to declare, "The Word [became] . . . flesh, and dwelt among us, (and we beheld his glory, the glory as of the only begotten of the Father,) full of grace and truth" (John 1:14).

Amplification

Amplify by exalting the person of our wonderful Lord. The test of every true character is, first of all, purity, and second, influence upon mankind. Judged by both these tests Jesus Christ is unique, incomparable, and utterly other. Concerning his purity, he could look into the faces of friends and foes and say, "Which of you convinceth me of sin?" (John 8:46). And they dared not raise a voice. The evil spirit said, "I know . . . who thou art, the Holy One of God" (Mark 1:24). Judas said, "I have . . . betrayed the innocent blood" (Matt. 27:4). "In him is no sin," say the apostles; He "did no sin"; He "knew no sin" (1 John 3:5; 1 Peter 2:22; 2 Cor. 5:21). And as for his influence upon mankind, no one has influenced literature, art, music, culture, education, science, and the human personality like Jesus Christ, the Son of God.

B. His Perfect Foliage

"I am the true vine" (John 15:1). As the vinedresser examines the foliage of the grapevine, with its almost translucent leaves, he looks for health and loveliness, green and thrifty growth. Artists will tell you that, because of their sheer beauty, magic, and intrinsic worth as aesthetic objects, vine leaves and the bloom on a grape cluster are among the most challenging and appealing subjects of art throughout history.

As we look at Jesus Christ through the words of this wonderful book, we find that of all the persons who have ever lived he is the only perfect one. Of course, if we are blind in sin, conceited and proud, and have never been united to the living vine, we may be like the Jewish people of his day who saw "no beauty that [they] . . . should desire him" (Isa. 53:2). But having eyes anointed by the Holy Spirit, we have to declare, in the words of the Song of Solomon, "He is altogether lovely . . . the chiefest among ten thousand" (Song. 5:16, 10). In him there is beauty, grace, and fragrance. Throughout the world the vine is recognized as a symbol of fruitfulness, nourishment, and beauty. God has chosen this as the symbol of the loveliness of the Lord Jesus.

Illustration

The following is a translation of a letter sent by Publius Lentulus to the Roman senate during the Roman Empire period. "There appeared in these days a man of great virtue, named Jesus Christ, who is yet among us; of the Gentiles accepted for a prophet of truth; but his disciples call him the Son of God. He raiseth the dead, and cureth all manner of disease. A man of stature somewhat tall and comely, with a very reverend countenance, such as the beholder must both love and fear.

"In reproving, he is terrible; in admonishing, courteous and fair-spoken; pleasant in conversation, mixed with gravity. It cannot be remembered that any have seen him laugh, but many have seen him weep; in speaking, very temperate, modest, and wise; a man of singular beauty, surpassing the children of men."[1]

C. His Perfect Fruitfulness

"I am the true vine" (John 15:1). The grapes of Eshcol were so enormous that they could weigh anywhere from twelve to fifteen pounds a cluster. When Joshua, Caleb, and the other ten explorers went into the valley of Eshcol and cut those clusters of grapes, two men had to carry their immense weight on a pole. As you know, crushed grapes make a wonderful drink, and dried grapes make a wonderful feast. In our Lord Jesus Christ there is complete sustenance for everyone who will come to him. He is the true vine, perfect in formation, in foliage, and fruitage.

Amplification

Amplify by underscoring the perfections of Christ. Jesus said, "I am the . . . vine [the perfect]; and my Father is the husbandman" (John 15:1). Consider the words of God the Father, who is infallible in his judgment, searching in his wisdom, and inscrutable in his discernment. On two occasions he broke into time to speak concerning his Son. Looking back over his private life, at the age of thirty, when he was baptized in Jordan, God could say of him, "This is my beloved

Son, in whom I am well pleased" (Matt. 3:17). Three years later, after his public ministry had been scrutinized by foe, fiend, and friend, on the Mount of Transfiguration, God could declare yet once again, "This is my beloved Son, in whom I am well pleased; hear ye him" (Matt. 17:5).

II. The Dependency of the Vine

"I am the vine, ye are the branches" (John 15:5). Although he is the perfect vine, he is dependent upon us as the branches for the human expression of his life. He longs to see reproduced in us as individuals, and the church as a corporate body, all that he was in his incarnate perfection. Because of sin this perfection will not be consummated until we see him in glory. In the meantime, however, he continues his sanctifying work in us day by day. How we reveal his life depends on what kind of branches we are.

A. *The Fruitful Branch*

"Every branch that beareth fruit, he purgeth it, that it may bring forth more fruit" (John 15:2). The function of the branch is to bear fruit, and so it needs to be pruned to become more and more fruitful.

How often men and women have come to me and said, "I am interested in being a Christian, but there is one problem that haunts me. Why is it that Christian people seem to suffer so much? If they are God's own people, why does he not protect them from suffering?"

God has his heavenly logic and purpose in our suffering. Says George MacDonald: "Jesus Christ, the Son of God, suffered, not that we might be saved from suffering, but that our suffering might be like His." If the world is going to know a redemption, it must be through the work of the cross, and that means death—an unpopular but necessary doctrine for Christian people. There must be a Calvary before there can be a Pentecost. There must be a cutting back of the self-life, so that the Christ-life may burst forth.

Illustration

Dr. John Wilson, writing in *The Christian*, said that he once "heard Booth-Tucker say that he preached in Chicago one day, and out from the throng a burdened toiler came and said to him, before all the audience: 'Booth-Tucker, you can talk like that about how Christ is dear to you and helps you; but if your wife was dead, as my wife is, and you had some babies crying for their mother, who would never come back, you would not say what you are saying.'

"Just a few days later, he lost his beautiful and nobly gifted wife in a railway wreck, and the body was brought to Chicago and carried to the Salvation Army barracks for the funeral service. Booth-Tucker at last stood up after the funeral service and said: 'The other day when I was here, a man said I could not say Christ was sufficient if my wife were dead and my children were crying for their mother. If that man is here, I tell him that Christ is sufficient. My heart is all crushed. My heart is all bleeding. My heart is all broken, but there is a song in my heart, and Christ put it there.'

"That man was there, and down the aisle he came, and fell down beside the casket, and said, 'Verily, if Christ can help us like that, I will surrender to Him.' He was saved there and then."[2]

B. The Barren Branch

"Every branch in me that beareth not fruit he taketh away" (John 15:2). If the fruitful branch represents the spiritual man, the barren branch speaks of the carnal man. There are too many carnal Christians who are not prepared for the knife, for the suffering that brings the glory. But notice the solemn words, "He taketh away" (v. 2). This is not a reference to eternal damnation, for these words are spoken of the Christian, but rather a warning concerning a possible cutting off of the physical life.

Exegesis

Explain "taketh away." "The word may mean this literally (as "remove" in [John] 11:39) and would therefore be a reference to the physical death of fruitless Christians [Acts 5:6, 10]; 1 Cor. 11:30, [and 1 John 5:16]; or it may mean lift up (as "picked up" in [John] 8:59) which would indicate that the vinedresser encourages and makes it easier for the fruitless believer, hoping he will respond and begin to bear fruit."[3]

C. The Withered Branch

"If a man abide not in me, he is cast forth as a branch, and is withered; and men gather them, and cast them into the fire, and they are burned" (John 15:6). Notice that when Jesus speaks here of the withered branch, he does not say "Every branch *in me.*" It is a branch, evidently, which has a defect; a branch that is not properly secure in the vine. There is a blockage, or a breakage, and the life of the vine is not flowing through it.

What happens to the withered branches? They are burned. The symbolism here is terrifying, if you take it seriously, and there is no other way to take it. Who gathers the branches, how they are burned, and what it means, is left in silence, without any explanation. All we know is that Scripture expounds Scripture, and if we are to understand this picture at all we have to remember that there is a place for withered branches: it is separation forever from the presence of God. It is spoken of as "the lake of fire" (Rev. 20:14) that burns with inextinguishable flame. If the horrifying symbolism of that does not cause us to fear in the presence of God, may he have mercy on our souls!

Amplification

How then may we be united to the vine and become fruitful branches? Jesus replies, "Abide in me, and I in you" (John 15:4). This simply means *the acceptance of Christ*—"I in you" (v. 4). You must open the door of your heart, and receive the Lord Jesus into your life now. "He that is joined unto the Lord is one spirit" (1 Cor. 6:17). With the acceptance of Christ there must be *the reliance on Christ*— "Abide in me" (John 15:4). Before there can be communion there must be union.

Union is the acceptance of Christ, and communion continues by reliance on Christ. In order to abide in Christ you must feed upon his Word and get to know him; then bask in the sunshine of his love, drawing from him the resources, the very life, of the vine.

III. The Fertility of the Vine

"Herein is my Father glorified, that ye bear much fruit; so shall ye be my disciples" (John 15:8); and again: "Ye have not chosen me, but I have chosen you, and ordained you, that ye should go and bring forth fruit, and that your fruit should remain" (v. 16). The whole purpose of the fertility of the Vine is that God should be glorified. Indeed, that is the whole purpose of our lives. We are to "glorify God, and to enjoy him for ever." There are two ways in which God is glorified, in relation to the fertility of the vine. The first is:

A. Christian Discipleship

"Herein is my Father glorified, that ye bear much fruit; so shall ye be my disciples" (John 8). A disciple is a person who receives not only the authority, but the sovereignty, of his Lord; one who disciplines his life in obedience, to bear fruit to the glory of God. Jesus Christ wants men and women who will follow him closely, loyally, cost what it will, even if it means the pruning knife.

Illustration
Henry Drummond, preacher and author, once introduced an address to a select West End club in London with these words: "Ladies and gentlemen, the entrance fee into the kingdom of heaven is nothing: the annual subscription is everything."[4]

B. Christian Apostleship

"Ye have not chosen me, but I have chosen you, and ordained you, that ye should go and bring forth fruit, and that your fruit should remain" (John 15:16). Christian apostleship is one of the great needs in the Christian church today. The biblical use of this word "apostle" is confined to the New Testament where it occurs seventy-nine times. It literally means "to send." Christ was an apostle, a "sent one"; the twelve were apostles. Paul and others were apostles, and it is clear from the Word of God that we can be apostles today.

Alongside the distinctive and more technical use of the word is the employment of it in the sense of the messenger (Phil. 2:25; 2 Cor. 8:23). Right through to the end of time God needs messengers who will go out to bring forth fruit that will remain.

Illustration

While David Brainerd, one of the most celebrated of our missionaries, was laboring among the poor, benighted Indians on the banks of the Delaware, he once said, "I care not where I live, or what hardships I go through, so that I can but gain souls to Christ. While I am asleep, I dream of these things; as soon as I awake, the first thing I think of is this great work. All my desire is the conversion of sinners, and all my hope is in God."[5]

Conclusion

We conclude as we started, with the thought of Christ the perfect vine. Just as he could reveal the Father perfectly in his incarnation, so we are called upon to reveal our Savior through our mortal bodies. The only way in which this can be accomplished is by abiding in him, so that his life and fruit may be seen in us. God save us from being barren, or withered, branches! God make us fruitful branches, bearing not only "fruit," "more fruit," but "much fruit" (15:2, 8).

Part 2
GOD ALIVE IN MIRACLES FROM THE GOSPEL OF JOHN

8

The Changing of Water into Wine:
The Glory of Christ
John 2:1-11

Introduction

The miracles of the New Testament are recorded to illustrate the glory of our Lord Jesus Christ. Particularly is this so in the gospel of John, where we read of seven miracles before the resurrection and one after the resurrection. These miracles John calls "signs," because they each have special significance and a message to teach.

Out of all the miracles our Lord performed it is significant that the first one had to do with a wedding. This is because marriage, at its best, is one of the highest points of human realization. God's great design is consummated when a man and woman are made one in fellowship, joy, and blessing. At this point of highest achievement and realization, however, there was a threatened failure. Indeed, that is often the case, for as the psalmist says, "Verily every man at his best state is altogether vanity" (Ps. 39:5, KJV). It was at this point that the Lord Jesus broke into the scene and turned what would have been gloom into glory.

I. The Presence of Christ in Human Life

"Both Jesus was called, and his disciples, to the marriage" (John 2:2). When Jesus first appeared in his ministry, it was not at a synagogue or church, nor at a funeral, but at a wedding. There, in the midst of human joys, he showed that the Gospel speaks to the happiest and gladdest experiences of life, for the Gospel of our Lord Jesus Christ is "Good News." It is the Good News spelled out to needy men and women.

Notice, in the context of the previous chapter, that the presence of the Lord Jesus manifesting his glory was the presence of "grace and truth." "The Word was made flesh, and dwelt among us, (and we beheld his glory, the glory as of the only begotten of the Father) full of grace and truth" (John 1:14, KJV).

A. His Presence Always Elevates

"The only begotten of the Father, full of grace" (John 1:14, NKJV). "Grace" brings liberation and salvation. "The grace of God that bringeth salvation hath appeared to all men" (Titus 2:11); and again: "Sin shall not have dominion over you: for ye are not under the law, but under grace" (Rom. 6:14). Grace always saves and elevates. The presence of the Lord Jesus lifted that scene of threatened sorrow and tragedy into a wedding that has become known through history as an example of joy and celebration because of his miracle-working presence.

Illustration

Africaner, the notorious Hottentot chief, was the terror of the whole country. He carried on a cruel and constant warfare with his neighbors, stealing cattle, burning kraals, capturing women and children, and killing his enemies. When Robert Moffatt, as a messenger from the Prince of Life, started for Africaner's kraal, friends warned him that the savage monster would make a drum-head of his skin and a drinking cup of his skull, that no power could change such a savage. But Moffatt went to the chief and spoke to him the word of life. It entered the heathen heart and Africaner lived. He left the environment of death, was loosened from the bands of the grave, and became a Christian chief. When a Dutch farmer, whose uncle Africaner had killed, saw the converted Hottentot he exclaimed: "Oh God, what cannot thy grace do! What a miracle of thy power!"[1]

B. *His Presence Always Educates*

"The only begotten of the Father, full of . . . truth" (John 1:14, NKJV) If grace saves, then truth sanctifies; and the presence of the Lord Jesus at that wedding was a sanctifying influence. He brought the happy experience of that young couple right up to the standard of his immediate presence. Nothing happened at that feast without his approval and control.

In his high priestly petition, the Lord Jesus prayed, "Sanctify them through thy truth: thy word is truth" (John 17:17). If your life is to be lived at the highest level; if you want the sweetness and sanctifying power of God to operate, then you must invite the Lord Jesus into your life. His grace will save, his truth will sanctify.

Illustration

"If we work upon marble, it will perish; if on brass, time will efface it; if we rear temples, they will crumple into dust; but if we work upon immortal minds, and imbue them with principles, with the just fear of God and love of our fellow men, we engrave on those tablets something that will brighten to all eternity."[2]

II. The Power of Christ in Human Life

"This beginning of miracles did Jesus in Cana of Galilee" (John 2:11). "The miracles of Jesus are called signs by John in order to emphasize the significance of the miracles rather than the miracles themselves. They revealed [the] various aspects of the person or work of Christ (here His glory), and their purpose was to encourage faith in His followers."[3] The glory of Christ's power was demonstrated in a threefold manner:

A. *He Restored Order*

"They have no wine" (John 2:3). It seems that Mary was there before Jesus (the tense used in the Greek suggests that she was already there); and it is possible that she was in charge of the wedding festivities. Therefore, a failure would be a reflection on her, and for a moment she panicked. "They have no wine. The wine has failed!" she said to Jesus—and she expected a miracle of him. He was her son, it was true, but she had already pondered much in her heart what kind of man he was. She knew that he was none other than the Son of God, the Messiah, so she broke in upon him and said, "Won't you do something about it?" "Woman," he said, "leave it to me. My hour is not yet come. Be confident that I have a plan for all of this, and at the right moment I will act."

> **Exegesis**
> John 2:4. The word "woman" (*gunē*) is used of a female, unmarried or married. As employed in our text it carries no tone of reproof or severity, but of endearment and respect. The Lord Jesus used the same form of address when he spoke from Calvary's cross and said, "Woman, behold thy son!" and to the disciple, "Behold thy mother!" (John 19:26-27).

There was panic and chaos at the wedding, but the Lord Jesus brought order out of it. And when he comes into a life he brings order out of chaos. God had a plan for his Son, and he walked every moment and hour according to that divine program. He has a plan for your life, too. Have you that divine sense of direction and destiny in your life?

> **Illustration**
> The minister who was drilling Sunday school students in

catechism asked, "What is a miracle?" A little girl put up her hand and replied, "Something we can't do, but Jesus can."

So often when faced with a chaotic situation we throw up our hands and say, "I quit." This is when we ought to remember that Jesus specializes in bringing order out of chaos. We can't, but he can!

B. He Released Nature

"Draw out now, and bear unto the governor of the feast" (John 2:8), and even as they drew the water it turned to wine. Having been told to "fill the waterpots with water" (v. 7), the servants filled them to the brim in complete obedience. Then the miracle happened. As the water was poured out it could be seen that it had turned to wine!

What Jesus did here was to speed up the processes of nature. What is wine but the dew and rain of heaven sucked up through the roots and branches into the cluster of grapes until it reddens to the wine we all recognize? It took Jesus only an instant, not a season, to produce that wine. He released nature from its bondage of time.

Why is the universe slowed down and delayed in its unfolding of natural beauties and wonders? Because of the bondage of corruption (Rom. 8:21). When Adam sinned in the Garden he brought the curse of sin upon creation, and ever since, creation has groaned under the bondage of corruption, awaiting that glad day when, released from bondage, nature will perform as God intended it to do.

Illustration

William Jennings Bryan was once eating a piece of watermelon and was struck by its beauty. He relates: "I took some of the seeds and weighed them and found that it would require some 5,000 seeds to weigh a pound. And then I applied mathematics to a forty-pound melon. One of these seeds, put into the ground, when warmed by the sun and moistened by the rain goes to work; it gathers from somewhere 200,000 times its own weight and forcing this raw material through a tiny stem, constructs a watermelon. It covers the outside with a coating of green; inside of the green it puts a layer of white, and within the white a core of red, and all through the red it scatters seeds, each one capable of continuing the work of reproduction.

"Everything that grows tells a like story of infinite power. Why should I deny that a divine hand fed a multitude with a few loaves and fishes when I see hundreds of millions fed every year by a hand which converts the seeds scattered over the field into an abundant harvest? We know that food can be multiplied in a few months' time. Shall we deny the power of the Creator to eliminate the element of time, when we have gone so far in eliminating the element of space?"[4]

C. He Reversed Failure

"When the ruler of the feast had tasted the water that was made wine, and knew not whence it was: (but the servants which drew the water knew;) the governor of the feast called the bridegroom, And saith unto him, Every man at the beginning doth set forth good wine; and when men have well drunk, then that which is worse: but thou hast kept the good wine until now" (John 2:9-10). The Lord Jesus turned failure into success, crisis into creativity, tragedy into triumph, poverty into plenty, water into wine.

When man provides anything, he always supplies the best at first, and then an inferior quality. But when Jesus Christ comes into a life he starts with the best, and then continues to do "above all that we ask or think" (Eph. 3:20). He alone can turn failure into victory.

III. The Purpose of Christ in Human Life

"This beginning of miracles did Jesus in Cana of Galilee, and manifested forth his glory; and *his disciples believed on him*" (John 2:11). The Lord Jesus had just influenced five men. John the Baptist had pointed him out, saying, "Behold, the Lamb of God" (John 1:29), and right away two of them followed Jesus. Simon, Philip, and then Nathanael followed him, but at first were puzzled as to his identity. Then they saw the glory of his presence, full of grace and truth, and the glory of his power, restoring order, releasing nature, reversing failure, and they looked at one another and said, "This is he of whom the prophets wrote; the Messiah indeed!" And they believed on him. So the glory of Christ's purpose is:

A. *The Establishment of a Divine Relationship*

"He came unto his own, and his own received him not. But as many as received him, to them gave he power to become the sons of God, even to them that believe on his name" (John 1:11-12). They believed on him, and the glory of the Gospel was manifested in the establishment of a divine relationship. From that moment onward, those followers were the children of God by faith in him.

And so it is with us. We become the children of God by receiving the Lord Jesus and believing in him. That is more than believing *about* him. It is more than intellectual assent: it is heart consent. It is the commitment of the mind, heart, and will to Jesus Christ as Savior and Lord.

Illustration

A. T. Schofield, the Harley Street physician, was fifteen when he started school at a private academy in Rhyl, North Wales. When his new roommate inquired, "Are you a Christian?" Schofield replied that he was not, for, although he had been religiously brought up, his parents' teaching had fallen on deaf ears. Then his companion asked, "Would you like to be one?" A. T. Schofield replied, "It's no use liking. I know well I never shall be a Christian."

His young mentor went off to a prayer meeting to pray for the new boy, and on his return tumbled into bed and fell asleep. But A. T. Schofield could not rest, knowing that the lad who shared the room with him was all right and he was all wrong. He tossed in uneasy sleep till nearly 2:00 A.M. , asking himself why he could not rest like the boy in the next bed. Suddenly there came to his mind the words, "Because you won't take it." He realized then that he was very sick with the sin disease when all the time the medicine to heal his disease was within reach. The remedy was true personal belief in Christ, his Savior. To simply believe in the medicine would do him no good: *he must take it.* There and then he prayed from his heart, "O God, I take Thy Son, Jesus Christ, to be my Savior this night," and dropped off to sleep.

The next morning a teacher came and sat beside him, and said, "We prayed for you last night. I'm so sorry you are not a Christian." "But I am one," he said to the master and related how he received the Lord at two o'clock in the morning. In telling his story, Dr. Schofield then added, "I rushed out of the house, threw my cap into the air, and ran around the play-ground to let off, as it were, some of the steam."[5] Herein is the glory of the Gospel!

B. The Experience of a Divine Fellowship

"Truly our fellowship is with the Father, and with his Son Jesus Christ" (1 John 1:3). From the moment those disciples believed in the Lord Jesus they were in his circle. They prayed together, lived together, slept together, talked together, traveled together, and worked miracles together: He, the leader and divine Son; and they, not only his children by faith, but his followers and friends (John 15:14).

Illustration

Among the Dutch, roses were sometimes cultivated by planting an inferior rose close to a rose of superior quality. The lesser rose was carefully watched, and its anthers removed to avoid self-pollinization and permit pollinization by the superior rose. Gradually the rose thus treated demonstrated the superior characteristics of its companion. This is indeed a beautiful illustration of the blessing that comes to the life that knows the companionship of Jesus. If our lives are pollinized, as it were, by his righteousness; if his life-transforming truth is received into the heart, if self is sacrificed to make room for the incoming of his superior life, it is inevitable that gradually the life will lose its own inferior characteristics and develop the characteristics of the blessed life of him who is himself the rose of Sharon.

It is wonderful to trace the development in the lives of the disciples from that day in Cana of Galilee through to the day of Pentecost. Truly, they were changed into his likeness, from glory to glory.

Do we know a fellowship like that in our lives? If not, we can have it, for it is all bound up in the glory of Christ as demonstrated in this miracle.

Conclusion

Jesus was called to the marriage and he came. We never hear of an invitation given to him that he refused. Have you invited him into your marriage, your home, your church, and, what is even more personal and relevant, have you invited him into your heart?

9

The Healing of the Nobleman's Son:
Faith in Christ
John 4:43-54

Introduction

If the first miracle recorded in John's gospel illustrates the glory of Christ, the second miracle illustrates the reality of faith in Christ. It is interesting that there are three expressions in this story that relate to faith. Twice it is specifically stated that the nobleman "believed" (4:50, 53); and again, he "besought" Jesus (4:47). The word "besought" in the Greek is stronger than the words "to ask" or "to petition" and conveys the idea of "pleading in faith." These steps of faith illustrate the movements in the process of an individual's salvation. No one can be truly saved through faith in Christ alone until he has progressed through these three movements of faith.

I. The Creation of the Nobleman's Faith

"When he heard that Jesus was come out of Judea into Galilee, he went unto him, and besought him that he would come down, and heal his son: for he was at the point of death" (4:47). As we read through this story we notice the progression of this man's approach to Christ. First he heard, then he came, finally he sought. Christian faith grows from these three essentials.

A. *He Heard of Christ*

"When he heard that Jesus was come out of Judea into Galilee, he went unto him" (John 4:47). He had been told of the mighty work of Jesus and had come to understand that he was no ordinary person. Perhaps he even glimpsed, intellectually, that here was the Son of God, the Messiah, and he figured that if ever a miracle was going to be performed upon his son it would have to be done by this Jesus.

Many people ask why missionaries go out to the foreign field and disturb the culture, thinking, and practices of people of another nation. The man who understands the sovereignty of God in redemption, as revealed through all the followers of Jesus Christ, realizes that we are committed to a task of evangelism that knows no national barriers. "How then shall they call on him in whom they have not believed? and how shall they believe in him of whom they have not heard? and how shall they hear without a preacher? . . . So then faith cometh by hearing, and hearing by the word of God" (Rom. 10:14, 17). A more literal translation would be, "Faith cometh by hearing, and hearing by the Gospel of Christ."

B. *He Came to Christ*

"When he heard that Jesus was come out of Judea into Galilee, he went [came] unto him" (John 4:47). When faith is created in the human heart by the Word of God, there is a movement toward Christ. Inertia is replaced by action, the voluntary response of the mind, heart, and will.

Many people imagine that they can drift into an experience of Christ when the appropriate but undefined time arrives, but this is a delusion. There is nothing fortuitous about a personal confrontation with Jesus Christ. Christianity is not "the opiate of the people," it is rather a deliberate choice, a rational and responsible encounter with the Son of God. The Lord Jesus made this very clear when he preached the gospel of the kingdom. To some he said, "*Come* unto me" (Matt. 11:28); to others he commanded "*Follow* me" (Luke 9:23), and to those who tended to hesitate he urged "*Strive* [or "agonize"] to enter in at the strait gate" (Luke 13:24)—all active verbs that call for a vigorous response.

C. He Asked of Christ

He "besought him that he would come . . . and heal his son" (John 4:47). The word "besought" means "asked," "besieged," "desired," "entreated," or "prayed." We have made this whole matter of salvation so cheap and easy that people have forgotten the great travail of soul through which men and women in past generations have had to go in order to come to Christ. The modem generation sits passively in church and expects the Lord to come and do them a favor. True salvation from sin demands of us a deep, heart exercise. God wants to see this earnestness in terms of repentance, faith, and obedience. We know that salvation is "not of works, lest any man should boast" (Eph. 2:9), but at the same time it is an active, appropriating faith.

Illustration

In order to clarify what faith involved, C. H. Spurgeon used to employ this illustration. Suppose there is a fire on the third floor of a house, and a child is trapped in a room there. A huge, strong man stands on the ground beneath the window where the child's face appears, and he calls "Jump!" "It is a part of faith," Spurgeon would say, "to know that there is a man there; still another part of faith to believe him to be a strong man; but the essence of faith lies in trusting him fully and dropping into his arms." Thus it is with the sinner and Christ.[1]

II. The Conviction of the Nobleman's Faith

"Then said Jesus unto him, Except ye see signs and wonders, ye will not believe" (John 4:48). Though the nobleman was in anguish and tears, the Lord did not spare him. He had to believe first, and then see the touch of healing upon his son. Two demands were made upon his faith:

A. *Obedience to the Word*

"Go thy way; thy son liveth. And the man believed the word that Jesus had spoken unto him, and he went his way" (John 4:50). The conviction of faith that follows the creation of faith will come when there is obedience to the Word. Paul had this in mind when he wrote the Epistle to the Romans and talked about "the obedience of faith" (Rom. 16:26). James implied it when he wrote, "Faith without works is dead" (James 2:26). Dietrich Bonhoeffer, in his book, *The Cost of Discipleship*, writes: "Faith is not faith unless it leads to obedience." Jesus said to this nobleman, "Go thy way; thy son liveth. And the man believed the word that Jesus had spoken unto him, and he went his way" (John 4:50).

There is no substitute for obedience, either in sinner or saint, for as we have seen already, faith that does not lead to obedience is not faith at all.

Illustration

Through United Press comes the report that termites have eaten through a large stack of pamphlets entitled, *Control of Termites,* in the mailing room of the University of California at Berkeley. It is one thing to have in a pamphlet the information concerning the control of termites, and quite another thing to make a practical application of that information! On speaking to His disciples on one occasion, the Lord Jesus said regarding the things He taught them, *"If ye know these things, happy are ye if ye do them"* (John 13:17).[2]

B. Dependence on the Lord

He "himself believed, and his whole house" (John 4:53). When the man discovered that his son had been healed it affected not only his own life, but that of his entire household. As we shall see in a moment, he became an open follower of the Lord Jesus. From that moment on he lived by faith and not by sight. He had learned the lesson that Thomas needed to learn after the resurrection, when he insisted, "Except I shall see in his hands the print of the nails, and put my finger into the print of the nails, and thrust my hand into his side, I will not believe (John 20:25). Jesus had to say to him, "Blessed are they that have not seen, and yet have believed" (John 20:29). This is the message that Habakkuk, Paul, and Martin Luther preached, namely, "The just shall live by faith" (Hab. 2:4; Rom. 1:17).

Illustration

Martin Luther, as a monk, "happened on a volume of the Scriptures. He knew it only as a forbidden book. He read it furtively until he came to the place where it is written, 'There is none other name under heaven given among men, whereby we must be saved.' He read, 'By the deeds of the law there shall no flesh be justified . . . . What the law could not do, in that it was weak through the flesh, God sending his own Son . . . .' The light began to break.

He [went] to Rome. He determined on penance by climbing . . . the Sacred Stairway on his knees. Half way up he seemed to hear a voice saying, 'The just shall live by faith!' and the day broke. He stood erect, a believer in Christ as his only Savior from sin."[3]

III. The Confession of the Nobleman's Faith

"So the father knew that it was at the same hour, in the which Jesus said unto him, Thy son liveth: and himself believed, and his whole house" (John 4:53). The Bible teaches that the Christian faith is a confessional faith. Christ never called for secret disciples. This explains why the early Christians were publicly baptized right after their conversion. Baptism is the outward expression of an inward experience of personal faith in Christ. The confession of faith has a twofold aspect:

A. *Confession to God*

"That if thou shalt confess with thy mouth the Lord Jesus, and shalt believe in thine heart that God hath raised him from the dead, thou shalt be saved" (Rom. 10:9); and again: "For whosoever shall call upon the name of the Lord shall be saved" (Rom. 10:13). Somewhere along that long journey (25 miles) to his home, the nobleman must have committed himself to the Lord Jesus Christ in an act of faith. And this is how it should be. Anything less than this is hypocritical and unreal. We cannot confess outwardly what we do not know inwardly of personal faith in Jesus Christ.

B. *Confession to Men*

"So the father knew that it was at the same hour, in the which Jesus said unto him, Thy son liveth: and himself believed, and his whole house" (John 4:53). So real was this man's experience of faith in Christ that he was able to influence his whole household. His confession to God was matched by his confession to men—and this is how it should be. The Lord Jesus said, "Whosoever therefore shall confess me before men, him will I confess also before my Father which is in heaven" (Matt. 10:32).

On the day of Pentecost we see this twofold confession dramatically exemplified. After Peter had preached his God-anointed sermon there was, first of all, *conviction of sin.* The hearers cried out, "Men and brethren, what shall we do?" (Acts 2:37). Then followed *conversion of life.* Peter said, "Repent, and be baptized every one of you in the name of Jesus Christ for the remission of sins" (Acts 2:38), and that issued in *confession of faith*—"They that gladly received his word were baptized: and the same day there were added unto them about three thousand souls" (Acts 2:41). This demonstration of enthusiastic faith is the evidence of the genuine working of God in the human soul.

Illustration

Henry J. Heinz, of the fifty-seven varieties fame, wrote his will as follows: "Looking forward to the time when my earthly career will end, I desire to set forth at the very beginning of this will, as the most important item in it, a confession of my faith in Jesus Christ as my Saviour. I also desire to bear witness to the fact that throughout my life, in which were the usual joys and sorrows, I have been wonderfully sustained by my faith in God through Jesus Christ. This legacy was left me by my consecrated mother, a woman of strong faith, and to it I attribute any success I have attained."[4]

Conclusion

This living miracle of the healing of the nobleman's son has taught us an important lesson about faith in Christ. We have seen what is meant by the creation of faith, the conviction of faith, and the confession of faith. Where true faith is born in a person's life he is never apologetic. On the contrary, his walk and talk reflect joy and confidence. Faith is to believe what we do not see; and the reward of this faith is to see what we believe.

10

The Making Whole of a Crippled Life:
The Complete Cure
John 5:1-15; 7:23

Introduction

Here is a story that beautifully illustrates the completeness of
the cure which the Lord Jesus can effect in the lives of men and
women who are afflicted by the disease of sin. The setting for
this event was the city of Jerusalem at the time of "the feast"
(some manuscripts include the article *he*— "the first") which
would naturally mean the Passover; but there is no way of being
certain what feast it was that Jesus attended here. Ever aware of
the needy souls around him, he made his way to the pool of
Bethesda, near the sheep market. The name means "the house
of mercy," and there lay a great multitude of sick people—
blind, crippled and withered. Among the most desperate of all
was a man who had been an invalid for thirty-eight years. Time
and again, he had tried to avail himself of the healing waters
bubbling up from an underground spring, but without success.

Disappointed and frustrated, he lay there, unable to move. Then the Lord Jesus appeared on the scene and spoke words that instantly brought about a complete cure.

I. The Word of Divine Diagnosis

"Wilt thou be made whole?" (John 5:6). "Do you know what is really wrong with you? Do you want to be rid of this complaint?" he asked. The piercing eyes of the Lord Jesus had looked beyond the external, and by his question he brought home to the man's heart just what his condition was. The words that the Savior spoke revealed:

A. The Health He Needed

"Jesus saw him lie, and knew that he had been now a long time in that case" (John 5:6). Sin ultimately affects physical health, and Jesus Christ coupled this man's malady with his sinful life. "Sin no more, lest a worse thing come unto thee" (v. 14), were his parting words to him.

And this is true of men and women today. However fit they may appear to be at the moment, if they refuse the complete cure which is available in Jesus Christ, sin will bring them to the place of ultimate ill health—death (1 Cor. 11:30).

Illustration

"Sin" really does exist, according to Dr. Karl Menninger. The famous psychiatrist is distressed that modern society tries to figure out its problems and talk about morality without ever mentioning the word "sin." He is convinced that the only way to raise the moral tone of present-day civilization and deal with the depression and worries that plague clergy, psychiatrists, and ordinary folk is to revive an understanding of what "sin" is.[1]

B. The Help He Needed

"Sir, I have no man, when the water is troubled, to put me into the pool" (John 5:7). Sin affects not only the physical, but the social life. Here was someone who was alone and lonely. No one would pity him or help him. Perhaps his manner of sinful living had turned even his best friends against him. Like the psalmist, he had to cry, "No man cared for my soul" (Ps. 142:4).

The Scriptures show that though there is a confederacy of sin, the time comes when sin separates even worldly friends from each other.

Illustration

Cite the story of the prodigal son (Luke 15:11-32), and emphasize the words "and no man gave unto him" (v. 16).

C. The Hope He Needed

"Sir, I have no man, when the water is troubled, to put me into the pool: but while I am coming, another steppeth down before me" (John 5:7). He had lost all hope. And the Bible speaks of men and women "having no hope, and without God in the world" (Eph. 2:12).

Sin affects the physical, social, and the spiritual realms of the human personality. This man had a diseased body, a defiled soul, and a dead spirit. In theological terms, we speak of man's "total depravity"; and by that we mean that sin has invaded the entire being. It is no wonder, then, that Jesus addressed him with the words, "Wilt thou be made whole?" (John 5:6). Jesus said, "They that be whole need not a physician, but they that are sick" (Matt. 9:12).

Exegesis

It is important to point out that verse 4 is missing in the oldest and best manuscripts. In all probability it was added, like the clause in verse 3, to make clear the statement in verse 7. The Jews explained the healing virtue of the intermittent springs by attributing it to the ministry of angels.

Illustration

Dr. Walter Wilson, ever on the alert to speak to men about their souls and need of the Saviour, asked an attendant at a service station who had filled his car with gas: "How did sin get in Sinclair?" pointing to the lighted sign atop the gas pump. "I do not know, sir, how sin got into Sinclair; but, sir, I have wished many times that I knew how to get sin out of my life!" It was then that Dr. Wilson had the opportunity to tell the young man of the One who is the sinner's friend and of whom it is written: "And thou shalt call his name JESUS: for he shall save his people from their sins" (Matt. 1:21)[2]

II. The Word of Divine Deliverance

"Rise, take up thy bed, and walk" (John 5:8), were the Savior's words. And the man realized that he was in the presence of one whose eyes shone with the glory of heaven, and who spoke with the voice of authority. Such was the redemptive power of the word spoken that a threefold deliverance took place in this man's life:

A. A Spiritual Deliverance

"Rise" (John 5:8). This was the word that quickened his dead spirit; and the Lord Jesus always starts with the spirit. Later he could say to him, "Behold, thou art made. .. [well]: sin no more, lest a worse thing come unto thee" (v. 14). Writing to the Ephesians, Paul could say, "You hath he quickened, who were dead in trespasses and sins" (Eph. 2:1). This is the nature of spiritual deliverance. It involves not only the remission of past sins, but the regeneration of our spirits; a mighty deliverance indeed!

Illustration

When the lame man and the healing pool and the Master came together, there was health and hope. When the little lad and the few loaves and fishes and the Master came together, there was sufficiency and even abundance. A thirsty woman, an ancient well, and the Master, and there were streams of living water flowing into human hearts. A rugged fisherman, a broken net, and the Master, and there was discipleship, and a story to tell. Wherever a human need and a sincere faith and the Master meet, there is transformation and consecration. If we bring our lives, weak and insufficient, to the Master, He will remake us.[3]

B. A Moral Deliverance

"Take up thy bed" (John 5:8). At that command the man rolled it up and put it on his shoulder. Someone has said that he did this in order to show that he was making no provision for a relapse!

It may be that you have been laid low by temptation again and again. You may have tried discipline and reformation, but without the delivering word of Jesus Christ you will never know moral deliverance.

It is a wonderful day when we can pick up and carry away the very thing that symbolizes our moral defeat. Observe that this man had the courage to carry his pallet (the bed of the very poor), even on the Sabbath day. Carrying furniture on the Sabbath was the kind of work prohibited by the rabbis in their strict interpretation of the fourth commandment. When we know the deliverance of Christ we fear no one but God.

Illustration

A painter once painted the devil playing a game of chess with a young man whose eternal soul was at stake. The scene showed the devil with a look of glee on his face as he checkmates the young man whose look of despair acknowledges defeat. There appears no other move for him to make. A great chess player came across the work of art, and after carefully studying the game, he set up a chessboard with the pieces in a similar position. After much thought and time, he saw that defeat could be turned into victory. By making just one certain move on the young man's behalf, the devil was placed in a position of utter defeat.

In the game of life, youth has no chance against the wiles of the devil who is determined to ruin the soul. But at Calvary the Lord Jesus intervened and made a "move" that enables [all] who trust [him] to have complete victory. "Thanks be unto God who giveth us the victory through our Lord Jesus Christ."[4]

C. A Physical Deliverance

"Rise, take up thy bed, and *walk*" (John 5:8). New life was flowing through him as he walked through the streets of Jerusalem that day. And it is God's will for us, apart from the mystery of suffering, that we should be quickened in our mortal bodies, and glow with abundant life and vigor. One day we shall have perfect, incorruptible bodies, like our Lord's. In the meantime, however, God intends that we should know his supernatural strength, even when we are weak. The apostle Paul knew something of this during his life and ministry. Even though afflicted by a thorn in the flesh, he could rejoice in his many afflictions, and declare, "When I am weak, then am I strong" (2 Cor. 12:10).

> **Exegesis**
>
> "Rise, take up thy bed, and walk" (John 5:8). Notice that the present active imperative of *egeirø* is a sort of exclamation like our "get up!" The first active imperative (*arøn* or *airø*) means "to pick up the pallet and go on walking." This present continuous verb underscores the magnitude of deliverance that Jesus can effect in our lives.

III. The Word of Divine Direction

"Afterward Jesus findeth him in the temple, and said unto him, Behold, thou art made whole: sin no more, lest a worse thing come unto thee" (John 5:14). Observe that it is in the temple that Jesus gives divine direction. That is why the church exists, not for the world but for the family of God. The world is to be evangelized by an outgoing church. The church is the hospital for the sick, the home for the lonely, and the school for the uninstructed in the family of God. Jesus found this man in the temple and told him to do three things:

A. *Live a Life of Radiant Certainty*

"Afterward Jesus findeth him in the temple, and said unto him, Behold, thou art made whole" (John 5:14). This is the first thing we should teach those who have recently come to Christ. One of the devices of the devil is to rob us of radiant certainty. John could write to his converts and say, "These things have I written unto you that believe on the name of the Son of God; that ye may know that ye have eternal life" (1 John 5:13).

When God says to us, "You are made whole," it is not something to question, or even debate; it is something to believe and rejoice in. So many Christians lose their joy because they become morbidly introspective. C. H. Spurgeon warned against this when he said, "I looked to Jesus, and the dove of peace came into my soul; I looked at the dove and it flew away." The secret of certainty is keeping our eyes on Jesus.

Illustration

At a certain church a boy of ten years of age was examined for membership. After he had spoken of his sense of guilt, came the question, "What did you do when you felt yourself so great a sinner?" and the eyes of the boy brightened as he answered, "I just went to Jesus and told Him how sinful I was, and how sorry I was, and asked Him to forgive me." "And do you hope at times that Jesus heard you and forgave your sins?" "I don't only hope so, sir, I know He did." "How do you know it, my son?" Every eye was intent on the little respondent. "He said He would," said the boy, with a look of astonishment, as if amazed that anyone should doubt it.[5]

B. *Live a Life of Radiant Victory*

"Sin no more" (John 5:14). Jesus would never have said such a thing to tantalize a man if it were not possible. Jesus not only gives the command, but also the enabling. And we have promises to support this glorious truth: "For sin shall not have dominion over you: for ye are not under the law, but under grace" (Rom. 6:14); "thanks be unto God, which always causeth us to triumph in Christ" (2 Cor. 2:14); "in all these things we are more than conquerors through him that loved us" (Rom. 8:37). Someone has said that the victorious Christian life is the victorious Christ in us.

Illustration

Hudson Taylor at thirty-seven, already a mighty man of faith and a great missionary warrior, was longing for a victory he did not have. He was often restless and irritated, defeated in his prayer life, a struggling Christian, wondering if there was not something better for him. He read a letter from a fellow missionary of the China Inland Mission, one little known, who told his director out of a full heart how he had come into joy and peace and victory. Hudson Taylor "saw it in a flash," he writes, and his "exchanged life" began: the miracle of Christ working out through him.[6]

C. Live a Life of Radiant Loyalty

"Sin no more, lest a worse thing come unto thee" (John 5:14). The life of faith is a life of utter dependence on the Lord Jesus to do in and through us what we cannot achieve of ourselves. God ordained it that way to teach us that there is only one place of victory, and that is in Christ. Peter could walk on the water while he kept his eyes on his Master, but the moment he looked at the boisterous waves he began to sink.

Loyalty means following the Lord Jesus in undeviating obedience and steadfast love. When the Lord Jesus said, "Sin no more, lest a worse thing come unto thee" (John 5:14), he was issuing a serious warning. To fail at this point in his life was to invite a worse disaster than the thirty-eight years of illness from which he had been just delivered! He would now be sinning against the light that he had just received. Loyalty is not optional, in the life of a Christian: it is obligatory, if we are to please our Savior and to enjoy the fullness of his blessing.

Illustration

A magnificent monument was erected in England soon after the close of World War II and was dedicated to the memory of three women who had served their country as secret agents at the cost of their lives. One of them had been terribly tortured by the enemy before her death, as they sought to obtain information that was locked away in her mind. Misunderstood, hated by their own countrymen, their lives in constant hazard, the noble three had gone on until each in turn was apprehended and put to death, with honor coming to them posthumously, driven on by their noble sense of loyalty that was a fundamental part of their characters. "Be thou faithful unto death, and I will give thee a crown of life" (Rev. 2:10)[7]

Conclusion

We have studied together a story that illustrates the Savior's power to cure completely. The Lord Jesus never does things by halves; he always goes all the way. His is not only the double cure, it is the triple cure: He heals the spirit, soul, and body. Let our prayer be:

> Out of my bondage, sorrow and night,/Jesus, I come, Jesus, I come;/Into Thy freedom, gladness, and light,/Jesus, I come to Thee;/Out of my sickness into Thy health,/Out of my want and into Thy wealth,/Out of my sin and into Thyself,/Jesus, I come to Thee.
> William T. Sleeper

11

The Feeding of the Five Thousand:

The Satisfying Savior

John 6:1-14

Introduction

One of the fascinating features of Christ's earthly ministry was his way with crowds of people. Over and over again we find him followed by multitudes, or speaking to multitudes.

It is true, of course, that the salvation experience is an individual encounter; God does not save people en masse—even though the history of evangelism and missions shows that vast numbers have turned to Christ in times of revival. People enter the kingdom one by one, yet Christ also appeals to the crowds. The phenomenon of mass evangelism in the past, and in modern times, more than substantiates this.

In the story before us, we have an outstanding illustration of our subject. The feeding of the five thousand is recorded in each of the four gospels (Matt. 14:13-21; Mark 6:30-44; Luke 9:10-17; John 6:1-13). It is well to read each of the accounts in order to get the full picture; but the main points we want to make are clearly here in the passage before us.

I. The Crowd Saw the Attraction of Christ

"A great multitude followed him" (John 6:2). There was something about the Lord Jesus that attracted people. Mark has a beautiful line in his record that reads, "they came to him [the Lord Jesus] from every quarter" (Mark 1:45). Even though his enemies, the Jewish leaders, despised him and eventually rejected him, they could not stop the common people from converging on him whenever they had an opportunity. As we study the gospels, we see three things that created this attraction in Christ:

A. *Christ's Magnetism*

"The people . . . followed him: and he received them" (Luke 9:11). A little child's reaction to a person is a good test of that person's character. This was particularly true of the Lord Jesus. Children loved to run into his arms. This is why the Master had to rebuke his disciples when they attempted to shield him from the "intrusion" of little ones.

Even sinners found it easy to come to him and tell him their problems and seek his help. This attraction to Christ was evident in the case of individuals, as well as the multitudes. In him people saw the irresistible qualities of grace and truth; hearts responded to the grace, with its warmth, and truth, with its strength—and that is still true today. Jesus prophesied: "And I, if I be lifted up from the earth, will draw all men unto me" (John 12:32).

Illustration

A man's life is always more forcible than his speech; when men take stock of him they reckon his deeds as [dollars] and his words as [cents]. If his life and his doctrine disagree the mass of lookers-on accept his practice and reject his preaching.[1]

Illustration

I was once asked to explain Billy Graham's magnetism. I said that there were three qualities that attracted people. First, he is a man with charisma. When the anointing of the Spirit is upon a man, God gives him an acceptance among the people. Second, he is a man of courage. All over the world he is known as a preacher who punctuates every sermon with the words, "The Bible says." Even in a day when the authority of the Word of God is being challenged, people long to hear a man speak with authority. Third, he is a man of compassion. Even his critics admit that he really cares for people. He proved this in the days of the civil rights struggle as well as his visits to disaster areas of the world and his concern for social injustice today. Like his Master, he exudes both truth and grace, and this is what makes him a magnetic personality.

B. Christ's Message

"The people . . . followed him: and he received them, and spake unto them of the kingdom of God" (Luke 9:11). People have always flocked to listen to a man with a real message. And such was the significance, authority, and challenge of the Savior's words that the people—great or small, simple or educated—thronged to him. They discerned the difference between him and the scribes and Pharisees, and "wondered at the gracious words which proceeded out of his mouth" (Luke 4:22). On one occasion, when soldiers were sent to apprehend him, they turned and went back; and when asked for a reason their reply was, "Never man spake like this man" (John 7:46). Here was a man who had something to say, and he said it with such authority that it "rang a bell" in the souls of men and women. They knew instinctively that this was a word from heaven, something that could not be denied.

Illustration

If preachers insist on competing with psychiatrists as counselors, with physicians as healers, with politicians as statesmen and with philosophers as speculators, then these specialists have every right to tell them how to preach. If a minister's message is not based on "Thus saith the Lord," then as a sermon it is good for nothing but to be cast out and trodden under foot of the specialists in the department with which it deals.[2]

C. Christ's Miracles

"A great multitude followed him, because they saw his miracles which he did on them that were diseased" (John 6:2). Here was one who not only spoke, but acted. Had his ministry ended with his words he would have ultimately lost his audience, for most people are shrewd enough to discard preaching that doesn't result in practicing. That is why our politicians are constantly challenged about their campaign promises with the verbal barb, "All smoke and no fire."

Our Savior, however, was known not only for what he said, but what he did. A great theologian came to meet him one night. Looking into his face, he said, "(Master), we know that thou art a teacher come from God: for no man can do these miracles that thou doest, except God be with him" (John 3:2). In other words, he was saying, "There is authority not only in your message, but in your miracles."

II. The Crowd Sensed the Compassion of Christ

"Jesus then lifted up his eyes, and saw a great company come unto him" (John 6:5). We read in Matthew and Mark that when Jesus saw the multitude he was moved with compassion. That word "compassion" means "to enter into another's deep anguish," "to feel sympathy," "to have pity." One authority has pointed out that it conveys the idea of "getting into the skin of another." This is the way the Lord Jesus felt about individuals and multitudes.

A. His Compassion Was Born of Vision

"Jesus then lifted up his eyes, and saw a great company come unto him" (John 6:5). Here was one who saw men and women as no one else saw them.

There is a type of man who sees a crowd of people in terms of population. He thinks only of their numerical strength. Another type looks at a large group and counts them as hands. He thinks in terms of the labor force. And there is yet another whose first thought is that of popularity: "I must be something when a crowd like this comes along to see me!" He thinks in terms of status.

But very few men today, outside of those who know the compassion of Jesus Christ, look upon people as he saw them. When he lifted up his eyes he saw them not so much as a crowd, but as individuals.

Illustration

The story is told of C. H. Spurgeon, who was billed to speak at the Crystal Palace. He went ahead of time to test out his voice and the hall's acoustics. Standing on the rostrum, in what he thought was a great empty auditorium, he quoted John 3:16: "For God so loved the world, that he gave his only begotten Son, that whosoever believeth in him should not perish, but have everlasting life." A workman hidden behind the platform (indeed, still erecting part of it) heard the words and was saved on the spot. When Spurgeon came back later that day to address the crowd, thirty thousand people had gathered, and as he stood up to speak, he had to pause and compose himself, so moved was he with the sight of those people.

B. His Compassion Was Born of Passion

"Jesus, when he came out, saw much people, and was moved with compassion toward them" (Mark 6:34). Jeremiah says, "Mine eye affecteth mine heart" (Lam. 3:51). A person who really sees human need *feels* human need. The multitudes who followed him recognized that Jesus not only saw them, but loved them. His heart went out to them in tenderness.

Illustrations

Among the first glimpses we get of our God is that of a Seeker: "Adam . . . Where art thou?" (Gen. 3:9). In commenting upon this question, a teacher said, "You can never be a preacher if you read it as though God were a policeman. Read it as though God were a brokenhearted Father looking for a lost child!"[3]

Great sermons begin in great hearts, and hearts are made great by tilling them with the needs of a brokenhearted, suffering world. Jesus' trained ears could hear a beggar's cry above the shouts of the throng.[4]

III. The Crowd Shared the Provision of Christ

"When Jesus then lifted up his eyes, and saw a great company come unto him, he saith unto Philip, Whence shall we buy bread, that these may eat?" (John 6:5). In Matthew, Mark, and Luke, Jesus said, "Give ye them to eat" (Matt. 14:16, Mark 6:37, Luke 9:13). How these words spell out not only the redemptive compassion of Christ, but his practical concern for men and women. After all, the Master had taken time with his disciples for refreshment and fellowship. Why should he bother with the thronging crowds at this time? Surely, they could wait for a more appropriate occasion. But that was not how Jesus thought. His compassion led him to action, and so we read of:

A. A Merciful Provision

"Whence shall we buy bread, that these may eat?" (John 6:5). These people had seen the Lord Jesus leading his disciples away to a solitary place across the lake for a time of relaxation and rest, a time to recapture true perspectives. The people outraced Jesus and his disciples and arrived before the ship reached the other side. There were at least five thousand men, women, and children, and they were tired and hungry. The disciples did not appear to have observed this, but Jesus made a thoughtful provision. Looking upon the multitude, he said to Philip, "We must feed this crowd. Whence shall we buy bread?" Philip, the "mathematician," began to work it out in terms of two hundred pennyworth, but what was that among so many? Then Andrew pointed out that there was a lad with a few loaves and fishes, but how could they ever be stretched to feed such a crowd? Jesus himself knew what he would do, and in his provision there was forethought and faithfulness.

Illustration

A theological student came to Charles Spurgeon one day, greatly concerned that he could not grasp the meaning of certain verses in the Bible. The noted preacher replied kindly but firmly, "Young man, allow me to give you this word of advice. Give the Lord credit for knowing things you don't understand."[5]

B. A Multiplied Provision

"Jesus took the loaves; and when he had given thanks, he distributed to the disciples, and the disciples to them that were set down; and likewise of the fishes as much as they would" (John 6:11). There is something profound and beautiful here. What has the Lord Jesus Christ done? He has taken into his holy hands the simple barley loaves and sardines from the little boy. Barley loaves were the food of the simplest and poorest people of the community. The rich man gave barley loaves to his horse, or mule, or ass.

The miracle here is not that of speeding up the processes of nature, as when the water was made into wine. Rather, it is based on the principle that what is good or sufficient for one is sufficient for all. If there were only one sinner in the whole world, he would still require the death of the Son of God at Calvary's cross. And what was food for one healthy boy was food good enough for everyone, in the Master's hands.

The Lord Jesus taking those five barley loaves in his hands illustrates the work of redemption. When he came from heaven he did not take the nature of angels, but was made in the likeness of men. He was incarnated in the simple material of human clay, and through it effected redemption. And in taking upon him humanity, he came as a little babe, born in a manger, to become the Savior of the world. Jesus took an insignificant boy in the crowd and made him the instrument of feeding five thousand. Taking the loaves into his hands, he gave thanks before distributing them. That was the Eucharist, the same thanksgiving as he uttered when he broke the bread to represent his broken body. It was a picture of Calvary, when the miracle of multiplication by subtraction began and has gone on ever since. Although there is only one Christ, he dwells in millions of people now.

Illustration

The story was told in the *Christian Herald* of a teacher in London, an unbeliever, who was telling her class the story of the five loaves and two fishes and trying to explain away the miracle in the account. "Of course you will understand, children, that it does not actually mean that Jesus fed all those people with such a small amount of food. That would be impossible. It means that He fed the people with His teaching, so that they lost all sense of bodily hunger and went home satisfied." But one little girl, not satisfied with that teaching asked, "But, teacher, what was it that filled the twelve baskets afterward, if it wasn't really food?" Good logic, and good faith![6]

C. A Ministered Provision

"Jesus said, Make the men sit down . . . . And Jesus took the loaves; and when he had given thanks he distributed" (John 6:10-11). They had to sit down and wait to be ministered to.

And the Lord Jesus Christ insists upon that today. Remember he has said: "I am the bread of life: he that cometh to me shall never hunger; and he that believeth on me shall never thirst" (John 6:35). If he would be your minister of this Bread of Life, he would condition you for two things: first, *to believe the blesser.* These people were conditioned for that. Their eyes were focused on him. They saw in the Lord Jesus such authority and sufficiency, and such a promise of blessing, that they believed. Secondly, they sat down ready *to receive the blessing*, and then the multiplication began. Through his disciples he ministered to them the bread and the fishes, and when they had eaten and were filled, we read that there were twelve baskets full of fragments. Such was the multiplied and ministered provision from the Savior's hands.

Amplification

Show that Christ met not only the needs of the multitude, but also of his disciples. Notice John 6:13, "They . . . filled twelve baskets with the fragments." Some have suggested that it was one basket for each of the apostles, but without doubt the lad had his share as well. God never gives sparingly.

Conclusion

Few passages of the Word of God could be more relevant to our day. We live in a world of unbelievable starvation and privation. There are countries such as the Far East and Africa where people are literally dying by the thousands each day. What is the church doing about this?

We have seen Christ's way with the crowds, and we have learned of an attraction, a compassion, and a provision which are so characteristic of our God. Is that same Savior living and working in and through us? What do people see, sense, or share when we minister to them? Remember that the Master still says today, as he said then, "Give ye them to eat" (Matt. 14:16).

12

The Walking on the Water:
The Christ of Today
John 6:16-21

Introduction

It is one of the sad features of modern preaching that so often the emphasis is placed entirely upon the Jesus of history. Stories such as this are used merely as lessons, and we are exhorted to imitate, in our own strength (or weakness) the Jesus of history who touched the heads of little children, fed the hungry, healed the leper, and caused the blind to see.

Such a doctrine, however, is not the teaching of the New Testament concerning the Christ of today, the Christ of Christianity. The apostle Paul clearly states in his second Epistle to the Corinthians: "Though we have known Christ after the flesh, yet now henceforth know we him no more" (2 Cor. 5:16). Why? Because he is no longer merely the Jesus of history. He is the risen Christ, the Lord of glory. His significance for us today lies not simply in the facts of his life and death in Israel, though those are historic facts upon which our faith is based. The relevance of God in Christ for a world of today is that Jesus lives, and is operative in the everyday world in which we find ourselves. This beautiful story helps to elucidate the ever-present ministry of the risen Christ. We have here three pictures of him. See him, first of all, as:

I. The Christ of Sympathy

"He departed . . . into a mountain himself alone" (John 6:15). John does not include the words "to pray," but Matthew does (14:23). Events that had just transpired were burdening the heart of the Lord Jesus, and he must take them to the place of prayer, the place of advantage, from whence he could intercede and intervene. John the Baptist had just been beheaded. Jesus had shared this news with the disciples, who were depressed beyond measure. That is why they took to the boat on the lake and spent a whole day there. The sight of the multitude, too, had made his heart heavy, for they were as sheep without a shepherd, confused and without direction or care. So the Savior had ministered to them in healing, preaching, and feeding. Again, the Lord Jesus was burdened as he looked upon his disciples. So often they disappointed him when they did not rise to the occasion. They wanted to send that hungry multitude away. Now they are on the lake. A storm has blown up, and they are toiling in rowing. The heart of the Savior goes out to them as he watches them, for he is the Christ of sympathy.

What happened historically, then, is, in fact, true today. The Christ of sympathy has ascended the mountain to the throne, where he shares all our experiences. "We have not an high priest which cannot be touched with the feeling of our infirmities; but was in all points tempted like as we are, yet without sin" (Heb. 4:15). There is no heartthrob or experience of life here upon earth that he does not feel from his throne.

A. *His Place of Intercession*

"Wherefore he is able also to save them to the uttermost that come unto God by him, seeing he ever liveth to make intercession for them" (Heb. 7:25). Someone may be saying, "I have no mother, father, Sunday school teacher, to pray for me," but there is one who is praying for you now. He is the one who, on that mountaintop that day, prayed for the vast multitude who wended their way into the darkness, to camp out, or to reach the villages beyond. He prayed, too, for his anxious disciples as they struggled against wind and tide: "Father, strengthen them; let not their faith fail; impress upon them the great truths I have sought to inculcate."

B. His Place of Intervention

"Whosoever shall call upon the name of the Lord shall be saved" (Rom. 10:13). From his vantage point the Lord Jesus could see the plight of his disciples and move to their aid. Seasoned fishermen though they were, they were unable to cope with the great storm that had blown up. They had reached the point of no return, halfway across the lake; a dangerous and frightening position to be in. It was in such a state that Jesus saw his disciples and came to their rescue.

So, today, from his vantage point, the sympathetic Savior sees and knows all about us and swiftly comes to our aid. The omniscient, omnipresent, and omnipotent Christ can touch the world at any and every point from his throne in heaven. His ear is ever open to our cry, and his arm is ready and able to save.

Illustration

Visitors to the famous Gallery in St. Paul's Cathedral, London, can hear a whisper travel around the whole dome, the sound bouncing back many times from the smooth walls.

A number of years ago, a poor shoemaker whispered to his young lady that he could not afford to marry her as he hadn't money enough to buy any leather, and his business was ruined. The poor girl wept quietly as she listened to this sad news.

A gentleman on the other side of the gallery, which is 198 feet across, heard this story and the shoemaker's whispered prayer, and he decided to do something about it. After finding out where he lived, the gentleman had some leather sent along to the shop. Imagine how delighted the poor man was! He made good use of this gift, and his business prospered so that he was able to marry the girl of his choice. It was not till a few years later that he learned the name of his unknown friend—the Prime Minister of Great Britain, W. E. Gladstone.

There is always one above who hears our whispered sorrowings and prayers, and will take action. No matter how low we whisper he can hear. We cannot always tell our human friends about things, but God always knows, so we can tell him all in prayer, and he will hear and answer.[1]

II. The Christ of Victory

"They see Jesus walking on the sea, and drawing nigh unto the ship" (John 6:19). It was about six miles across the lake, so assuming that their fishing boat was halfway across ("in the midst of the sea"—Mark 6:47), they were in a perilous position. Their boat might sink. To swim meant that they would have to cover some three miles—almost impossible in such a storm. This was indeed a crisis hour for that little group of men, but not for the Christ of victory. Consider, then:

A. *His Moment of Victory*

"And in the fourth watch of the night Jesus went unto them, walking on the sea" (Matt. 14:25). It was psychologically planned; not before or after time, but just at the moment of desperate need. God knows just when to move into a person's experience.

Matthew and Mark tell us that Jesus came to his disciples "in the fourth watch of the night," which is the darkest hour before dawn. Focus on that concept throughout the Scriptures. Think of the four hundred years of darkness before Jesus was born. Think of the delay prior to the death of Lazarus. Think of the timing before the rescue of the storm-tossed disciples. There is a point at which he must intervene—and it is always the right moment.

Illustration

Aquilla Webb asked a lifeguard at Newport, Rhode Island: "How can you tell when anyone is in need of help when there are thousands of bathers on the beach and in the water making a perfect hub-bub of noises?" He answered: "No matter how great the noise and confusion, there has never been a single time when I could not distinguish the cry of distress above them all. I can always tell it." Webb comments, "That is exactly like God. In the midst of the babel and confusion he never fails to hear the soul that cries out to him for help amid the breakers and storms of life."[2]

B. His Manner of Victory

"They see Jesus walking on the sea" (John 6:19). Bishop Dodderidge pointed out that in Egyptian hieroglyphics, the sign of two feet upon water is the symbol of sovereign power. The "Jesus of history" that our radical friends talk about is limited, but the Jesus of authentic Christianity is the Christ of sovereignty, the master of the elements. There is no situation over which he is not triumphant. He muzzles the winds and says to the angry waves, "Be still," and they obey.

The Christ of victory is equal to anything that threatens to overwhelm us—whether it be circumstances, or the attacks of Satan. Friends betrayed him, demons hurled their worst at him, and his enemies nailed him to a cross and disposed of him in a tomb, thinking he was finished with, but on the third day he emerged, victorious. The Christ of today is not a weak, emaciated Christ. He is no longer helplessly nailed to a crucifix. He is a virile, victorious, and valiant Christ.

Illustration

Hudson Taylor summed it up like this: "We are a supernatural people, born again by a supernatural birth; we wage a supernatural fight and are taught by a supernatural teacher, led by a supernatural captain to assured victory."[3]

C. *His Message of Victory*

"It is I; be not afraid" (6:20). It is a message that *quiets our fears.*
The storms are blowing around us, the wind hurling past our rig-
ging, and we feel as if we cannot go any farther. Then the Christ
of victory appears and says, "Be not afraid." It is a message that
quickens our faith— "It is I," said the Master. His presence makes
all the difference, and faith finds its anchorage in him.

Illustration

It is reported that the newspaper counselor, Ann Landers,
receives an average of 10,000 letters each month, and nearly
all of them from people burdened with problems. She was
asked if there was any one problem which predominates
throughout the letters she receives, and her reply was the one
problem above all others seems to be fear. People are afraid
of losing their health, their wealth, their loved ones. People
are afraid of life itself.[4] How wonderful to know that into this
kind of situation Jesus brings a message of victory, "It is I; be
not afraid" (John 6:20).

III. The Christ of Destiny

"Then they willingly received him into the ship: and immediately the ship was at the land whither they went" (John 6:21).
International leaders may have a lot to say about our world
today but in the last analysis the destiny of the nations, and of
individuals, is in the hands of one—and only one—the Christ
of today. Presently he is going to appear and wrap up this
aspect of world history in order to introduce the next drama
of his redemptive purpose.

Until that moment he waits, as the Christ of victory and of
destiny, to be received into our individual hearts and lives.

A. *He Assures Progress*

"Immediately the ship was at the land" (John 6:21). Nine
hours they had been rowing and had only gone three miles,
and were struggling in the center of the lake, like many of our

lives—going around in circles, getting nowhere. So many people imagine that through their own reading and studying they can plumb the great mysteries of life. They dip into philosophy, psychology, and other fields of knowledge, but seem to get nowhere. Only when they turn to the Lord Jesus Christ and put their faith in him do they realize a true sense of destiny.

There is nothing more pathetic than an aimless person. As someone has said, "Any dead fish can go with the stream. It takes a live one to swim against it." The Christ of destiny assures us of progress in our life.

Illustration

I was traveling by air from one city to another. I saw a man reading a book titled *A Round Trip to Nowhere*. When the opportunity came, I engaged the man in conversation about eternal issues and was able to share the Gospel of Christ who can tell us where we have come from, where we are, and where we are going.

B. He Assures Purpose

"Immediately the ship was at the land *whither they went*" (John 6:21). It was at Jesus' command that they had set out to reach Capernaum. And God has a plan for every life. There is design in all that he creates. But we fail to achieve his purpose for our lives until we receive Christ. The moment the Master was received into the ship there was progress, and soon after, the purpose of the voyage was realized.

Paul sets forth the life of purpose when he writes: "We are his workmanship, created in Christ Jesus unto good works, which God hath before ordained that we should walk in them" (Eph. 2:10). As Christians, we are not here by accident or chance. God has foreordained the path that we should walk. It is our privilege to find, follow, and finish the course that is laid out before us. For the believer, there is not only progress in the Christian life, but also purpose.

Conclusion

In this beautiful little story we have learned three things: that the Christ of today is the Christ of sympathy, who from his vantage point in heaven intercedes and intervenes. We have learned that he is the Christ of victory, coming at just the right moment with just the right message: "It is I; be not afraid" (John 6:20). And we have learned that he is the Christ of destiny: when he comes in, there is progress and purpose.

Will you do what the disciples did that day? They "willingly [or eagerly] received him into the ship" (John 6:21). If you do, he says, "I will come in" (Rev. 3:20). Will you ask him in now?

13

The Opening of a Blind Man's Eyes:

Darkness to Dawn

John 9:1-41

Introduction

Of all the handicaps that can curse men and women, blindness must be one of the saddest. Yet there is something infinitely worse than physical blindness: it is spiritual blindness. Indeed, so real and disastrous is this condition that God considered it necessary to send his Son to earth for the express purpose of opening the eyes of the blind and lightening the darkness of men.

I. The Blind Man's Night

"A man which was blind from his birth" (John 9:1). In a very real sense, here was a man who was sitting in the darkness of a physical night. This had been his condition from birth; he had never seen the light of day.

This story has been providentially preserved in order to

teach us the fact of our spiritual night by nature. As Dr. William Temple simply puts it, "The man 'blind from birth' is every man." No matter how youthful, beautiful, intellectual, or charming you may be, you have been born spiritually blind.

A. A Condition of Tragedy

"Jesus . . . *saw* a man which was blind from his birth" (John 9:1). The word "saw" means "to perceive mentally." In other words, he did not merely give a cursory glance as he passed; he saw something tragic. The disciples only glanced at the poor man and remarked, judgmentally, that he was receiving the due reward of his sins, or at any rate, that of his parents. But Jesus saw that this man in his blindness was a picture of every man who is born into the world, quite apart from personal or parental sins.

Similarly, we have to recognize that the moral blindness of men and women, boys and girls, is not something we can dismiss with an observation, a speculation, an opinion, or even a disagreement. It is a tragic fact.

B. A Condition of Poverty

After his eyes were opened, his neighbors asked, "Is not this he that sat and begged?" (9:8). A fifth of the world's pleasures and treasures were dead to him. How true this is of those who are still in the darkness of a spiritual night. The Bible tells us that "the natural man receiveth not the things of the Spirit of God: for they are foolishness unto him: neither can he know them, because they are spiritually discerned" (1 Cor. 2:14).

Illustration

A gentleman once tried to describe scarlet to a blind man. When he had done so, the blind man pathetically asked, "Is scarlet like the blast of a trumpet?" To the blind man, scarlet was an enigma; he could not discern it, for he was optically incapable.

So it is with spiritual things. Because men are blind to the things of the Spirit they merely dismiss the pleasures and treasures of the Christian life as foolishness, not realizing what they are missing.

II. The Blind Man's Sight

"Now I *see*" (John 9:25), cried the blind man, after he had encountered the Lord Jesus. But how did it all happen? The simple answer is that it was a miracle, and miracles cannot be explained. This was something that the religious bigots were not able to accept. All that the man could do was to describe *what* had happened and leave the *how* to Christ who had touched his eyes. As far as he was concerned, there was:

A. *The Divine Operation*

"He answered and said, A man that is called Jesus made clay, and anointed mine eyes, and said unto me, Go to the pool of Siloam, and wash: and I went and washed, and I received sight" (John 9:11). How simple and yet how profound! Whatever interpretations may be given of this act of the Master's, one thing is quite clear: the whole operation was not only real in itself; it was symbolic of an even deeper reality. This is the only recorded occasion on which Jesus took the initiative in restoring sight. This fact makes the symbolic act even more significant: just as Jesus voluntarily mixed his own spittle with the earth and then anointed the eyes of the blind, so he voluntarily came from heaven and entered an earthly body, in order that through the mixing of himself with human clay he might impart life to the dead eyes of men. We read in Hebrews: "Forasmuch . . . as the children are partakers of flesh and blood, he also himself likewise took part of the same; that through death he might destroy him that had the power of death, that is, the devil" (Heb. 2:14). This was the divine operation that Jesus performed, in order that we might be delivered from the blinding power of the devil.

Amplification

It is said that saliva in the East represents a man's essential nature or being. To use one's spittle in healing suggested profound sympathy.[1]

B. The Human Application

"I went and washed, and I received sight" (John 9:11), said the man who had been blind. Having anointed him with the clay, the Lord Jesus had told him to go to the pool of Siloam and wash.

Once again, the act is symbolic. The pool of Siloam, which John carefully tells us means "sent," was a specially provided pool of water for ceremonial drinking and cleansing. Jesus had already likened himself to these very waters, when he cried out on the last day of the Feast of Tabernacles, "If any man thirst, let him come unto me, and drink" (John 7:37). So the blind man went, washed, and received his sight. He accepted the divine operation, and then effected the human application, and forthwith he could see!

Similarly, if you would have light in your darkness, and sight for your blindness, you must accept the divine operation. You must believe that when Jesus died at the cross, he finally and completely handled the problem of spiritual blindness. Then, having accepted the divine operation in simple faith, you must effect the human application by taking the cure for blindness that Jesus makes available through his risen life.

Illustration

One of the miracles of modern surgery is the corneagrafting operation, which now gives sight to hundreds of blind people every year.

On Saturday, January 27, 1951, the *Daily Graphic* reported the thrilling story of one such person who received his sight. The man was Hendrik Botha, a thirty-year-old former clerk, who had been blind for ten years. At the expense of a little church in South Africa, he was sent to the famous Manhattan Eye Hospital. The day he arrived in New York a man died in

Michigan. At 2:00 a.m. the next morning the surgeon removed the cornea of the blind man's right eye and grafted in the replacement from the dead man. It was a success. Later that year a similar operation restored the sight of the left eye. With joy and thanksgiving that knew no bounds, the South African started back home to look for the first time upon a devoted wife and two small daughters. The startling headlines to this remarkable story carried these words: "He will see family through the eyes of a dead man!"

That is the gospel of spiritual sight. Jesus is not only the divine Surgeon, but also the one who has given his life that others might see. He has completed the operation, but you must effect that application by coming to him and receiving the sight that he makes available through his sacrificial life.

III. The Blind Man's Light

"I am the light of the world," Jesus said (John 9:5). No doubt this man had heard him and had wondered what that meant; but now he knew. He had passed from *darkness to dawn*. He now possessed:

A. *The Light of Positive Certainty*

"One thing I know, that, whereas I was blind, now I see" (John 9:25). How this man's eyes must have sparkled with joyous confidence, as he affirmed those words of certainty, "One thing I know." It is hard to argue with a man who refuses to budge from the facts of the case. He could not yet give an explanation of the character of the one who had opened his eyes; neither could he enter into the theological and philosophical arguments of those unbelieving Pharisees; but of one thing he was certain: a man called Jesus had opened his blind eyes.

Christianity is propagated by testimony rather than argument. Controversy, of which some are very fond, has done little for the cause of Christ, but testimony has done a great deal.

Illustration

Dr. S. D. Gordon tells of a Christian woman whose age began

to tell on her memory. She had once known much of the Bible by heart. Eventually only one precious bit stayed with her. "I know whom I have believed, and am persuaded that he is able to keep that which I committed unto him against that day" (2 Tim. 1:12, KJV). By and by part of that slipped its hold, and she would quietly repeat, "That which I have committed unto him." At last as she hovered on the borderline between this and the spirit world, her loved ones noticed her lips moving. They bent down and heard her repeating over and over again to herself the one word of the text, "Him, Him, Him." She had lost the whole Bible, but one word. But she had the whole Bible in that one word.[2]

B. The Light of Patient Constancy

"They reviled him" (John 9:28). "They cast him out" (v. 34). No one can claim the light of certainty without at once encountering unbelieving and bigoted enemies. So we read that the formerly blind man's parents, friends, and leaders cold-shouldered him and finally excommunicated him. To a Jew, such treatment constituted the greatest possible shame and ignominy. But in spite of it all, he remained constant and unshaken. In fact, he turned the very persecutions and accusations of his enemies into a most impressive and challenging witness to the Lord Jesus.

So often people say that they would be Christians if only they were assured of the courage and power not to fail when the going was hard. To such people this blind man has a complete answer. His is the light of patient constancy. It shines even when the clouds overhead are dark.

Illustration

Pliny, Roman governor in Asia Minor in the early second century, was so puzzled about the Christians brought before him for trial that he wrote his famous letter to the Emperor Trajan asking for his advice. This was the kind of thing he found himself up against:

A certain unknown Christian was brought before him, and Pliny, finding little fault in him, proceeded to threaten him.

"I will banish thee," he said.

"Thou canst not," was the reply, "for all the world is my Father's house."

"Then I will slay thee," said the governor.

"Thou canst not," answered the Christian, "for my life is hid with Christ in God."

"I will take away thy possessions," continued Pliny.

"Thou canst not, for my treasure is in heaven."

"I will drive thee away from man and thou shalt have no friend left," was the final threat. And the calm reply once more was, "Thou canst not, for I have an unseen friend from whom thou art not able to separate me." What was a poor, harassed Roman governor, with all the powers of life and death, torture and the stake at his disposal, to do with people like that?[3]

C. The Light of Progressive Clarity

"Now I see" (John 9:25). It is thrilling to read through the story and see how the light of perception and discernment grows brighter and brighter, as the blind man has strength to receive it. To start with, the Lord Jesus was "a man that is called Jesus" (v. 11). Then the blind man declared that he was "a prophet" (v. 17). Later he spoke of Christ as a "man . . . of God" (v. 33). Finally, he reached that moving climax when he met the Savior face to face and cried, "Lord, I believe," and worshiped him (v. 38).

Eye specialists tell us that after certain operations have been performed on the eyes, it is the procedure to bandage the eyes heavily, and then remove one bandage at a time, as the eyes gain the strength for increased light. In a similar way, God leads all those who come to him for spiritual sight. As they can take it, so he increases the light of clarity.

"But suppose I do not confess my blindness in sin?" you ask. The answer is that such an attitude is fatal. Jesus said, "For judgment I am come into this world, that they which see not [that is, they who own their blindness] might see; and that they which see [or refuse to own their blindness] might be made blind" (John 9:39). What serious words! May the Lord Jesus never have to say to you what he addressed to those unbelieving and proud Pharisees: "Ye say, We see; therefore your sin remaineth" (v. 41).

Conclusion

To say that you *see,* when you are in spiritual darkness, is to seal your doom in sin. God save you from such an end! Rather, may you come to Christ now and take advantage of his divine operation, and then seek the human application of the spiritual sight and light that he alone can give. So will your *darkness* be turned to *dawn,* and your testimony will be:

> Once I was blind, but now I can see;
> The Light of the world is Jesus.
> Philip P. Bliss

14

The Raising to Life of Lazarus:
The Destroyer of Death
John 11:1-44

Introduction

John records several miracles before the Crucifixion, and all are deeply significant. The raising of Lazarus is the last and greatest, for in this sign Jesus reveals himself as the destroyer of death, mankind's last and greatest enemy. If miracles are enacted parables, then the one before us is a magnificent demonstration of Christ's power to bring to life those who are dead in trespasses and sins.

I. Christ Confronts Death

"Our friend Lazarus sleepeth; but I go, that I may awake him out of sleep" (John 11:11). Scholars tell us that the Talmud often speaks of a rabbi's death as "sleep" (see Matt. 9:24; 1 Thes. 4:14). Homer refers to death and sleep as "twin sisters." Christ's conscious power to awaken Lazarus from sleep brings new meaning to these ancient concepts, for the Savior came into the world to abolish death. We see, then, that Jesus confronted death in a twofold manner:

A. *He Viewed Death Redemptively*

"This sickness is not unto death, but for the glory of God, that the Son of God might be glorified thereby" (John 11:4). Though Jesus knew that Lazarus was going to die, in his plan of redemption death was already conquered. There is only one in the universe who can view death like that. He looks at your life and sees the marks that death has made on you already, for men and women who are "dead in trespasses and sins" (Eph. 2:10) are in the process of perishing. But Christ knows that by virtue of his redemption a mighty, saving work can be effected in the sinner who truly believes.

B. *He Viewed Death Realistically*

"Our friend Lazarus sleepeth . . . . Lazarus is dead" (John 11:11, 14). Christ spoke of death as *undisturbed slumber.* He said, "Our friend Lazarus sleepeth" (v. 11).

Here is a sleep from which there is no awaking, unless the Lord Jesus himself intervenes, and what is true physically is even more true spiritually. This man had ears, but he could not hear; eyes, but he could not see; a heart, but he could not love; a will, but he could not act. And unless Jesus Christ awakens the sinner he will continue to sleep undisturbed. No other voice can awaken; no ingenious invention of philosophers, scientists or educators can ever quicken a dead spirit to life. David the psalmist showed his horror of this perpetual sleep when he cried, "Consider and hear me, O LORD my God: lighten mine eyes, lest I sleep the sleep of death" (Ps. 13:3).

Jesus also spoke of death as *unrelieved separation* —"Lazarus is dead" (John 11:14). Interpreting this in the light of the New Testament, we understand that "the body without the spirit is dead" (James 2:26). Only God can call back a departed spirit. All manner of claims have been made concerning resurrection, but there is no resurrection without divine intervention.

This physical fact has its spiritual counterpart; only God can quicken a dead spirit to life. This is what the apostle means when he says, "And you He made alive, who were dead in trespasses and sins"; and again: "God, who is rich in mercy, because of His great love with which He loved us, even when we were dead in trespasses, made us alive together with Christ (by grace you have been saved)" (Eph. 2:1, 4-5, NKJV).

Illustration

Let me recount the conversion of a young man who later spent four years in Italy as a missionary. In a subsequent conversation with him, the young man, Jack Kreider, looking back to his conversion, said, "I never cease to wonder at the miracle that took place. It was a Good Friday noon service, and I was brought to church by my aunt. Without any religious background, I was totally dead to spiritual things. As I listened to the message of the cross something happened which instantly changed me from a dead man to a live man in Christ Jesus. I did not even need counseling. I just knew that I was spiritually alive from the dead. The proof of it is that I have gone on to finish college and seminary and am now serving my Lord in the land of Italy. There I have seen those "dead in trespasses and sins" come to life, even as I was quickened by the Spirit of God."

II. Christ Condemns Death

"When Jesus therefore saw her weeping, and the Jews also weeping which came with her, he groaned in the spirit, and was troubled [or 'was moved with indignation']" (John 11:33). The reactions of our Lord Jesus in the presence of death are highly significant. The language employed highlights such emotions as agitation and indignation. The narrative demonstrates:

A. *The Depth of His Displeasure*

"He groaned in the spirit, and was troubled" (John 11:33). In the Greek, this constitutes "an incongruous combination." As

A. T. Robertson puts it: "The word means 'to snort with anger like a horse.' It occurs in the Septuagint (Dan. 11:30) for violent displeasure. The notion of indignation is present in the other examples of the word in the New Testament (Mark 1:43; 14:5; Matt. 9:30). . . . The presence of these Jews, the grief of Mary, Christ's own concern, the problem of the raising of Lazarus—all greatly agitated the spirit of Jesus .... He struggled for self-control."[1] It is my conviction that what moved the Savior to such indignation was the root cause of death, namely, *sin*. "When lust hath conceived, it bringeth forth sin: and sin, when it is finished, bringeth forth death" (James. 1:15). "The wages of sin is death; but the gift of God is eternal life through Jesus Christ our Lord" (Rom. 6:23). Death is the inevitable outcome of sin, and one cannot help feeling that with a backward glance through history the Lord Jesus gathered up in a moment the whole tragic story of man's sin. "Wherefore, as by one man sin entered into the world, and death by sin; and so death passed upon all men, for that all have sinned." (Rom. 5:12).

Amplification

S. D. Gordon says that there are seven simple facts that everyone ought to know about sin: The first is that "sin earns wages." The second, "sin pays wages." The third, "sin insists on paying." You may be quite willing to let the account go, but sin always insists on paying. Fourth, "sin pays its wages in kind." Sin against the body brings results in the body. Sin in the mental life brings results there. Sin in contact with other people brings a chain of results affecting those others. It is terribly true that 'no man sinneth to himself.' Sin is the most selfish of acts. It influences to some extent everyone whom we touch. Fifth, "sin pays in installments." Sixth, "sin pays in full, unless the blood of Jesus washes away the stain." Seventh, "sin is self-executive, it pays its own bills. Sin has bound up in itself all the terrific consequences that ever come . . . . The logical result of sin is death; death to the body, death to the mind, death to the soul!"[2]

B. *The Depth of His Distress*

"Jesus wept" (John 11:35). Those tears that trickled down his face were not only his expression of oneness and sympathy with Mary and Martha; he was weeping over the damage which sin had brought about. Here was yet another victim of death's relentless hand. All the sin, sorrow, and suffering of the world seemed focused within his spirit at that moment. His soul's outburst of grief condemned sin and death.

Illustration

One who knew [George] Whitefield well, and attended his preaching more frequently, perhaps, than any other person, said he hardly ever knew him go through a sermon without weeping; his voice was often interrupted by his tears, which sometimes were so excessive as to stop him from proceeding for a few moments. "You blame me for weeping," he would say, "but how can I help it when you will not weep for yourselves, though your immortal souls are on the verge of destruction, and for ought you know, you are hearing your last sermon, and may never more have an opportunity to have Christ offered to you?"[3]

III. Christ Conquers Death

"I am the resurrection, and the life: he that believeth in me, though he were dead, yet shall he live: and whosoever liveth and believeth in me shall never die" (John 11:25-26).

These words must have startled Martha, for Jesus was not expounding mere doctrine about future events, but rather exposing present realities. He was the resurrection and the life. With those words of triumph he approached the tomb of Lazarus with a fourfold word:

A. *The Word of Preparation*

"Take ye away the stone" (John 11:39). It would have been the easiest thing in the world for the Lord Jesus to have performed a triple miracle here. He could have rolled away the stone with a word, called Lazarus to life and commanded him to appear with a word. But he did not do so. Instead, he employed those who were standing around to prepare the way. And before he will call to life those who are "dead in trespasses and sins" (Eph. 2:1) he calls on us who are alive spiritually to "roll away the stone."

B. The Word of Intercession

"Jesus lifted up his eyes, and said, Father, I thank thee that thou hast heard me" (John 11:41). Jesus was never out of touch with heaven; and he is demonstrating here his close working relationship with his Father. As A. T. Robertson points out:

> Clearly Jesus had prayed to the Father concerning the raising of Lazarus. He has the answer before he acts. "No pomp of incantation, no wrestling in prayer even; but simple words of thanksgiving, as if already Lazarus was restored" (Dods). Jesus well knew the issues involved on this occasion. If he failed, his own claims to be the Son of God (the Messiah), would be hopelessly discredited with all. If he succeeded, the rulers would be so embittered as to compass his own death.[4]

Archbishop Trench says, "Prayer is not overcoming God's reluctance, it is laying hold of his highest willingness."

C. The Word of Resurrection

"Lazarus, come forth" (John 11:43). He called out strongly with the word of authority, the voice of the Son of God. "It is just as well he named Lazarus," said an old puritan, "or the whole graveyard would have turned out!" Show me an audience in which the preparation has been done, and a preacher who is in touch with heaven, and I will show you a context in which the word of resurrection brings men and women to life.

Illustration

Dr. A. T. Schofield tells of an occasion when, crossing the English Channel by boat, he heard the loud voice of a small, dirty-looking boy standing near the engine-room. Though Schofield could not hear what was said, he could feel the great paddle wheels slowing down. Again the clear tones were heard, and suddenly the motion of the engines was reversed and the paddles began to turn in an opposite direction. At first it appeared as if the boy had taken control of the vessel. The orders he gave were with authority and the utmost confidence. On getting closer to him the mystery was explained. His eyes were intently fixed on the bridge overhead where the captain stood, giving the orders. He seldom spoke, and then but a word, and yet the boy kept shouting down below as if moved by some unseen power. At last Schofield realized the captain was giving his orders by short, sharp movements of the hand. Unintelligible as they were to the passengers, to the boy every movement had its meaning, and the mighty engines moved in obedience. Pondering this incident, Schofield added: "We wished we were more like the captain's boy. The boy was (like John the Baptist of old) simply 'a voice,' but as the Baptist's voice derived all its importance because it was the Lord's, so did the boy's because it was but an echo of the captain's." In a similar way, Jesus could say, "The Son can do nothing of himself, but what he seeth the Father do: for what things soever he doeth, these also doeth the Son likewise" (John 5:19)[5]

D. The Word of Liberation

"Loose him, and let him go" (John 11:44). What a startling sight—a man stumbling out of the grave! The heart had started again, the arteries had begun to pulse, and the muscles to operate. So he shuffled out of the tomb, bound hand and foot. That he came out was almost as great a miracle as that he was called to life.

Some of you have been called to life and can remember the day you were converted. But what about the graveclothes that still hamper you—those relics of your past life? You cannot see properly because there is a napkin around your eyes, you cannot work efficiently because your hands are bound.

You cannot walk well because the graveclothes still bind your feet. Jesus' word to you is: "Be loosed!"

Observe the three things that proved that Lazarus was alive. There was *communion*— "Lazarus was one of them that sat at the table with him" (John 12:2). Here is a beautiful picture: Mary at Jesus' feet, Martha serving, and Lazarus sitting at table with him. One of the evidences that a person is quickened to life is a worshiping heart, whether in private devotions or at the table of communion. There was *commotion*— "The chief priests consulted that they might put Lazarus also to death" (John 12:10). Where there is spiritual life there is commotion and conflict. It happened in the early church, and throughout the centuries. Jesus told his disciples it would be so (see Matt. 5:11-12; John 15:20). There was *confession*— "By reason of him many of the Jews went away, and believed on Jesus" (John 12:11). One look at Lazarus and they had to believe in Jesus. Here was a man alive from the dead! The evidence of omnipotence is irresistible. The Jews were always seeking after a sign—and here was one in living color. What convinced these unbelievers was not so much what Lazarus had to say, but rather what he was: a man alive from the dead.

Illustration

Many years ago when the great missionary Adoniram Judson was home on furlough, he passed through the city of Stonington, Connecticut. A young boy playing about the wharves at the time of Judson's arrival was struck by the man's appearance. Never before had he seen such a light on any human face. He ran up the street to a minister to ask if he knew who the stranger was. The minister hurried back with him, but became so absorbed in conversation with Judson that he forgot all about the impatient youngster standing near him. Many years afterward that boy. . . became the famous preacher Henry Clay Trumbull. In a book of memoirs he penned a chapter entitled: "What a Boy Saw in the Face of Adoniram Judson." That lighted countenance had changed his life.[6]

Conclusion

The central message of this remarkable miracle is: Jesus the destroyer of death—confronting death redemptively and realistically; condemning death by the depth of his displeasure and distress; and conquering death by the words of preparation, intercession, resurrection and liberation. Throughout the centuries the words still sound: "the dead shall hear the voice of the Son of God: and they that hear shall live" (John 5:25). Will you respond to that voice now?

ENDNOTES

Preface

1. John R. W. Stott, "Paralyzed Speakers and Hearers," *Christianity Today* (Mar. 13, 1981), pp. 44-45.

Chapter 1

1. Constance Barnett, quoted in A. Naismith, *1,200 Notes, Quotes and Anecdotes* (Marshall Pickering, an imprint of HarperCollins Publishers), p. 176.

2. Quoted in ibid., p. 73.

3. *The New Scofield Reference Bible* (New York: Oxford University Press, 1967), pp. 128-29. See also Stephen F. Olford, *The Tabernacle: Camping with God* (Neptune, N.J.: Loizeaux Brothers, 1971).

4. Paul Lee Tan, *Encyclopedia of 7,700 Illustrations* (Dallas: Bible Communications, 1979), p. 170.

5. David Livingstone, quoted in ibid., p. 1611.

6. Naismith, *1,200 Notes, Quotes and Anecdotes*, p. 211.

7. ibid., p. 198.

8. Tan, *Encyclopedia of 7,700 Illustrations*, p. 750.

Chapter 2

1. David L. Currents, quoted in Paul Lee Tan, p. 503.

2. A. Naismith, p. 120.

Chapter 3

1. A. Naismith, p. 108.

2. ibid., p. 49.

3. *Evangelical International High School Quarterly*, quoted in Walter B. Knight, *Knight's Master Book of New Illustrations* (Grand Rapids: Eerdmans, 1956), pp. 235-36.

Chapter 4

1. Tan, p. 496.
2. ibid., p. 498.
3. Naismith, p. 181.
4. The *Ryrie Study Bible* (Chicago: Moody Press, 1978), p. 1620.

Chapter 5

1. Naismith, p. 53.
2. *Gospel Trumpet*, quoted in Walter B. Knight, *Knight's Master Book of New Illustrations* (Grand Rapids: Eerdmans, 1956), p. 566.
3. Quoted in ibid., p. 562.

Chapter 6

1. *Zion's Herald*, quoted in Walter B. Knight, *3,000 Illustrations for Christian Service* (Grand Rapids: Eerdmans, 1952), p. 584.
2. Marvin R. Vincent, *Word Studies in the New Testament* (Grand Rapids: Eerdmans, 1957), p. 241.
3. *Adventures With God*, quoted in Paul Lee Tan, pp. 186-87.
4. *The Australian Baptist*, quoted in ibid., p. 737.

Chapter 7

1. Foster, quoted in Paul Lee Tan, p. 648.
2. Naismith, p. 29.
3. The *Ryrie Study Bible* (Chicago: Moody Press, 1978), p. 1630.
4. Naismith, p. 55.
5. Tan, p. 1316.

Chapter 8

1. Aquilla Webb, *1001 Illustrations for Pulpit and Platform* (New York: Harper & Brothers, 1926), p. 96.
2. Daniel Webster, quoted in Tan, p. 373.

3. The *Ryrie Study Bible,* p. 1603.

4. Walter B. Knight, *3,000 Illustrations for Christian Service* (Grand Rapids: Eerdmans, 1952), p. 438.

5. Naismith, pp. 44-45.

Chapter 9

1. Naismith, p. 66.

2. *Now,* quoted in Knight, p. 471.

3. Burrell, *Christ and Progress,* quoted in ibid., p. 251.

4. Quoted in ibid., p. 248.

Chapter 10

1. *Pastor's Manual,* quoted in Tan, pp. 1284-85.

2. Willis Cook, quoted in ibid., p. 1284.

3. *The Upper Room,* quoted in Knight, p. 250.

4. *Youth for Christ Magazine,* quoted in Naismith, p. 204.

5. *Earnest Worker,* quoted in Knight, p. 18.

6. *Sunday School Times,* quoted in ibid., p. 716.

7. G. Franklin Allee, *Evangelistic Illustrations for Pulpit and Platform* (Chicago: Moody Press, 1961), p. 243.

Chapter 11

1. C. H. Spurgeon, quoted in Knight, p. 372.

2. Tan, p. 1075.

3. Al Bryant, quoted in ibid., p. 496.

4. Quoted in ibid., p. 1081.

5. ibid., p. 504.

6. G. Franklin Allee, *Evangelistic Illustrations for Pulpit and Platform* (Chicago: Moody Press, 1961), p. 162.

Chapter 12

1. Naismith, p. 155.

2. Tan, p. 504.

3. Knight, p. 716.

4. *The Bible Friend,* quoted in Tan, p. 434.

Chapter 13

1. Naismith, p. 187.
2. *American Holiness Journal*, quoted in Tan, p. 239.
3. Quoted in ibid., p. 993.

Chapter 14

1. A. T. Robertson, *Word Pictures in the New Testament*, vol. 5 (Nashville: Broadman Press, 1960, renewed 1988), p. 202.
2. *Earnest Worker*, from Knight.
3. Tan.
4. Robertson, p. 205.
5. Naismith, adapted.
6. Tan.

FOR FURTHER READING

Part 1: God Alive in Discourses from the Gospel of John

Barclay, William. *Daily Study Bible* (John). Rev. ed. Philadelphia: Westminster Press, 1975-1976.

Ironside, H. A. *Addresses on the Gospel of John.* Neptune, N.J.: Loizeaux Brothers, Inc., 1942.

Morgan, G. Campbell. *The Gospel According to John.* Westwood, N.J.: Fleming H. Revell Co., 1933.

Tasker, R. V. G. *The Gospel According to St. John.* Tyndale New Testament Commentaries. Grand Rapids: Wm. B. Eerdmans Publishing Co., 1960.

Tenney, Merrill C. *John: The Gospel of Belief.* Grand Rapids: Wm. B. Eerdmans Publishing Co., 1948.

Westcott, B. F. *The Gospel According to St. John.* Grand Rapids: Wm. B. Eerdmans Publishing Co., 1950.

Part 2: God Alive in Miracles from the Gospel of John

Bruce, Alexander Balmain. *The Miracles of Christ.* Minneapolis: Klock and Klock Christian Publishers, 1980.

Hendriksen, William. *A Commentary on the Gospel of John.* 2 vols. New Testament Commentary. Grand Rapids: Baker Book House, 1953.

Laidlaw, John. *Studies in the Miracles of Our Lord.* Minneapolis: Klock and Klock Christian Publishers, 1982.

Lewis, C. S. *Miracles: A Preliminary Study.* New York: Macmillan Publishing House, 1947.

Lockyer, Herbert. *All the Miracles of the Bible: The Supernatural in Scripture, Its Scope and Significance.* Grand Rapids: Zondervan Publishing House, 1961.

MacDonald, George. *The Miracles of Our Lord.* Wheaton, Ill.: Harold Shaw Publishers, 1980.

Morris, Leon. *Studies in the Fourth Gospel.* Grand Rapids: Wm. B. Eerdmans Publishing Co., 1969.

————. *The Gospel of John.* New International Commentary of the New Testament. Grand Rapids: Wm. B. Eerdmans Publishing Co., 1970.

Pink, Arthur W. *Exposition of the Gospel of John.* Grand Rapids: Zondervan Publishing House, 1975.

Ryrie, Charles Caldwell. *The Miracles of Our Lord.* Nashville: Thomas Nelson Publishers, 1984.

Scroggie, William Graham. *Guide to the Gospels.* London: Pickering & Inglis, 1962.

Spurgeon, Charles H. *Sermons on the Miracles.* Vol. 3. Library of Spurgeon's Sermons, ed. Charles T. Cook. Grand Rapids: Zondervan Publishing House, 1958.

Taylor, William Mackergo. *Miracles of Our Saviour.* Grand Rapids: Kregel Publications, 1975.

Trench, Richard Chenevix. *Notes on the Miracles of Our Lord.* London: Pickering & Inglis, 1953.

SECTION 3

Committed to Christ and His Church:

Teachings on Discipleship and Membership

PREFACE

The priority program on heaven's agenda is the calling out and completion of the church, the body of Christ. When Jesus declared, "I will build My church, and the gates of Hades shall not prevail against it" (Matt. 16:18, NKJV), he launched a movement that no devil in hell or angel in heaven can ever thwart. Notwithstanding its many failures and factions, the true church of redeemed and regenerated souls will prevail. One day soon she will be raptured and presented before the presence of the Savior himself "a glorious church, not having spot or wrinkle or any such thing" (Eph. 5:27, NKJV).

It follows, therefore, that our main task as pastors, teachers, and leaders is to "[warn] every man and [teach] every man in all wisdom, that we may present every man perfect in Christ Jesus" (Col. 1:28, NKJV). To this end we need to give ourselves to a church-family ministry.

This third part of *Basics for Believers* focuses on this "family ministry." We start with a series on "The Demands of Discipleship." This is an in-depth examination of New Testament discipleship. One reason we are witnessing such defections from our local churches today is because we have forgotten the demands of discipleship in our ministry of follow-up.

This leads quite naturally to another series on "God's Blueprint for Church Membership." These sermon/lectures contain material I have consistently used in our membership classes in all the churches I have served. No one received "the right hand of fellowship" without attending each class and signing the Covenant of Membership (before an elder board) at the conclusion of the stated number of weeks.

As you expand and expound these sermon outlines, make sure that you preach "in demonstration of the Spirit and of power, that [the faith of your people] should not be in the wisdom of men but in the power of God" (1 Cor. 2:4-5, NKJV).

So I exhort you to "preach the word . . . do the work of an evangelist, [and] make full proof of [your] ministry" (2 Tim. 4:2, 5, KJV). God richly bless you!

Part 1
THE DEMANDS OF DISCIPLESHIP

1

The Disciple's Relationship

Matthew 10:16-27;

Luke 6:35-42; John 13:1-17

"A disciple is not above his teacher, but everyone who is perfectly trained will be like his teacher" (Luke 6:40, NKJV).

Introduction

The term *disciple* is used consistently in the four gospels to describe the relationship between Christ and his followers. Jesus used it in speaking of them, and they employed it when referring to one another. The term did not pass out of use in the days following Pentecost; on the contrary, the word runs throughout the Acts of the Apostles (see 9:1, 26; 20:7, 30; 21:16). In fact, the members of the early church were known as disciples before they were first called "Christians" at Antioch (see Acts 11:26). The word signifies "a taught or trained one." Jesus is the teacher and we are the learners. He has all knowledge of the ultimate purposes of God for us, and we are the seekers after truth. As a teacher, the Lord Jesus is not merely a lecturer, from whose dissertations we may deduce certain lessons; nor, indeed, is he only a prophet who delivers his burden and then leaves us with the issues. Rather, he is the teacher who bends over his pupils with the set purpose of training them step by step, until they become identified with the teacher himself. The gospels teach that:

I. The Disciple Is One who Is Identified with the Master's Discipline

"A disciple is not above his teacher, nor a servant above his master" (Matt. 10:24, NKJV; see also vv. 16-27). The context shows that the Lord Jesus had been misunderstood and misinterpreted, and he warns his disciples that they will suffer in a similar manner since the disciple is not above his master, nor the servant above his Lord. As a son, Jesus Christ "learned obedience by the things which He suffered" (Heb. 5:8, NKJV); and in this regard we must follow in his steps. The greatest privilege you and I can have is to be identified with the Master in his discipline. Such discipline will be one of:

A. *Personal Persecution*

"You will be hated by all for My name's sake" (Matt. 10:22, NKJV). No one can be a genuine disciple without encountering some form of personal persecution. Jesus promised this: "If they persecuted Me, they will also persecute you" (John 15:20, NKJV). In the face of such persecution, however, the Lord Jesus promises *the power of utterance:* "Do not worry about how or what you should speak. For it will be given to you in that hour what you should speak" (Matt. 10:19, NKJV).

Under the fires of persecution, one of the greatest disciplines is that of controlling our thoughts, tempers, and tongues. Left to our own resources, we should fail miserably and bring dishonor to the name of our Lord. This is where the Master promises the power of the Holy Spirit to control thoughts, tempers, and tongues. How wonderfully this was illustrated in the Master's life —particularly when he suffered under Pontius Pilate. *What discipline of speech and silence he exercised on that momentous occasion!* No wonder the apostle Paul uses this event in the experience of our Lord as the basis of his call to a life of discipline and control. Note his words to Timothy: "I urge you in the sight of God who gives life to all things, and before Christ Jesus *who witnessed the good confession before Pontius Pilate,* that you keep this commandment without spot, blameless until our Lord Jesus Christ's appearing" (1 Tim. 6:13-14, NKJV).

Under the pressure of persecution, the Lord Jesus also promises *the power of endurance:* "He who endures to the end will be saved" (Matt. 10:22, NKJV). The patience and longsuffering required at times like this are only possible when the believer knows the discipline of the master in his life. It was said of the Savior that "for the joy that was set before Him [He] endured the cross, despising the shame, and has sat down at the right hand of the throne of God" (Heb. 12:2, NKJV).

Illustration

The following incident is related by Mrs. Charles Spurgeon, who suffered greatly for more than a quarter of a century: "At the close of a gloomy day I lay resting on my couch as night drew on. Though all was bright within my cozy room, some of the external darkness seemed to enter my soul and obscure its spiritual vision. In sorrow of heart I asked, 'Why does my Lord deal thus with his child? Why does he permit lingering weakness to hinder the sweet service I long to render to his servants?" For awhile silence reigned in the little room, broken only by the crackling of the oak log burning in the fireplace. Suddenly she heard a sweet, soft sound, a little clear musical note like the tender trill of a robin, and wondered what it could be. Surely, no bird would be singing outside at that time of the year and night. Suddenly she realized it was coming from the log on the fire; the fire was letting loose the imprisoned music from the old oak's inmost heart. Perhaps the tree had garnered up this song in the days when all was well, when birds twittered merrily on its branches, and sunlight decked the tender leaves with gold. Mrs. Spurgeon thought, "When the fire of affliction draws songs of praise from us, then we are truly purified and God is glorified." As she mused on this her soul found comfort. Singing in the fire! If that is the only way for God to get harmony out of these hard, apathetic hearts, then let the furnace be heated seven times hotter than before![1]

B. Spiritual Opposition

"If they have called the master of the house Beelzebub, how much more will they call those of his household!" (Matt. 10:25, NKJV). Spiritual opposition is the deliberate failure to rightly understand and interpret the work of God. Such opposition often tends to distress and depress the disciple, but Jesus reassures his own by telling them:

"Do not fear them. For there is nothing covered that will not be revealed, and hidden that will not be known" (Matt. 10:26, NKJV). The Savior says that however unjustly we may be opposed by misunderstanding and misinterpretation, there is going to be a day of disclosure and vindication. Our business is to press on regardless, speaking in the light what God has taught us in the darkness of persecution and opposition; preaching from the housetops what he has whispered to us in the time of discipline.

We must learn that if we would rise to the measure of true discipleship we must count it a joy to suffer for Christ. It is recorded of those early disciples that after persecution and opposition "they departed from the presence of the council, rejoicing that they were counted worthy to suffer shame for His name" (Acts 5:41, NKJV). God gives us the grace to be willing to suffer likewise. Only thus shall we know a true identification with the Master's discipline.

Illustration

Adoniram Judson, the renowned missionary to Burma, endured untold hardships trying to reach the lost for Christ. For seven heartbreaking years he suffered hunger and privation.

During this time he was thrown into Ava Prison, and for seventeen months was subjected to almost incredible mistreatment. As a result, for the rest of his life he carried the ugly marks made by the chains and iron shackles that had cruelly bound him. Undaunted, upon his release, he asked for permission to enter another province where he might resume preaching the gospel. The godless ruler indignantly denied his request, saying, "My people are not fools enough to listen to anything a missionary might say, but I fear they might be impressed by your scars and turn to your religion!"

II. The Disciple Is One who Is Identified with the Master's Discernment

"A disciple is not above his teacher, but everyone who is perfectly trained will be like his teacher" (Luke 6:40, NKJV; see also vv. 35-42). A consideration of this portion reveals that there are two elements in this discernment:

A. The Maturity of Knowledge

"A disciple is not above his teacher, but everyone who is perfectly trained [or made mature in knowledge] will be like his teacher" (Luke 6:40, NKJV). Our Lord had just quoted a well-known proverbial parable: "Can the blind lead the blind? Will they not both fall into the ditch?" (v. 39, NKJV). Virtually he was saying that the blind cannot lead the blind, any better than the blind man can guide himself; the inference being that until a man is perfect, he will abstain from needless, hasty, and uncharitable judgment of others.

The purpose of the master teacher is to develop his disciple in knowledge, both academically and experimentally. Only by such perfection of knowledge can the disciple be identified with the master's discernment. It was with this thought in mind that Jesus said, "A disciple is not above his teacher, but everyone who is perfectly trained will be like his teacher" (Luke 6:40, NKJV).

Illustration

Peter Waldo, the probable leader of the pious Waldensians, was a rich merchant of Lyons, France. He was converted through the death of a friend at a feast. He then had the Scriptures translated by two erudite scholars into his own tongue, and thereafter gave up all his wealth and followed his Lord. Everywhere he went he preached the claims of Christ, using the words "Look to Jesus! Listen to Jesus! Learn of Jesus!" These are the prerequisites of discipleship.[2]

B. The Authority of Judgment

"Why do you look at the speck in your brother's eye, but do not perceive the plank in your own eye?" (Luke 6:41, NKJV). The principle the Savior is teaching here is that what we judge in others is invariably what we are guilty of ourselves. We see the speck (splinter) in our brother's eye, but forget that we are even more blind because of the planks in our own eyes.

Illustration

A lady in Switzerland brought a small package of greatly aged cheese. Putting it in her handbag, she continued her shopping in different stores. She was greatly repelled at what she thought was the malodor of the different clerks encountered. Her thoughts ran something like this: "How can these ill-smelling clerks maintain their positions?" Imagine her embarrassment when opening her handbag to discover that it was she, not others, who was responsible for the offensive odor![3]

Judgment, born of the maturity of knowledge, must be characterized by:

1. CAUTIOUSNESS

"Judge not, and you shall not be judged. Condemn not, and you shall not be condemned. Forgive, and you will be forgiven" (Luke 6:37, NKJV). An evidence of immaturity is hasty judgment and destructive criticism. Authoritative judgment, on the other hand, will be marked by a cautiousness that withholds condemnation until the possibility of forgiveness is thoroughly explored. The fact that we are not to condemn, but to forgive, does not mean that we are not to judge; that would be a contradiction of Scripture. The warning, rather, is that of cautiousness and constructiveness in judgment.

2. GRACIOUSNESS

"Be merciful, just as your Father also is merciful" (Luke 6:36, NKJV). Authoritative judgment is always tempered with grace. The goodness and severity of God are not at variance. This is why the psalmist could say, "I will sing of mercy and justice" (Ps. 101:1, NKJV); and the prophet could say: "In wrath remember mercy" (Hab. 3:2, NKJV).

3. BOUNTEOUSNESS

"Give, and it will be given to you: good measure, pressed down, shaken together, and running over will be put into your bosom. For with the same measure that you use, it will be measured back to you" (Luke 6:38, NKJV). With the cautiousness and graciousness, there must be bounteousness in judgment. If graciousness speaks of largeheartedness, then bounteousness is a token of largemindedness. This is the kind of authoritative judgment that takes all relevant facts into account. Someone has defined wisdom as "the right application of knowledge to any given situation in the light of all the verified facts." Such wisdom is bounteous judgment. Phillip Brooks once prayed, "Let me not lose faith in my fellow men. Keep me sweet and sound of heart, in spite of ingratitude, treachery, or meanness. Preserve me from minding little stings or giving them." What a rare grace this is today!

III. The Disciple Is One who Is Identified with the Master's Devotedness

"I have given you an example, that you should do as I have done to you. Most assuredly, I say to you, a servant is not greater than his master; nor is he who is sent greater than he who sent him" (John 13:15-16, NKJV; see also vv. 1-17). An examination of the context reveals that Jesus had just performed an act of superlative selflessness—that of washing the disciples' feet. Although this act of devoted service was performed hours before the agony of Gethsemane, the cruelty of the cross, and the desertion of his disciples, the Savior refused to be deflected from humbling himself to attend to the needs of his unworthy disciples. How easy it is to be taken up with our own sufferings or successes and so become self-centered or indifferent to the needs of others. As far as our Lord was concerned, however, his devotedness was complete. Consider:

A. The Reality of Such Devotedness

"[Jesus] . . . rose from supper and laid aside His garments, took a towel and girded himself. After that, He poured water into a basin and began to wash the disciples' feet, and to wipe them with the towel with which He was girded" (John 13:4-5, NKJV). To wash the feet of guests at a feast was the work of a slave; but notwithstanding this he willingly made himself a bondslave, "taking the form of a bondservant" (Phil. 2:7, NKJV). This reality of devotedness to "slave" for others was characteristic of the Savior throughout his ministry. He could say, "The Son of Man did not come to be served, but to serve, and to give His life a ransom for many" (Matt. 20:28, NKJV).

Illustration

A young woman who had left home because of her drunken father later became a Christian. Thereafter she announced her intention of returning and doing what she could to reclaim him. "But what will you do when he finds fault with all your efforts to please him?" someone asked. "Try a little harder," she answered with a light in her eyes. "Yes, but when he is unreasonable and unkind you will be tempted to lose your temper, and answer him angrily. What will you do then?" "Pray a little harder," came the answer. The discourager had one more arrow: "Suppose he should strike you as he did before. What could you do but leave him again?" "Love him a little harder," said the young Christian steadily. Her splendid perseverance conquered. Through love, prayer, and patient effort, her father was not only reclaimed from his besetting sin, but proved Christ's power to save. To what extent are we identified with this characteristic in our devotedness?[4]

B. The Morality of Such Devotedness

Having lovingly, voluntarily, and perfectly washed his disciples' feet, Jesus said to them, "I have given you an example, that you should do as I have done to you. Most assuredly, I say to you, a servant is not greater than his master; nor is he who is sent greater than he who sent him" (John 13:15-16, NKJV). Christ supremely demonstrates the devotedness of a disciplined life. He calls us to demonstrate a quality of life so that those who follow us will emulate the example of Christ. To what extent are others led into a life of devotedness because of what they see in us?

Illustration

When Catherine Booth, "Mother of the Salvation Army," died in 1890 of cancer, her body lay in state in Congress Hall. The poorest of the poor mingled with members of Parliament as they filed past the casket; all were eager for a last look upon the face they loved. Ruffians passed her weeping. Prostitutes turned from her side and begged to be taken to some home where they could begin a new life. "That woman lived for me," an alcoholic cried in anguish. They drew him aside, and down on his knees he accepted pardon and promised that her God should be his. Three men knelt together one night at the head of the coffin, repented of their sins, and left the hall saved. Another said, "I've come sixty miles to see her again. She was the means of saving my two boys." What a thrilling testimony to one who had exemplified the qualities of a Christian![5]

Conclusion

The three experiences that perfect our relationship as disciples are identification with Christ in his discipline, discernment, and devotedness. Such identification matures only as we daily bring our lives under the mastership of his personal tuition. So may our prayer ever be:

> At the feet of Jesus
> Is the place for me;
> There, a humble learner,
> I would choose to be.
> P. P. Bliss

2

The Disciple's Responsibility

John 8:31-36

"If you abide in My word, you are My disciples indeed. And
you shall know the truth, and the truth shall make you free"
(John 8:31-32, NKJV).

Introduction

When the right relationship has been established in the
School of Discipline, there is a lifelong responsibility that
emerges for every true disciple of Jesus Christ. It is comprehended in the words of our text: "If you abide in My word, you
are My disciples indeed. And you shall know the truth, and the
truth shall make you free" (John 8:31-32, NKJV). The disciple's
responsibility must be regarded as threefold:

I. Continuance in the Word of Truth

"If *you* abide in My word" (John 8:31, NKJV). The emphasis is
on the pronoun "you." This is significant because the Lord
Jesus was addressing leaders of religious life who were nominal believers—men who did not possess the conviction or

courage to rank themselves openly as the disciples of Christ. True discipleship demands:

A. Continuance in the Truth as It Is in Christ

He had just said, "Even if I bear witness of Myself, My witness is true" (John 8:14, NKJV). The Jews required the testimony of two witnesses before they accepted a record as valid. This requirement was based on the imperfection of individual knowledge and the untrustworthiness of individual testimony. With Christ, however, there was no imperfection or untrustworthiness. So as to give men no excuse to doubt his Word, he declared, "I am One who bears witness of Myself" (v. 18, NKJV). In other words, he claimed to represent the two required witnesses since he was one with the Father in *speaking*, as well as *being*, the truth. To grasp such a claim is to be willing to continue in the truth as it is in Jesus Christ.

B. Continuance in the Whole Truth as It Is in Christ

"If you abide in My word" (John 8:31, NKJV). Notice that the Lord speaks of "My word" in the singular. In Chapter 15:7 we have the opposite form of the thought where he says, "If you abide in Me, and My words abide in you." The reason for the singular form in this context is that Christ was demanding continuance in the truth in its entirety from would-be disciples. By the term *my word*, Jesus was conveying the idea of the full revelation of God as it is in himself. It is easy to be selective in our loyalty to truth, but such selectiveness is not worthy of discipleship.

Illustration

When bankers are trained to learn the difference between a counterfeit bill and a real one they are told not to waste time studying the counterfeit; they study the real thing until they know it upside down, backwards and forwards. Then, when a counterfeit bill comes along, it stands out like a sore thumb. In like manner, we must study the real thing—Christ and his life. Only then shall we continue in the truth.

C. *Continuance in Nothing but the Truth as It Is in Christ*

"If you abide in My word" (John 8:31, NKJV). The human tendency is to cease to "abide" in the Word and to be led astray by our own opinions and preconceived ideas. We must ever remember that truth is the objective apprehension of the revelation of Christ, as distinguished from human speculations distorted by desires and special interests. To continue in the truth, the whole truth, and nothing but the truth, is to be guided wholly by the Word of God and governed wholly by the Spirit of God in all matters of faith and practice. This constitutes true discipleship.

> Since truth is always true
> And only true can be,
> Keep me, O Lord, as true to truth
> As truth is true to Thee.[1]
> T. Baird

II. Obedience to the Word of Truth

"And you shall *know* the truth" (John 8:32, NKJV). The Lord Jesus left us in no doubt as to what he meant by knowing the truth. In this very gospel he says, "If anyone wills to do [God's] will, he shall know concerning the doctrine, whether it is from God . . ." (John 7:17, NKJV). Willingness to do God's will is the secret of progressive knowledge in divine things. Someone has put it:

Light obeyed bringeth light; Light rejected bringeth night.

A. *There Must Be Obedience of Mind*

Paul speaks of "bringing every thought into captivity to the obedience of Christ" (2 Cor. 10:5). This calls for the casting down of our own carnal imaginations and proud rationalizations so that the Word of God may dwell in us richly in all wisdom. In terms of practical experience, this involves reading the Bible every day. Repeatedly, the Master had to turn to his disciples and ask, "Have you not read?" (Matt. 12:3, NKJV; see also

19:4; 21:16; 22:31, etc.). The apostle Paul exhorted Timothy to "give attention to reading" (1 Tim. 4:13, NKJV). More than just the public reading of Scripture, Paul was concerned that Timothy might become neglectful of this holy habit in his personal life. As martyrdom drew perilously near, that apostle admonished Timothy again: "Be diligent to come to me quickly; . . . [and] Bring . . . the books, *especially the parchments*" (2 Tim. 4:9, 13, NKJV). Think of it! Here Paul was in prison. Death was near and heaven was soon to open to receive him, but this man of God felt the need for more reading, especially the parchments—the Holy Scriptures. What an indictment on our reading of the Word in these days of rushed living.

But along with the reading there should be the searching of the Word of God every day. "Search the Scriptures," said our Lord to the religious leaders of his day, "for in them you think you have eternal life; and these are they which testify of Me" (John 5:39, NKJV). Bishop B. F. Westcott points out that this word *search* is in the imperative mood; that is to say, our Lord was insisting that to find the Savior, men must *search* the Scriptures. In their blindness, however, the scribes and Pharisees hopelessly failed to make this discovery, even though they were engaged in the most intense investigation of the Scriptures. They did not realize that searching, like reading, must be under the control of the Holy Spirit if Christ is to be revealed. The Bible says, "Eye has not seen, nor ear heard, nor have entered into the heart of man the things which God has prepared for those who love him. But God has revealed them to us through his Spirit. For the Spirit searches all things, yes, the deep things of God . . . . no one knows the things of God except the Spirit of God" (1 Cor. 2:9-11, NKJV; see also vv. 12-14). So to know the truth there must be the obedience of our minds to the Word of God in *reading* and *searching* the truth until Christ is revealed by the Holy Spirit.

Illustration

In these days of selected readings and favorite passages, wrested texts, and promise boxes, here is helpful counsel. It was given by Dr. T. T. Shields to his students when he concluded a series of lectures on the Pentateuch. He told them: "I urge you to read consecutively through the entire Bible. Open your hearts to the martial strength of Joshua; the individual heroism of Judges; the sylvan beauty and domestic loveliness of Ruth; the philosophy of history, the sequence of cause and effect in the historical portions of the Old Testament; the philosophy of tears in the poetry of Job; the universality of the experimental utterances of David; the practical wisdom of Proverbs; the Preacher's appraisal of the vanity of things under the sun; the holy passion of the Canticles; the seraphic fire of Isaiah; the threnodies of Jeremiah; the supernal splendor of Ezekiel's visions of God; the foresight of Daniel; the pathos of Hosea; and the periscopic and telescopic discernment of all the minor prophets, until you open the New Testament and read, 'When Jesus was born in Bethlehem of Judea in the days of Herod the King.' [Here] you will breathe the atmosphere of Genesis, and find principles reminiscent of Exodus, and feel as well as reason that the same Author speaks in every book. Read the Gospels, read the story of the Crucifixion and of the Resurrection, and gather with the apostles as the Holy Spirit descends. Read through the Acts. One by one the witnesses slip away, while their history recurs in part in the Epistles. Then read John's vision on the Isle of Patmos, and on through the book of Revelation, and you will hear the same Voice which has been speaking through all the Temple of Truth, saying, 'Surely I come quickly,' and you will be able to respond, 'Even so, come, Lord Jesus.' When you have finished it all, I know you will say, 'it is God's book. Nobody but God could speak like that.'"[2]

B. There Must Be Obedience of Heart

The apostle reminds his readers at Rome that they were once slaves to sin, but now they *"obeyed from the heart* that form of doctrine to which [they] were delivered" (Rom. 6:17, NKJV). To obey with the heart means more than just believing the truth.

So many of us *assent* to truth but we do not *consent* to it! Just as a sinner can never be born into the kingdom of God without receiving what he believes, so no saint can progress in the life of discipleship without receiving what he believes. James says: "Therefore lay aside all filthiness and overflow of wickedness, and *receive* with meekness the implanted word, which is able to save your souls" (James 1:21, NKJV). We must not fool with God. If we mean business, then with docility and humility we must obey the truth of God from the heart.

Amplification

One of J. W. Chapman's rules for Bible study was this: "Live the truth you get in the morning through each hour of the day." Ultimately, it is not a matter of how often we go through the Bible, but how often the Bible goes through us. Some books are produced for our information. The Bible was produced for our transformation. There is nothing in the Bible that benefits you unless it is transmuted into life, unless it becomes a part of yourself, just like food. Unless you assimilate it and it becomes body, bone, and muscle, it does you no good.[3]

C. There Must Be Obedience of Will

A phrase in Philippians 2:8 sums up the obedience of will: It is "obedient to the point of death" (NKJV). Before this could happen in the life of God's Servant, he had to pray, "Father, . . . not My will, but Yours, be done" (Luke 22:42, NKJV). The cross represents the fulfillment of God's redemptive purpose for every life. Therefore, obedience is never valid until it becomes obedience unto death. This involves willingness to obey God—cost what it will—until the divine will is accomplished.

Illustration

Two friends were out walking in the mountains. Following hard at the heels of his master was a faithful dog. The dog's ears and eyes were listening and watching for words of command from his master. In conversation, the master began gesturing. He raised his arm in the direction of a precipice. The faithful dog, thinking that his master was giving a word of command to him, instantly leaped to his death over the precipice. Oh, that we were as quick to obey our master's commands, to have our ears "tuned to hear his slightest whisper," and then to obey from the heart—even unto death!

III. Experience of the Word of Truth

"The truth shall make you free" (John 8:32, NKJV). If there is faithful continuance in the truth and soulful obedience to the truth, there will be joyful experience of the truth. This experience is summed up in one word: freedom (v. 32). These words were addressed to people who claimed political freedom but, in reality, they were the slaves of Rome. They claimed religious freedom, but instead were slaves to the letter of the law. They claimed moral freedom, but in point of fact were slaves to sin. Nevertheless, it was to slaves like these that Jesus said, "The truth shall make you free" (v. 32, NKJV). The Savior was offering them—and men and women ever since:

A. *Personal Freedom*

"If the Son makes you free, you shall be free indeed" (John 8:36, NKJV). The Jews had just remarked to Christ, "We are Abraham's descendants, and have never been in bondage to anyone. How can you say, 'You will be made free'?" (v. 33, NKJV). People have been saying this since the dawn of time to cover up their bondage to people. All of us are dominated by what others think and say. H. G. Wells once stated that the voice of our neighbors sounds louder in our ears than the voice of God; and it was Solomon who stated that "The fear of man brings a snare" (Prov. 29:25). Jesus can set you free from such bondage through the Word of God and the Spirit of God. The reason we are not the radiant and fearless witnesses we ought to be is because of our bondage to men.

One of the Reformers was told, "All the world is against

you," to which he replied, "Then I am against the world." The epitaph on the tomb of John Knox reads: "Here lies the man who never feared the face of clay."

B. Literal Freedom

"The truth shall make you free" (John 8:32, NKJV). The divine law without the divine life is bondage; the Word of God without the Spirit of God is slavery; but when the truth is obeyed in mind, heart, and will, it sets men free. The law of God becomes a way of life, the Word of God becomes a path of life, the Gospel of God becomes the aim of life. Literal freedom is the liberty to speak, preach, and write with confidence and conviction. Once a person has been set free in this area there is no influence for good that he cannot exert.

C. Spiritual Freedom

"The Spirit of life in Christ Jesus has made me free from the law of sin and death" (Rom. 8:2, NKJV). Jesus had just told his listeners that "Whoever commits sin is a slave of sin" (John 8:34, NKJV). How true this is! Discipleship breaks the chains that bind us to our sins and enables us to be the persons we know we ought to be. Discipleship implies freedom through the Son of God, by the Word of God, and in the power of the Spirit of God.

Illustration

Herod could incarcerate John the Baptist and finally behead him, but John was free while his captor was a slave, although he was called king; Nero was the slave while Paul was God's free man, shouting, "I can do all things through Christ who strengthens me," in a Roman prison. King James could imprison that humble tinker, John Bunyan, for preaching on the streets of Bedford, but Bunyan was free in a soul that reveled in spiritual visions and delights. Madame Guyon was imprisoned in the lonely Bastille prison, but she was free in heart.

Do you know this spiritual freedom, or are you under the

dominion of sin, compelled to give way to evil tempers and lusts—a servant of the experience of Romans 7? If so, move over into the eighth chapter and shout, "The law of the Spirit of life in Christ Jesus has made me free from the law of sin and death."[4]

Conclusion

Here, then, is the threefold responsibility of true discipleship: continuance in the truth, obedience to the truth, and experience of the truth, as revealed by the Spirit of God and released by the Son of God. Christ says to us again: "If you abide in My word, you are My disciples indeed. And you shall know the truth, and the truth shall make you free" (John 8:31-32, NKJV). God make us disciples indeed!

3

The Disciple's Requirements

Luke 14:25-35; 9:57-62

"Whosoever doth not bear his cross, and come after me, cannot be my disciple . . . likewise, whosoever he be of you that foresaketh not all that he hath, he cannot be my disciple" (14:27, 33, KJV).

Introduction

The School of Discipline has its responsibilities, but it has also its requirements—which are vigorous and demanding. It is willingness to meet those requirements that distinguishes the nominal believer from the committed disciple. So we find that Jesus addressed the requirements of discipleship to the individual within the crowd. While great multitudes were following him, the Master's call was to "any man" (Luke 14:26). What a challenge there is in these requirements of discipleship! In the first place, discipleship requires:

I. No Rival in the Life for Christ

"If any man come to me, and hate not" (Luke 14:26).

Christian discipleship means giving one's first loyalty to the Lord Jesus Christ; anything less than this is virtual treason if Jesus is truly Lord. There is no other response than that of full submission to his sovereignty. This is the only explanation to the master's use of the word "hate." Since there is no place in Jesus' teaching for literal hatred, he must have intended to convey the quality of love that he expected of his followers. Anything less than this would be hatred by comparison.

There is a deeper meaning here. I believe that Jesus is making a clear distinction between redemptive love, which is divine, and possessive love, which is human. If our relationship to our loved ones does not flow out of redemptive love, it will not last. This is why possessive love is basically selfish, and therefore doomed to failure. When Jesus Christ is unrivaled in our lives then we love him first, and the overflow of that love reaches out to family, friends, and even foes. In practical terms, this means:

A. We may have a father and enjoy his loving attention, but he cannot rival the Lord Jesus.

B. We may have a mother and enjoy her loving affection, but she cannot rival the Lord Jesus.

C. We may have a wife and enjoy her loving devotion, but she cannot rival the Lord Jesus.

D. We may have children and enjoy their loving submission, but they cannot rival the Lord Jesus.

E. We may have brothers and sisters and enjoy their loving friendship and fellowship, but they cannot rival the Lord Jesus.

F. We may have self-life and enjoy its loving ambition, but it cannot rival the Lord Jesus.

Illustration
When V. Raymond Edman was a missionary in Ecuador he knew an earnest and effective layman who felt called to the

ministry, but his wife would not hear of it. She threatened all manner of reprisal if he should leave his lucrative employment to become a servant of Jesus Christ. One evening he came to Brother Edman with a bundle under one arm, and tears in his eyes. The good doctor read to him from Mark 10:29-30: "Verily I say unto you, There is no man that hath left house, or brethren, or sisters, or father, or mother, or wife, or children, or lands, for my sake, and the gospel's, But he shall receive an hundredfold now in this time, houses, and brethren, and sisters, and mothers, and children, and lands, with persecutions; and in the world to come eternal life." After prayer and tears, Edman inquired what the man had in the bundle. "It contains my working clothes," he replied. "I left my employment today."

He had counted the cost, and had set himself to leave all, and to face whatever persecutions might come; only that he might be Jesus' disciple. Do we wonder that he won his wife to full allegiance to the Master, and that together they have become pillars in the house of God?[1]

God has declared that "In all things [Christ must] have the preeminence," (Col. 1:18). Can I, therefore, give him any less? A thousand times NO! For in doing so I would reveal that I have a rival in my life, and am a traitor to Christ. Discipleship demands that Christ should reign unrivaled in my heart, having preeminence in my thinking, speaking, and acting. If you, my friend, have a rival in your heart, God help you to pray:

Jesus, Thy boundless love to me
No thought can reach, no tongue declare;
Then [bend] my wayward heart to Thee,
And reign without a rival there.
Paul Gerhardt

II. No Refusal in the Life for Christ

"Whosoever doth not bear his cross, and come after me, cannot be my disciple" (Luke 14:27). The disciples, no doubt, had seen a man take up his cross, and they knew what it meant. It was a one-way journey; he would never come back. Taking up the cross means the utmost in self-denial. Dietrich Bonhoeffer reminds us that when Jesus Christ calls us to follow him, he calls us to die.[2] In the final analysis, bearing the cross means kneeling in Gethsemane and saying an eternal yes to all the will of God.

This is the path the Master trod, Should not the servant tread it still?

To understand the deeper significance of saying yes to the implications of the cross, we need to study what Paul has to say about the cross in our daily lives, as set out in his epistle to the Galatians. Three important verses should be noted:

A. Bearing the Cross Means No Refusal to Die to the Principle of the Old Life

"I am crucified with Christ" (Gal. 2:20). The old principle was "Not Christ, but I"; the new principle is "Not I, but Christ"; that is, a life with the "I" crossed out, and God's will supreme in everything.

In Gethsemane, the Lord Jesus could say, "Not my will, but thine, be done" (Luke 22:42). He could say throughout his lifetime, "Lo, I come: in the volume of the book it is written of me, I delight to do thy will, O my God: yea, thy law is within my heart" (Ps. 40:7-8). Once we have learned this application of the cross to our self-life we have solved the problem of making the right decisions in our lives. We no longer ask, "Should I do this, or go there, or marry so-and-so?" The issue is not what we want to do, but rather what Christ wants to do in us and through us.

B. Bearing the Cross Means No Refusal to Die to the Passions of the Old Life

"They that are Christ's have crucified the flesh with the affections and lusts" (Gal. 5:24). Instead of responding to the calls of the old nature, we set our affections on things above; that is, we transmute, or sublimate, those very passions, desires, and hungers that have gone through death and the grave, to the higher purpose of the RISEN life. This means that Christ reigns in our passion life, and we "make [no] provisions for the flesh, to fulfil the lusts thereof" (Rom. 13:14).

Illustration
My Soul Is All I Have

I am resolved I will not be/The dupe of things I touch and see;/These figured totals lie to me—/My soul is all I have.

Illusive cheats are goods and gold:/These chattels that I have and hold/Are preys of moth, and rust, and mold;/My soul is all I have.

A builder, I, but not with stone;/The self I am, nor flesh nor bone:/My house will 'dure when stars are gone;/My soul is all I have.

For me to traffic with my soul/Would make me brother to the mole;/The whole world's wealth were but a dole;/My soul is all I have.

I must take care I do not lean/T'ward what is sordid, false, or mean;/I must not touch the thing unclean;/My soul is all I have.

Oh, Keeper of the souls of men,/Keep mine for me from hurt or stain,/For, should it slip my hand—what then?/My soul is all I have!

T. O. Chisholm

C. Bearing the Cross Means No Refusal to Die to the Program of the Old Life

"God forbid that I should glory, save in the cross of our Lord Jesus Christ, by whom the world is crucified unto me, and I unto the world" (Gal. 6:14). The old program was "Go *with* the world"; the new program is "Go *into* the world"; no longer pandering to the world, but preaching to the world and entering into the risen Christ's thought for the world when he said,

"Go ye into all the world, and preach the gospel to every creature" (Mark 16:15).

Bearing the cross, therefore, means no refusal to die to the
principle, passions, and program of the old life. Christ is
supreme in my life: controlling the *principle-room* of my will,
the *passion-room* of my heart, and the *program-room* of my mind.
This is the secret of dynamic discipleship.

III. No Retreat in the Life for Christ

"Whosoever he be of you that forsaketh not all that he hath, he
cannot be my disciple" (Luke 14:33). Forsaking all is following
the Lord Jesus without retreat. This is vividly illustrated in Luke
9, verses 57-62. Three vignettes are recorded there of would-be
followers of the Lord Jesus. In each case he made it clear that
forsaking all meant no retreat. In specific terms, this means:

A. No Tiring in the Life of Discipleship

"It came to pass, that, as they went in the way, a certain man said
unto him, Lord, I will follow thee whithersoever thou goest.
And Jesus said unto him, Foxes have holes, and birds of the air
have nests; but the Son of man hath not where to lay his head,"
(Luke 9:57-58). There was nothing wrong with the way this
young man offered his allegiance. His only problem was that he
did not reckon with the cost of discipleship. Animals and birds
have their places of habitation, but the Son of Man has nowhere
to lay his head (v. 58). What a glimpse this is into the life of our
Lord and the cost of the incarnation! It also teaches us that
while here on earth, we are not promised luxurious living, or
beds of ease. It is so easy to respond with enthusiasm at the outset, but are we prepared to follow him to the end?

B. No Trifling in the Life of Discipleship

"And [Jesus] said unto another, Follow me. But he said, Lord,
suffer me first to go and bury my father. Jesus said unto him,
Let the dead bury their dead: but go thou and preach the
kingdom of God" (Luke 9:59-60). With a little understanding

of the background it becomes evident that this young man's father had not just died. The Jews counted a burial ritual as most important. The duty of burial took precedence over the study of the Law, the temple service, the observance of circumcision, and the reading of the Megillah.[3] What the young man was actually implying was a little more subtle. In effect, he was suggesting that he would gladly follow the Lord Jesus once his father was dead and he had entered into his inheritance. This would ensure that he had financial security to fall back on, should Christ's cause not succeed. The Master's response was sharp and searching:

"Let the dead bury their dead: but go thou and preach the kingdom of God" (Luke 9:60). The young man was talking the language of the unregenerate, which was in direct contrast to the demands of the kingdom. Jesus could not wait for all the conveniences of the young man's self-interest.

Illustration

John MacNeil, the Scottish evangelist, was once talking about the excuses people make for not completely following Christ. Referring to the man who wished to first go and bury his father, he exclaimed with disgust, "Why, this poor fellow wanted a gravedigger's shovel, when our Lord was trying to give him a resurrection trumpet!" God's choices for us may be difficult, but we may be sure that they are the best. Are we willing to "leave all" and go on to the "more abundant life" of discipleship?[4]

C. No Turning in the Life of Discipleship

"And another also said, Lord, I will follow thee: but let me first go bid them farewell, which are at home at my house. And Jesus said unto him, No man, having put his hand to the plough, and looking back, is fit for the kingdom of God" (Luke 9:61-62). This third man, like the first, offered his services, but he interposed a condition that he must say farewell to those at home. At first this seems reasonable enough, but in this case it evidently concealed some reluctance on his part to take the decisive step. So Jesus points out that the kingdom of God has no room for those who look back when they are called forward.

Illustration

Often when converts from Hinduism inform their parents of their intention to be baptized it is not long before mother and father travel to the mission house and plead, with tears and threats, that they not take a step so fatal. Failing by this means to shake their children's resolutions, they become resigned to the fact. Their only stipulation is that the convert pay them one parting visit—to "bid them farewell which are at home at [his] house." The request seems reasonable. After all, to refuse is to wound parental feeling. So though his heart is with his spiritual brothers and he announces his soon return, the convert goes—*but never returns.* How often a farewell at home proves to be a farewell to Christ![5]

The cause of failure in true Christian discipleship can be traced to this problem of turning back. For example, Lot's wife retreated and became a monument to uselessness and shame (see Gen. 19:26). On the other hand, Jephthah would not go back and became a monument of usefulness and sacrifice (see Judg. 11:35).

Conclusion

The issue of this message, then, is our willingness to meet these requirements of discipleship. They are going to cost; but before you say "too costly," view them in the light of Calvary love, and then with soberness and sincerity say:

Dear Lord, in full surrender at Thy feet,/I make my consecration vows complete:/My life I yield to Thee;/ Henceforward, there shall be/No rival, no refusal, no retreat.

Stephen F. Olford

4

The Disciple's Recognition

John 13:33-35

"Love one another . . . . By this all will know that you are My
disciples" (John 13:34-35, NKJV).

Introduction

Every truth in the Word of God has its importance, so that it
is impossible to pit one against the other. An aspect of teaching which calls for urgent expression in daily life is this matter
of the disciple's recognition. When the Savior urged his disciples to "love one another" it was to be the hallmark by which
his followers were to be recognized throughout all time. The
threefold sense in which this mark is to be recognized may be
formulated as follows:

I. Disciples Must Always Be Known by Redemptive Love

"Love one another," commanded the Savior, "as I have loved
you"(John 13:34, NKJV). When the Lord Jesus uttered these
words he had just exemplified redemptive love by humbling
himself to wash the feet of Judas, who was to betray him; of

Peter, who was to deny him; and of the rest, who were to forsake him. But notwithstanding their failures and faults, he loved them all "to the end" (John 13:1, NKJV). Such love is more than human love, it is essentially divine, and is only made available through the redemption that is in Christ Jesus.

John, in his first epistle, contrasts the difference between the absence of redemptive love and the presence of redemptive love:

A. The Absence of Redemptive Love

"In this the children of God and the children of the devil are manifest: Whoever does not practice righteousness is not of God, nor is he who does not love his brother" (1 John 3:10, NKJV). Note again: "He who does not love his brother abides in death. Whoever hates his brother is a murderer" (1 John 3:14-15, NKJV). By the word "hate" John is thinking of Cain, who is the prototype of jealousy and inward hatred which an unregenerate man can feel against his brother. "If someone says, 'I love God,' and hates his brother, he is a liar" (1 John 4:20, NKJV). Absence of redemptive love can lead to unrighteousness and hatred, in relation to others.

Illustration

There is a tradition that 300 priests with their trumpets and 300 rabbis with their scholars once gathered in the Temple court to curse the Samaritans with all the curses in the Law of Moses. Nor were the Samaritans less eager in hating and annoying. At the Passover it was the Jews' custom to light bonfires on the Mount of Olives, a signal for other fires, till the Euphrates was reached, to send the message to exiled Jews. The Samaritans lighted rival bonfires on other days to confuse the watchers.[1]

B. The Presence of Redemptive Love

John continues, "We know that we have passed from death to life, because we love the brethren" (1 John 3:14, NKJV); and again: "He who loves his brother abides in the light" (1 John 2:10, NKJV); and "let us love one another, for love is of God; and everyone who loves is born of God" (1 John 4:7, NKJV). Redemptive love is the result of being born of God, receiving eternal life, and abiding in the light. Human love may superficially impress men with its words and wag of the tongue, but it is only Calvary love that can express itself in action and in reality.

Illustration

Reuel Howe illustrates love in the story of a mother and her eight-year-old daughter. The girl did something that caused her to feel alienated from her mother. Although her mother tried her best to help, the daughter finally ran out of the room in anger and went upstairs. Seeing her mother's new dress laid out for a party that evening, she found scissors and vented her hostility by making incisions, thereby seeking to injure her mother. Later the mother came upstairs, saw the ruined dress, and wept. Soon the small daughter came into the room and whispered, "Mother." But there was no reply. "Mother, Mother," she repeated. Still no reply. "Mother, Mother, please," she continued. The mother responded, "Please what?" "Please take me back, please take me back," pleaded the girl. That is what love does; it takes people back. "Love never ends." It reaches out until redemption is realized.

II. Disciples Must Always Be Known by Reciprocal Love

"Love one another" (John 13:34, NKJV). The world that knows only human love may talk about a person who is "unsociable," or speak of "that mean woman," but this attitude must never characterize a follower of our Lord. You may feel there are certain Christians you could never love, or you may avoid those who belong to a different denomination. Such thinking is unknown in the circle of true discipleship, for reciprocal love means:

A. *Love Shared in Christ*

Paul describes such sharing when he expresses his deep desire for the Colossians that their hearts might be "knit together in love" (Col. 2:2, NKJV). The word *knit* conveys two ideas, in the original: the first is that of "bringing together"; the second, of "carrying along," as an audience would be carried along by a convincing argument. When the Lord Jesus becomes the center of our shared love, we are brought together and carried along by a love which knows no differences, no distinctions, and no disharmonies.

Illustration

In her book, *Living with Love,* Josephine Robertson tells of a youthful clergyman, the Rev. Joe Roberts, who arrived by stagecoach in a blizzard to minister to the Shoshone tribe of Wyoming. Soon after his arrival the son of the chief was shot by a soldier in a brawl, and the chief vowed to kill the first white man he met. Thinking this could lead to a long, bloody feud, Roberts decided to take action. Seeking out the tepee, fifteen miles away in the mountains, Roberts stood outside and called the chief's name. When the chief appeared, Roberts said, "I know that the other white men have families, but I am alone. Kill me instead." Amazed, the chief motioned him inside his tent, where he asked, "How do you have so much courage?" Joe Roberts told him about Christ: His death, His teachings. When Joe left, the chief of the Shoshones had renounced his vow to kill and resolved to be a Christian. He had seen love in action. Every group that calls itself Christian should decide what it can do to make love visible in the home, the church, and the world. For unless love becomes visible it is not love at all.

B. Love Shown in Christ

"Love one another" (13:34, NKJV). Such love is the unstinted giving of ourselves for the good of others—spiritually, ethically, and practically.

Spiritually, Christ "laid down His life for us. And we also ought to lay down our lives for the brethren" (1 John 3:16). Think of the occasion when the crowds so thronged to him that he and his disciples had no time to eat (see Mark 3:20); but he continued to give of himself in preaching, teaching, and healing. Or recall the story in John 4 of the weary Savior who went miles out of his way in order to talk to one sin-sick soul (see John 4:4). Paul, like his Lord, knew what it meant to lay down his life for the brethren. He could say, "I will very gladly spend and be spent for your souls; though the more abundantly I love you, the less I am loved" (2 Cor. 12:15). Epaphroditus put the welfare of others before his own. Paul says of him, "For the work of Christ he came close to death, not regarding his life" (Phil. 2:30).

Illustration

When Wycliffe translator, Doug Meland, and his wife moved into a village of Brazil's Fulnio Indians, he was referred to as "the white man," an uncomplimentary term, since other white men had exploited them, burned their homes, and robbed them of their lands. But after the missionaries learned the language and began to help the people with medicine and in other ways, they began to call Doug "the respectable white man." When the Melands began adopting the customs of the people, the Fulnio spoke of Doug as "the white Indian." Then one day, as Doug was washing the dirty, bloodcaked foot of an injured boy, he overheard a bystander say, "Who ever heard of a white man washing an Indian's foot before? Certainly this man is from God!" From that day on, whenever Doug entered an Indian home, it would be announced, "Here comes the man God sent us."[2]

Reciprocal love is then shown *ethically*. It is John who says, "He who loves his brother abides in the light, and there is no cause for stumbling [or scandal] in him" (1 John 2:10, NKJV). This means that the true disciple *thinks love*. The central note in Paul's "Song of Love" is the clause, "[Love] thinks no evil" (1 Cor. 13:5, NKJV). Rather, he *speaks love*. A world of mischief and madness can be created by the uncontrolled tongue. James tells us that the tongue can set on fire the whole course of nature (see James 3:6). But the Christian who lives in the power of the ungrieved Spirit can bear "with one another in love," speak "the truth in love," and edify the body "in love" (Eph. 4:2, 15-16, NKJV).

Illustration
A newspaper in Wales once carried this headline: "Poison Pen Sends a Woman to Death." The article went on to say that the lady committed suicide after receiving poisonous and anonymous letters and postcards for nine months.

The true disciple supremely acts love. Peter says, "Above all things have fervent love for one another, for 'love will cover a multitude of sins'" (1 Peter 4:8, NKJV). To "cover a multitude of sins" does not imply compromise or weakness, for we are told to "rebuke [those who are sinning] in the presence of all, that the rest also may fear" (1 Tim. 5:20, NKJV). The idea behind Peter's words is rather that of the "elastic" love that stretches over the shortcomings of our brethren. This is the love that is more ready to forgive than to expose and judge.

Reciprocal love is also shown *practically.* John asks the question, "Whoever has this world's goods, and sees his brother in need, and shuts up his heart from him, how does the love of God abide in him?" (1 John 3:17, NKJV). This was no theoretical idealism in the early church. Think of the beginning of the church. We read that "all who believed were together, and had all things in common, and sold their possessions and goods, and divided them among all, as anyone had need" (Acts 2:44-45, NKJV). Then consider the church as established at Jerusalem. We read: "And great grace was upon them all. Nor was there anyone among them who lacked . . . and they distributed to each as anyone had need" (Acts 4:33-35, NKJV). Once more, reflect on the churches throughout Macedonia. We read "that in a great trial of affliction the abundance of their joy and their deep poverty abounded in the riches of their liberality" (2 Cor. 8:2, NKJV).

What was true of the churches was also true of individuals.

Think of Barnabas who, "having land, sold it, and brought the money and laid it at the apostles' feet" (Acts 4:37, NKJV).

From these illustrations of reciprocal and practical giving we must not deduce a wrong conception of our responsibility in stewardship. God does not call us to sell up and distribute our goods without demand or discrimination. He does, however, challenge our love in relation to its *willingness*. If and when the occasion demands, we must be ever ready to give that willingness practical expression.

John Wesley's rule for Christian living was just this: "Do all the good you can, by all the means you can, in all the ways you can, in all the places you can, at all the times you can, to all the people you can, as long as ever you can. "[3]

III. Disciples Must Always Be Known by Reflected Love

"By this all will know that you are My disciples," said Jesus (John 13:35, NKJV). Followers of great teachers have their distinctive marks. The world outside recognizes a given teacher by that which is reflected in his students. This was true of the disciples of Jesus. They had to reflect redemptive and reciprocal love in a manner that would convince the world that they were his disciples. This was to be expressed outwardly in two ways; first, through:

A. *The Reflected* Oneness *of Love*

Jesus prayed that this oneness might be fulfilled in his disciples so that the world would believe that he had been sent by the Father and that they were also loved by him (see John 17:21-23). The apologists of the first centuries delighted in appealing to the striking fact of the common love of Christians, which was a new thing in the history of mankind; and while the Church has sometimes forgotten the characteristic, the world never has. Tertullian records in a famous passage how "the heathen were wont to exclaim with wonder, 'See how these Christians love one another!'"

Illustration

Dolly Madison, wife of the fourth president of the United States, was one of the most popular women in American history. Wherever she went she charmed and captivated everyone. Asked to explain the secret of her power over others, she exclaimed, "I have none, I desire none. I merely love everyone." Those who love are richly rewarded by love returned.

B. *The Reflected* Witness *of Love*

John reminds us: "If we love one another, God abides in us, and His love has been perfected in us. . . . And we have seen and testify that the Father has sent the Son as Savior of the world" (1 John 4:12, 14, NKJV). Nothing is so universal in its appeal, so powerful in its impact, and so wonderful in its effect, as the *witness* of love. The world is starved for love and waits eagerly for church members to reflect the love of Christ. The tragedy is that there is so little reflected oneness, and therefore no convincing witness. Even Chrysostom, in his day, lamented that division among Christians was hindering the conversion of the heathen.

How easy it is to lose our first love. May God rekindle his love in all our hearts! The witness of love is not only a ministry to the church, it is a service to the world. Men and women will never believe our message until they see and sense our genuine love for them.

Illustration

A Christian woman working among the prostitutes of London found a young girl desperately ill in a cold and bare room. She ministered to her by changing her bed linen, supplying food and medicine, and making the place warm and cheerful. When she thought she had gained the confidence of the girl, the worker offered to say a prayer, but was rebutted with the words, "No, you don't care for me; you're doing this just to get to heaven." Weeks went by in which God's servant worked tirelessly to restore the girl to full health. One day the woman worker said, "My dear, you are nearly well now, and I must leave you to tend the needs of others. Before I go, I want to kiss you goodbye." The pure lips that had known only prayer and holy words met the lips defiled by oaths and lustful caresses. In that moment the girl's heart broke. Love conquered and another soul was won for the kingdom.

Conclusion

God's way is love's way. May we be characterized by the redemptive, reciprocal, and reflected love of Christ, and so be known always as the disciples of Jesus.

5

The Disciple's Realization

John 15:7-16

"By this My Father is glorified, that you bear much fruit; so you will be My disciples" (John 15:8, NKJV).

Introduction

When Jesus said these words he was revealing the disciple's great realization. If fruitfulness glorified God, then nothing less than abundant fruitfulness should constitute the realization of every true disciple. Most commentators agree that the clause, "By this My Father is glorified" (NKJV), coordinates three aspects of fruitfulness, in verses 7, 8, and 16, or what we shall call:

I. Fruitfulness in the Prayer Life

"If you abide in Me, and My words abide in you, you will ask what you desire, and it shall be done for you" (John 15:7, NKJV). This statement of the Savior makes it clear that fruitfulness in the prayer life must be commensurate with:

A. *The Harmony of Requests in Prayer*

"If you abide in Me, and My words abide in you, you will ask" (John 15:7, NKJV). This means that if our wills are to be harmonized with God's will in requests that we make, we shall have to abide in Christ and allow his words to abide in us. Fruit ripens for picking as it abides in the sun and takes into its nature the cleansing and enriching rays. The same applies to our requests in prayer. They ripen for picking while we abide in Christ and in the process we take into our beings the cleansing and enriching properties of his Word.

B. *The Constancy of Replies to Prayer*

"You will ask what you desire, and it shall be done for you" (John 15:7, NKJV). Constant replies to prayer are the fruit of God's will brought to birth in our lives. This is why God is glorified in a fruitful prayer life. Jesus made this plain when he said, "And whatever you ask in My name, that I will do, that the Father may be glorified in the Son" (John 14:13, NKJV). Remember that God is our Father and, therefore, longs to answer prayer. The measure in which he is glorified is the measure in which he can righteously answer bigger and bigger requests from us.

Illustration

No more sublime story has been recorded in earthly annals than that of David Brainerd. No miracle attests, with diviner force, the truth of Christianity than the life and work of this godly man. Alone in the savage wilds of America, struggling day and night with a mortal disease, unschooled in the care of souls, having access to the Indians for a large portion of time only through the bungling medium of a pagan interpreter, with the Word of God in his heart and in his hand, his soul fixed with the divine flame, a place and time to pour out his heart and soul to God in prayer, he fully established the worship of God and secured great results. After spending a whole week in prayer he spoke with such power that countless numbers of Indians were led to yield their lives to God. The Indians were changed from the lowest besotments of heathenism to pure, devout, intelligent Christians.

Brainerd lived a life of holiness and prayer: by day and by night he prayed. Before preaching and after preaching he prayed. Riding through the interminable solitude of the forest he prayed. On his bed of straw he prayed. Morning, noon, and night he communed with God. Little wonder he had such power—God was with him mightily because he lived in the presence of God.[1]

Is your prayer life a fruitful one? Are you conscious of bringing to birth, in everyday life, God's will by the requests you offer and the answers you receive? If not, then you are not abiding in Christ, and discipleship, in all its fullness, is not being realized in your life.

To glorify God, in the second instance, means that the disciple must realize:

II. Fruitfulness in the Personal Life

"By this My Father is glorified, that you bear much fruit"(15:8, NKJV). The fruit we are expected to produce in personal life is spirituality. The apostle Paul describes this fruit as one cluster: "the fruit of the Spirit is love, joy, peace, longsuffering, kindness, goodness, faithfulness, gentleness, self-control" (Gal. 5:22-23, NKJV). In this cluster we have:

A. The Essence of Spirituality in Personal Life

"Love, joy, peace" (Gal. 5:22, NKJV). Each of these three graces is fundamental to a personal experience of God in Christ. Love is the evidence of relationship to Christ, while joy and peace are the evidence of fellowship in Christ. Where relationship to Christ and fellowship in Christ do not exist there cannot be genuine spirituality. This may sound devastating, but it is true. Let me illustrate what I mean.

A man may be resplendent. He may possess all conceivable

intellectual endowments, he may speak with the eloquence of angels, he may subdue the material world by conquering physical forces, and personally, he may embody the most charming combination of disposition and temperament—and yet not possess true spirituality. The reason for this is because natural endowments are distinct from the fruit of the Spirit. How important, then, that we should be sure of true essence of spirituality, namely, "love, joy, peace" (Gal. 5:22, NKJV).

B. The Expression of Spirituality in Personal Life

"Longsuffering, kindness, goodness" (Gal. 5:22, NKJV). While the essence of spirituality has to do with God, the expression of spirituality has to do with our fellow men. In the home, the church, and the world, we are to be known by our longsuffering, gentleness, and goodness. *Longsuffering* is that quality of patience, in the face of provocation, and the ability not to surrender or succumb under trial. *Kindness* is the spirit of serviceableness under all conditions, while *goodness* is the benevolence and generosity of the disciple at all times. Do others know us by our longsuffering, kindness, and goodness?

Illustration

Known as the "Bishop of the South Pacific," John Selwyn had at one time been recognized for his boxing skill. Touched by the Holy Spirit's convicting power, however, he later became an outstanding missionary. One day this saintly leader reluctantly gave a stern but loving rebuke to a man who regularly attended the local church. The disorderly one resented the advice and angrily struck Selwyn a violent blow in the face with his fist. In return the missionary folded his arms and humbly looked into the man's blazing eyes. With his boxing skill he could easily have knocked out his antagonist. Instead, he turned the other cheek and waited calmly to be hit a second time. This was too much for the assailant, who, greatly ashamed, fled into the jungle. Years later, the man accepted the Lord as his Savior and gave his testimony before the church. It was customary at that time for a believer to choose a Christian name for himself after conversion, and he chose the name John Selwyn, adding, "He's the one who taught me what Jesus Christ is really like." Longsuffering had made the missionary's witness effective.

C. The Exercise of Spirituality in Personal Life

"Faithfulness, gentleness, self-control" (5:22-23). The exercise of spirituality has to do with the discipline of self, or the inward faithfulness, humbleness, and temperateness of life. To fail in this inward exercise is to spoil the balance and symmetry of the whole cluster of fruit.

Dr. J. Hamilton tells us that chemists have analyzed the fruit of the vine and found that there are nine ingredients that make up the grape juice we know so well. The extraordinary thing about this juice, however, is that it cannot be made up of one, or even two, grapes. It can be produced only from the best specimens where the cluster is complete.

If God is to be glorified in the fruitfulness of our personal life, then the cluster of fruit must be complete. In other words, fruitfulness must be the essence, expression, and exercise of spirituality in us. Such fruitfulness will never be crude: it will always be finished, for it is not a process, but the result of many processes, the ultimate product of many forces working together.

Illustration

Imagine someone without experience sitting down before Raphael's famous picture of the transfiguration and attempting to reproduce it! How crude and lifeless his work would be! But if such a thing were possible that the spirit of Raphael should enter into the man and obtain mastery of his mind and eye and hand, it would be entirely possible that he could paint this masterpiece, for it would simply be Raphael reproducing Raphael. And this in a mystery is what is true of the disciple filled with the Holy Spirit. Christ by the Spirit dwells within him as a divine life, and Christ is able to image forth Christ from the interior life of the outward example.[2]

One more aspect of fruitfulness must engage our attention. For God to be glorified, the disciple must realize:

III. Fruitfulness in the Practical Life

"You did not choose me, but I chose you and appointed you that you should go and bear fruit, and that your fruit should remain" (John 15:16, NKJV). Observe that fruitfulness in practical life is:

A. *Appointed Service*

Said the Savior: "I chose you and appointed you that you should go and bear fruit" (John 15:16, NKJV). We see that while personal fruitfulness relates to spirituality, practical fruitfulness has to do with service. Despite this distinction, however, it is important to recognize that practical fruitfulness is an extension of personal fruitfulness. Indeed, without personal fruitfulness practical fruitfulness would be impossible. Such fruitfulness is God's purpose of vocation for every Christian. So many people are confused and perplexed about life's vocation. They imagine that unless they are especially called to do what is termed "full-time Christian work," or to engage in some other spectacular employment, they are not fulfilling life's vocation. Nothing could be further from the truth. Study the Savior's words in connection with other relevant Bible teaching and you will see that vocation is Christ working through his disciples in whatever sphere they are found. In this sense, every disciple is chosen, appointed, and sent to bear fruit to the glory of God. Bearing fruit is allowing the essence, expression, and exercise of the fruit of the Spirit in personal life to have its full impact within the context of our daily work and witness.

"But what about the mission field, or some other specific Christian vocation?" someone asks. The answer to that question is that direction to such fields of labor is the strategic placing of those who already are fulfilling a ministry. The responsibility of thrusting out laborers and distributing manpower is God's. Our business is to accept the work at hand as a vocation in the spirit of discipleship and "stay put" until he directs otherwise.

Illustration

Every Christian should think of himself as having a divine call. L. C. Hester of Whitehours, Texas is a plumber. Every time he goes out on a job he packs a New Testament in with his tools. Consequently, he has earned the title "the witnessing plumber." A minister said of him: "That witnessing plumber has won hundreds to Christ since he became a Christian. Many will listen to a working man who will not listen to a preacher."

B. Abiding Service

"Your fruit should remain" (John 15:16, NKJV). If our fruit is to remain we must be very careful to distinguish between fruit and fungus! We must surely affirm with all honesty that much activity that goes on in the name of fruit is really nothing more than fungus, and fungus is a parasite which is not only foreign to God's work, but actually saps its very life.

Illustration

In Mexico and the tropical zones of South America a so-called "strangler" fig grows in abundance. The Spanish-speaking people refer to it as the *matapalo,* which means "the tree killer." The fruit is not palatable except to cattle and the fowls of the air. After the birds eat it, they must clean their beaks of the sticky residue. They do this by rubbing them on nearby trees. The seeds of the small fig have a natural glue which makes them adhere to the branches. When the rainy season arrives, germination takes place. Soon tiny roots make their way down into the heart of the wood and begin to grow. Within a few years the once lovely palms have become entirely covered with the entangling vines of the parasitic growth. Unless the tree is set free through the removal of these "strangler" figs, it finally begins to wither, dropping one frond after another until it is completely lifeless. The only way to stop the killing process is for someone to take a sharp knife and cut away the invader.

The only fruit that remains is that which is produced within the orbit of God's will. John declares, "He who does the will of God abides forever" (1 John 2:17, NKJV). Without doubt, the reason why so many evidences of D. L. Moody's work for God remain with us today is because that text made a tremendous impression upon his life; in fact, it appeared on a plaque in his office and also on his tombstone.

If we want to see our fruit in service abide the day of testing and reward let us see to it that we are consciously fulfilling our vocation in the will of God. Such fruitfulness in practical life will glorify God, not only in eternity, but now in time.

Conclusion

We have seen that the disciple's realization is the glory of God in a fruitful prayer life, a fruitful personal life, and a fruitful practical life. Jesus taught that such fruitfulness has degrees of abundance: namely, "fruit," "more fruit," and "much fruit" (John 15:2, 5, 8, NKJV). What glorifies the Father is clearly the "much fruit"; that is, *much* fruit in the prayer life, *much* fruit in the personal life, and *much* fruit in the practical life. This "much fruit" is what completes discipleship, both in realization and manifestation. God make us all developed disciples for his glory! To achieve this realization we must know what it is to be consciously, constantly, and conspicuously filled with the Holy Spirit. Only as the Spirit fills will love, joy, peace, longsuffering, kindness, goodness, faithfulness, gentleness, and self-control be seen in our practical lives. Only then will our Father in heaven be glorified.

Part 2
GOD'S BLUEPRINT FOR CHURCH MEMBERSHIP

6

Christian Certainty

Romans 8:12-17, 26-39

"The Spirit Himself bears witness with our spirit that we are children of God" (8:16, NKJV).

Introduction

It is possible to be a Christian and yet not enjoy Christian certainty. One of the devil's main devices is to rob the Christian of the *joy* of salvation—because he knows he cannot rob him of the *fact* of salvation. God's purpose for us is that we should know not only the fact, but the *fullness* of salvation.

It was a great day when you committed your life to Christ, but again and again the devil brings doubts into your mind as to whether or not that experience was genuine. Here's how you can be sure that you are a child of God:

I. The Word of God

Christian certainty is the faith that accepts and rests on the Word of God. A study of the Bible reveals that:

A. *The Word of God Presents Christian Certainty*

"These [signs] are written that you may believe that Jesus is the Christ, the Son of God, and that believing you may have life in His name" (John 20:31, NKJV); and again: "These things I have written to you who believe in the name of the Son of God, that you may *know* that you have eternal life, and that you may . . . believe in the name of the Son of God" (1 John 5:13, NKJV). God has preserved this precious Book throughout the centuries so that we may have something upon which to rest our faith. God has spoken through this revelation, and he tells us that to believe on the name of his Son is to *know* that we have eternal life.

D. L. Moody once remarked, "I believe hundreds of Christians have not got the assurance of salvation just because they are not willing to take God at his Word."

B. *The Word of God Produces Christian Certainty*

Three verses from the New Testament show this: "Of His own will He brought us forth by the word of truth, that we might be a kind of firstfruits of His creatures" (James 1:18, NKJV); "having been born again, not of corruptible seed but incorruptible, through the word of God which lives and abides forever" (1 Peter 1:23, NKJV); "by which have been given to us exceedingly great and precious promises, that through these you may be partakers of the divine nature, having escaped the corruption that is in the world through lust" (2 Peter 1:4, NKJV). Look at the combined significance of these verses. The first says that God effects the miracle of the new birth through his Word. The second tells us that it is like seed that is carried into our hearts; faith lays hold of it and life begins. The third verse shows that as God's promises are applied to our lives we become "partakers of the divine nature" (2 Peter 1:4, NKJV).

C. *The Word of God Promotes Christian Certainty*

"Faith comes by hearing, and hearing by the word of God"

(Rom. 10:17, NKJV); "whatever things were written before were written for our learning, that we through the patience and comfort of the Scriptures might have hope" (Rom. 15:4, NKJV). The more we read, hear, and heed the Word of God, the stronger becomes our faith, love, hope, patience, and testimony.

So Christian certainty is based on the Word of God. It does not depend on feelings; those are merely by-products. Feelings change, depending on our temperament, background, and circumstances. It is not a question of feeling, but a matter of fact.

Illustration

Three people were walking up a mountainside. The one in front was called Mr. Fact; the middle one, Mr. Faith; and the third, Mr. Feelings. When Mr. Faith looked at Mr. Feelings he stumbled and made no progress. Then someone called to him: "Keep your eyes on Mr. Fact, not Mr. Feelings!" He obeyed and made the grade and soon reached the summit.

Don't worry if the devil comes and whispers that this or that is not true. Remember that you never had doubt before—which is one of the evidences that you are converted. In that sense doubts are healthy, but they become dangerous when you allow them to conceive and bring forth unbelief.

Illustration

A little boy had been gloriously converted. Before going to bed that night he read the text the evangelist had given him: "He who has the Son has life; he who does not have the Son of God does not have life" (1 John 5:12, NKJV). "I have life," he said, "for I have received the Son." A voice seemed to say from somewhere underneath the bed, "No, you haven't." "Yes, I have," he replied. "No, you haven't" the voice insisted. And so the argument went back and forth. Finally, Johnny got up, put on the light, and found the text. He read it aloud: "He who has the Son has life." Again he seemed to hear the voice saying, "No, you don't." Taking his open Bible, he pushed it under the bed and said, "There you are, read it for yourself!"

That is how the Lord Jesus met the devil in the wilderness. When the enemy came and tried to sow doubts in His mind, Jesus said, "It is written," "It is written," "It is written" (Matt. 4:4, 7, 10, NKJV).

II. The Work of Christ

Christian certainty is the faith that accepts and rests upon the work of Christ—all that he did for us on Calvary's cross and in resurrection triumph. The work of Christ guarantees the certainty of:

A. *The Believer's Justification*

"Being justified freely by His grace through the redemption that is in Christ Jesus" (Rom. 3:24, NKJV); "God demonstrates His own love toward us, in that while we were still sinners, Christ died for us. Much more then, having now been justified by His blood, we shall be saved from wrath through Him" (Rom. 5:8-9, NKJV). The word *justification* is a legal term and denotes "made right," or "made to appear before God in a favorable light." When addressing children, we sometimes say, "Justified means just as if I had never sinned."

The Bible reminds us that we are all sinners (see Rom. 3:23; 6:23) and stand condemned before the bar of God.

We are not only sinners by nature, but sinners by practice. Then we hear the Gospel—the Good News—that Jesus Christ, in love, came to pay the penalty for a broken law (see 1 Peter 2:24), and we believe and accept the pardon he has provided. Now we are justified, acquitted, made to appear before God in a favorable light, and God will never reverse that word of acquittal.

The act of justification positions the believer in Christ.

Illustration

A lady who possessed a valuable diamond ring was once walking along a street in Paris. In pulling off her glove she dislodged her ring, which rolled along the ground and dropped through a grating into a drain. Greatly distressed, she peered down into the catch basin, which was full of black, watery mud. She tried to retrieve her treasure with the end of her umbrella, but her efforts proved fruitless. In desperation, she finally rolled up her sleeve, plunged her arm deep into the black muck, and in a few minutes retrieved the ring. A Christian standing nearby was reminded of the Scripture in Psalm 40:2. He thought, "Has not Jesus done much more for me? I had nothing in me that was worthy; rather I was sinful, rebellious, and unlovely, but he was willing to come from heaven's glory, take me out of the horrible pit of sin, position me in Christ, and set me among the princes in glory. Yes, Jesus saves from the guttermost to the uttermost!"[1]

B. The Believer's Sanctification

"By that will we have been sanctified through the offering of the body of Jesus Christ once for all. . . . For by one offering He has perfected forever those who are being sanctified" (Heb. 10:10, 14, NKJV). The verb *sanctified* means "to make holy," or "to set apart for God," "to reserve for God." Whereas there is a progressive sanctification in the believer's life, the thought before us is the fact of our sanctification. The moment a person receives Christ as Savior and Lord he is sanctified, in God's sight, and no devil in hell, no man on earth, or angel in heaven, can change that fact. God writes across our lives "Reserved"; we are his.

The act of sanctification preserves the believer in Christ.

C. The Believer's Glorification

"We know that all things work together for good to those who love God, to those who are the called according to His purpose. For whom He foreknew, He also predestined to be conformed to the image of His Son, that He might be the first-born among many brethren. Moreover whom He predestined, these He also called; whom He called, these He also justified; and whom He justified, these He also glorified" (Rom.

8:28-30, NKJV). However long it takes to accomplish it, God sees us as those who have been made just like his Son, and one day we shall live with him in heaven.

An African was once asked, "Do you think you will ever get to heaven?" With confidence and a smile from ear to ear, he replied, "I am as sure of heaven as if I were already there." And he was right, for if we are resting upon the work of Christ then God says we are justified, sanctified, and glorified.

The act of glorification perfects the believer in Christ.

The work of Christ is a finished work; nothing can be added to it. So many people think they will get to heaven by giving, praying, going to church, or doing other good works. But that is not what the Bible teaches. The Lord Jesus Christ has finished the work, and we are to rest upon that work. Although we are going to serve him in devotion and love, and give him our time, talents, and all that we have, it still is a fact—so far as our eternal destiny is concerned—that we cannot do anything to earn our salvation; it is a completed work.

Illustration

An evangelist was trying to lead a cabinetmaker to Christ. This man was brilliant in his work, yet he felt he had to do something to earn his salvation. One day the evangelist visited him in his shop and admired a piece of work the man had just finished. With mischief in his eyes, the evangelist picked up a plane and said, "I'm going to see if I can ease off this corner and put a finishing touch to it." At that the cabinetmaker was horrified, and cried, "Man alive! Don't do that, it's a finished article!" "That's what I've been trying to teach you for the last few weeks," said the evangelist. "The work of Christ for your salvation is a finished work. You can't add anything to it. All you have to do is accept it." The man saw the point and decided for Christ there and then.

III. The Witness of the Spirit

God the Father, God the Son, and God the Spirit are involved in the work of redemption. Christian certainty is the faith that accepts and rests on the witness of the Spirit. His indwelling presence gives us:

A. A New Sense of Relationship

"As many as are led by the Spirit of God, these are sons of God. For you did not receive the spirit of bondage again to fear, but you received the Spirit of adoption by whom we cry out 'Abba, Father.' The Spirit Himself bears witness with our spirit that we are children of God" (Rom. 8:14-16, NKJV). If I were to ask you if you knew what it meant to be a Christian you might nod your head in a nominal way. But if I were to probe deeper you might reply: "If that is what it means to be a Christian, then I don't know anything about it." But if the Spirit of God tells your inward spirit that you are a child of God, then you have the assurance that you are related to him.

B. A New Sense of Resourcefulness

"And if children, then heirs—heirs of God and joint heirs with Christ" (Rom. 8:17, NKJV). An heir is a person who is entitled to an inheritance. Think of the inheritance we have in our Lord Jesus Christ! Not only pardon, peace, joy, victory, a sense of purpose, and eternal life, but heaven as well! You have sensed your weakness, and turning to Christ he has given you strength. You have sensed your emptiness, and turning to Christ he has given you fullness. You have sensed your aimlessness, and turning to Christ he has given you direction. In short, you have proved, and will continue to prove, that there is no demand made upon your life, as a young Christian, which is not a demand on the life of Christ in you. All the resources of heaven are at your disposal. Corrie ten Boom once said, "Too many Christians live as beggars. It grieves the Father when we do not live as rich as he is."

C. A New Sense of Responsibility

"If indeed we suffer with Him, that we may also be glorified together. For I consider that the sufferings of this present time are not worthy to be compared with the glory which shall be revealed in us" (Rom. 8:17-18, NKJV). There may have been times when you laughed and jeered at Christians, but now you take your stand for Christ, even though it involves misunderstanding and unpopularity with your unregenerate friends. You do not mind suffering for the Lord; indeed, you count it a privilege to do so, like the early disciples who rejoiced "that they were counted worthy to suffer shame for His name" (Acts 5:41, NKJV). You have discovered that you *now* have a new sense of responsibility to live for Christ; you want to win others to him. That is because the Spirit of God has come into your life. This is the witness of the Spirit.

Remember the Word of God extends to us Christian certainty, the work of Christ ensures for us Christian certainty, the witness of the Spirit effects in us Christian certainty.

Conclusion

Praise God, we can rest with confidence upon this threefold basis for the experience of Christian certainty. God grant us to sing and mean:

> Blessed assurance, Jesus is mine!
> Oh, what a foretaste of glory divine!
> Heir of salvation, purchase of God,
> Born of his Spirit, washed in his blood.
> Fanny J. Crosby

7

Daily Devotions

Deuteronomy 8:1-14

"Man shall not live by bread alone; but man lives by every word that proceeds from the mouth of the LORD" (8:3, NKJV).

Introduction

No one truly born of God would question that it is a commendable practice to have a daily quiet time with the Lord; in fact, it is absolutely vital to Christian growth and development. The Bible always associates the man or woman of God with a strictly disciplined devotional life. Writing to his son in the faith, Timothy, Paul says: "All Scripture is given by inspiration of God, and is profitable for doctrine, for reproof, for correction, for instruction in righteousness, that the man of God may be complete, thoroughly equipped for every good work" (2 Tim. 3:16-17, NKJV). When the Lord Jesus said, "Man shall not live by bread alone, but by every word that proceeds from the mouth of God" (Matt. 4:4, NKJV), he testified, once and for all, to the value of cultivating the devotional life. By "every word" he did not mean a casual reading of the Bible. The thought is rather "every spoken word," and it is only in the quiet place of communion and meditation that the child of God can hear (with the ears of the heart) the spoken Word. In order to help those who know nothing about a definite method in observing this necessary devotional habit, let me suggest some guidelines:

I. The Reasons for the Quiet Time

"Man shall not live by bread alone, but by *every word* that proceeds from the mouth of God" (Matt. 4:4, NKJV).

When the Lord Jesus spoke these words he testified, once and for all, to the value of the quiet time. What he was saying is that the whole Bible is for the whole man. Therefore, we cannot afford to miss any part of it, however difficult certain portions may be. Communion with God in the light of his Word is vital to:

A. Spiritual Constitution

"As newborn babes, desire the pure milk of the word, that you may grow thereby" (1 Peter 2:2, NKJV); and for those further on in the Christian life, the writer to the Hebrews reminds us: "solid food belongs to those who are of full age" (Heb. 5:14, NKJV). Peter is writing as a family man. He knew the experience of a father, or mother, waking up in the night to meet the cries of the young infant, the newly-born, who desires the milk by which he lives. God has built into every child at birth that insatiable desire for the very thing by which he lives. Peter implies that if there is no desire for "the pure milk of the word" then there is no new birth. It is impossible to subsist as a Christian without one's daily quiet time, because God has put into our spiritual life and nature a hunger for the Word.

For those who are more developed in the Christian life, it is even more important. So while there is milk for the very young there is meat for those who are full grown. It was because David realized the need for the spoken word for spiritual constitution and development that he prayed, "Strengthen me according to Your word" (Ps. 119:28, NKJV).

Illustration

S. L. Brengle, who worked with Gen. William Booth of the Salvation Army, once made this statement: "In eating, it is not the amount we eat, but the amount we digest that does us good; and just so it is in reading and studying. It is not the amount we read, but what we remember and make our own— that does us good."

B. Spiritual Correction

"All Scripture is given by inspiration of God, and is profitable for . . . correction" (2 Tim. 3:16, NKJV). Nothing will cleanse and correct the life like the Word of God. In one of his psalms, David asks a question: "How can a young man cleanse his way? By taking heed according to Your word" (Ps. 119:9, NKJV). It was because the Lord recognized the correcting and cleansing power of the Word that he said to his disciples, after one of his discourses, "You are already clean because of the word which I have spoken to you" (John 15:3, NKJV). The Word is the means by which we are being cleansed daily (see John 17:17).

Illustration

The Bible is man's living manual. When you buy an automobile or a washing machine, you receive a manual of operation for the machinery. It tells you how to operate it, how to service it, how to make necessary adjustments, what to look for if trouble develops, and so forth. The Bible is like that. . . . To ignore the Word of God is to face certain disaster. . . . God is the Master Mechanic; he made us and he can keep us operating effectively; he gave us an operator's manual to aid us in life and living.[1]

C. Spiritual Counsel

"All Scripture . . . is profitable . . . for instruction in righteousness" (2 Tim. 3:16, NKJV). "Give me understanding according to Your word," says David in Psalm 119:169 (NKJV). And in Psalm 73:24 (NKJV) the psalmist's constant assurance was, "You will guide me with Your counsel." The Bible is not so much a book of rules as a book of principles. The more we read the Word of God, the more his principles of righteousness are inculcated. No man can be guided by the Spirit who isn't a Bible-mastered man. The reason Christians are tentative and unsure about areas of decision is because they are not people of the Word of God. All wisdom and knowledge are embodied in Jesus Christ, and he is revealed in the pages of Scripture. "If any of you lacks wisdom, let him ask of God, who gives to all liberally and without reproach, and it will be given to him" (James 1:5, NKJV). God never gives wisdom that is contrary to the revealed Word. To know a guided life, we must know what it is to read the Word *day by day*.

D. Spiritual Conflict

"The sword of the Spirit . . . is the word of God," says Paul with victorious confidence (see Eph. 6:17).

The context of this passage is spiritual warfare (see 6:11-12), and in the light of these tremendous odds we are to have our defensive armor on, which is "Christ in his totality" (Chrysostom). The offensive weapons that Paul mentions are prayer and the Word of God (6:17-18). Prayer sights the enemy, while the Word fights the enemy.

How did the Savior overcome the devil in the wilderness? It was the spoken Word of God every time. No doubt his quotations from Deuteronomy were the very passages on which he had been meditating with his God during those forty days and nights. Isaiah tells us that every day his ear was open to hear the voice of his Father; he was not rebellious (Isa. 50:4-5). Three times the devil attacked him, and those temptations constitute every temptation with which man is confronted. Satan attacked him along the lines of the body, the soul, and the spirit. Each time he replied, "It is written," "It is written," "It is written" (Matt. 4:4, 7, 10), and with those Spirit-thrusts he defeated the enemy. As God of very God, he could have pulverized the devil, once for all, but he didn't. He reserved the right to withhold the prerogatives of his deity and, as

man—depending on the Word of God and the Spirit of God—
he beat the devil.

II. The Requirements for the Quiet Time

These are purely suggestive and practical, needless to say:

A. A Good Bible

Use a Bible with clear print, and one in which you can enter a
few notes. Remember, though, that too many notes on the
page of Scripture tend to confine your thoughts to old medi-
tations. Alongside of your Bible have a notebook and pen to
record nuggets of truth that God gives you. Jot down the date,
the Scripture reading, the text, and a few thoughts—something you will never regret, especially as you reflect upon them
in future days.

B. A Prayer List

It is preferable to use a loose-leaf notebook so that you can
always insert new pages. Put down the prayer requests of your
church, your friends, also the requests that are on your heart.
Here is a prayer cycle that you can use:

Monday: "M" is for missionaries.
Tuesday: "T" is for thanksgiving. That's when we give the Lord
special thanks for wonderful answers to prayer.
Wednesday: "W" is for Christian workers.
Thursday: "T" is for tasks—the ministry God has given.
Friday: "F" is for our families.
Saturday: "S" is for the saints—especially young Christians,
that Christ may be formed in them.
Sunday: "S" is for sinners, and, in particular, the gospel out-
reach in which we are involved.

C. A Quiet Place

With many this may be impossible at home. Such people may

want to use a nearby church, library, or some unused room, for an hour before business, or during lunchtime. Where there's a will, there's a way. In the summer, nothing is better than having one's quiet time in the park, under a shady tree. Remember that Jesus had nowhere to lay his head: he had no home of his own, but he never missed his quiet time—never! (See Mark 1:35.) Find a place without distraction to be totally alone with God.

D. A Definite Time

Most people agree that the morning is best, but this may not always be possible. A time should be fixed, however, and the appointment with the Lord punctually kept. The devil will see to it that the child of God never drifts into having a regular devotional period. It is imperative, therefore, that the place and time be arranged in the presence of the Lord and then jealously guarded above everything else.

E. An Expectant Spirit

The man of God receives what he expects in his quiet time. Such an attitude is usually determined by three factors:

1. A Physical One

You cannot keep late hours at night and expect to be fresh to meet with God in the morning (see 1 Cor. 9:27). Your life must be strictly disciplined if you are going to get the maximum blessing out of your daily devotions.

2. A Moral One

The Word says, "If I regard iniquity in my heart, The Lord will not hear" (Ps. 66:18, NKJV). This emphasizes the need for holiness. If you look with approval on anything out of adjustment to the will of God, you have wrecked your quiet time. Therefore, see that your life is morally clean—nothing between yourself and your brother. If there is, make it right and then come and offer your gift of prayer and meditation (see Matt. 5:23-24).

3. A SPIRITUAL ONE

This is the need for obedience. God conditions the revelation of truth on implicit obedience. Jesus declared: "If anyone wills to do [God's] will, he shall know concerning the doctrine, whether it is from God" (John 7:17, NKJV). As I obey, so God reveals; as I disobey, so God ceases to reveal. Or to put it another way, "Light received bringeth light; light rejected bringeth night." Obedience and revelation go hand in hand.

III. The Regulations for the Quiet Time

Once again, these are by way of suggestion. There are seven regulations that aid the believer in the quiet place of communion with God. Let me state them simply:

A. *Waiting*

Samuel Chadwick says in his book on prayer that "hurry is the death of prayer." Five minutes in quiet waiting upon God will yield far more than thirty hurried minutes. Silently wait on God to realize his presence. Seek cleansing, the power of concentration, and the illumination of the Spirit. Don't even open your Bible at this point. Just wait on God and be still.

Illustration
It is said that a piano can go out of tune by hard use. The constant striking of the strings may loosen them, and they need to be adjusted if they are to continue producing harmonious sounds. Someone has written, "in like manner all common experiences have an exhausting effect on us, even when we serve the Lord. . . . As we minister to others, as we strive and struggle, duty drains our life-fountain. We then need to come into God's presence for spiritual renewal. . . . In the quietness of that fellowship he tunes our lives and strengthens us for further service."[2]

B. Reading

Now open your Bible and begin to read the portion for the day. System and sequence must be observed. Plan your reading passage by passage. The whole value of Bible reading is lost with the "lucky dip" method of reading. A short portion well read is better than a chapter or more skimped.

Illustration

When I Read the Bible Through

I supposed I knew my Bible, reading piecemeal, hit or miss—/Now a bit of John or Matthew, now a snatch of Genesis;/Certain chapters of Isaiah, certain Psalms (the 23rd);/12th of Romans, 1st of Proverbs. Yes, I thought I knew the Word./But I found a thorough reading was a different thing to do,/And the way was unfamiliar when I read my Bible through./You who like to play at Bible, dip and dabble here and there/Just before you kneel aweary and yawn out a hurried prayer;/You who treat the Crown of Writing as you treat no other book,/Just a paragraph disjointed, just a quick impatient look;/Try a worthier procedure, try a broad and steady view;/You will kneel in very rapture, when you read your Bible through.[3]

C. Meditating

As you read, ask yourself: Is there a promise to claim, a lesson to learn, a blessing to enjoy, a command to obey, a sin to avoid; a new revelation of God, Christ, the Holy Spirit; a new thought about the devil? Such meditation, under the control of the Holy Spirit, never fails to yield some message to the soul.

D. Recording

Psychologists state that there is no impression without expression. It is well to test and confirm God-given impressions by expressing them on paper. Briefly record the thoughts gleaned in a personal and devotional form, and recognize that such thoughts, as illuminated by the Holy Spirit, are the spoken Word of God to your soul.

E. Praying

At this point turn the meditation into prayer and do it in this fashion: personal examination—let it search your heart. Then spiritual adoration. Praise God—even if he has rebuked you. Then turn it into general intercession. This will deliver you from stereotyped praying. Pray back to God what he has given to you until your will has been adjusted to all that the Holy Spirit has revealed to you.

F. Sharing

Leave the place of prayer determined to share the good of your quiet time with someone else during the day. As you do so it becomes doubly enriching. Not to use what the Lord has given is merely to acquire knowledge that puffs up. When the Israelites hoarded the manna during their wilderness journey, they found that it bred worms and stank. You don't lose by sharing, you gain.

G. Obeying

Rise from your knees with a determination to put into action what God has taught you.

Illustration

When Major C. H. Malan was a young officer in India, a Christian lady wrote to him, asking him to read and pray over his Bible. He did so, and it led to his conversion. Writing later, he said, "Herein I was helped by being a soldier, for I began to read my Bible as I read the Queen's regulations, as if all its instructions were intended to be followed out."

Conclusion

The barometer of one's Christian life is the quiet time. Do you have a quiet time, or have you let it slip? Be the man of God who "takes time to be holy, speaks oft with his Lord, abides in him only, and feeds on his Word" (William D. Longstaff, *Take Time to Be Holy*). God grant that this may be true of you.

8

Believers' Baptism

Matthew 28:16-20

"Go therefore and make disciples of all the nations,
baptizing them.. ." (28:19, NKJV).

Introduction

The practice of believers' baptism is not exclusive to Baptist
churches; it is New Testament doctrine. Much controversy has
raged over the mode of baptism, but baptism is the right of
every believer. This position is strengthened by the command
of the Lord Jesus Christ who said, "All authority has been
given to Me in heaven and on earth.

*Go therefore and make disciples of all the nations, baptizing them
in the name of the Father and of the Son and of the Holy Spirit"
(28:18-19,* NKJV). Observe:

I. The Institution of Believers' Baptism

"Go therefore and make disciples of all the nations, baptizing
them" (28:19, NKJV). With these words Jesus instituted believers' baptism. The word *baptism* occurs a number of times in

the New Testament without reference to believers' baptism. For instance, we read of:

A. *The Baptism of Moses*

"Moreover, brethren, I do not want you to be unaware that all our fathers were under the cloud, all passed through the sea, all were baptized into Moses in the cloud and in the sea" (1 Cor. 10:1-2, NKJV). Paul is illustrating here how the children of Israel were identified with their leader Moses. When passing through the Red Sea on dry ground, they were covered with a cloud and flanked on either side by water—a picture of baptism.

B. *The Baptism of John*

"I indeed baptize you with water unto repentance, but He who is coming after me is mightier than I, whose sandals I am not worthy to carry. He will baptize you with the Holy Spirit and fire" (Matt. 3:11, NKJV). This was known as the baptism of repentance. It was possible to have been baptized unto repentance and yet not to have received the Holy Spirit. When Paul went to Ephesus as a missionary he found twelve disciples who had been baptized unto the baptism of John [the Baptist]. They had repented of their sins, but had never believed in the name of Jesus, nor had they received the Holy Spirit (see Acts 19:1-5). They did not know there was such a person—so were evidently not regenerated. After hearing of Christ Jesus and believing on him, "they were baptized in the name of the Lord Jesus" (Acts 19:5, NKJV) and received the manifestations of the indwelling Holy Spirit.

C. *The Baptism of Jesus*

Though John the Baptist baptized him, Jesus did not have to repent, for he had no sins to confess. Yet he stepped into the waters of Jordan to identify himself with his messianic mission and to fulfill every demand of his Father (see Matt. 3:15). In a sense, if there were nothing else in all the

Scriptures concerning baptism, this verse would be sufficient to encourage us to follow Jesus Christ all the way.

D. The Baptism of the Cross

Contemplating the darkness of Calvary, Jesus said, "I have a baptism to be baptized with, and how distressed I am till it is accomplished" (Luke 12:50, NKJV). In that midday midnight, the fountains of God's holy wrath against sin were broken up, and our Savior was immersed in death for our salvation (see 2 Cor. 5:21).

E. The Baptism of the Holy Spirit

That happened at Pentecost, when the Holy Spirit was poured out by the risen Lord in accordance with the promise of the Father. The 120 disciples gathered in the upper room (and, potentially, the entire church throughout the centuries) was immersed into the one body. Paul, looking back, says, "By one Spirit we were all baptized into one body" (1 Cor. 12:13, NKJV). John Stott points out that this baptism is once and for all, and is synonymous with our incorporation into the body of Christ.[1] Dr. C. I. Scofield affirms that there is "one baptism, many fillings, constant anointing."

F. The Baptism of Judgment

John the Baptist spoke of it: "He will baptize you with the Holy Spirit [Pentecost] and fire [coming judgment]" (Matt. 3:11, NKJV). Let no one think that this world is going on indefinitely. God is going to break into history again. Just as he broke into history in grace, the next time he is coming in judgment (see Acts 17:31). That is going to be a baptism of fire, when the chaff will be burned with unquenchable fire.

Illustration

In Warren Wiersbe's *Meet Yourself in the Psalms,* he tells about a frontier town where a horse bolted and ran away with a wagon carrying a little boy. Seeing the child in danger, a young man risked his life to catch the horse and stop the wagon. The child who was saved grew up to become a lawless man, and one day he stood before a judge to be sentenced for a serious crime. The prisoner recognized the judge as the man who, years before, had saved his life; so he pled for mercy on the basis of that experience. But the words from the bench silenced his plea. "Young man, then I was your savior; today I am your judge, and I must sentence you to be hanged." One day Jesus Christ will say to rebellious sinners, "During that long day of grace I was the Savior, and I would have forgiven you. But today I am your Judge. Depart from me, ye cursed, into everlasting fire!"[2]

G. The Baptism of Believers

It is the Savior who instituted believers' baptism when he said, "All authority has been given to Me in heaven and on earth . . . make disciples . . . baptizing them in the name of the Father and of the Son and of the Holy Spirit" (Matt. 28:18-19, NKJV).

II. The Implication of Believers' Baptism

When a man or woman, boy or girl, is baptized, they publicly confess two things:

A. Acceptance of Christ as Savior

"Go into all the world and preach the gospel to every creature. He who believes and is baptized will be saved; but he who does not believe will be condemned" (Mark 16:15-16, NKJV). Our salvation is dependent upon believing, not necessarily on baptism. Baptism is the outward expression of this inward transaction. The penitent thief on the cross believed and was taken to paradise by the Lord who saved him, but he was not baptized. Baptism is the public confession of having accepted Christ as personal Savior.

B. Allegiance to Christ as Lord

"Go therefore and make disciples of all the nations, baptizing them" (Matt. 28:19, NKJV). Where there is discipleship there is lordship. There is no such thing as discipline without a master. At baptism we make known the fact that we have received Christ as Savior; we show to angels, principalities, and powers that we have acknowledged Christ as Sovereign. The Lord Jesus is looking for disciples, not names on church rolls or decision cards, but those who will own him as Lord and Master.

Illustration

Thomas Barclay labored for sixty years on Formosa as a missionary to the Chinese. Behind that life of service lay a covenant with God that he wrote when he was sixteen, and which he renewed every year. It read in part: "This day do I, with the utmost solemnity, surrender myself to Thee. I renounce all former lords that have had dominion over me, and I consecrate to Thee all that I have: the faculties of my mind, the members of my body, my worldly possessions, my time, and my influence over others; to be all used entirely for Thy glory, and resolutely employed in obedience to Thy commands, as long as Thou continuest me in life; with an ardent desire and humble resolution to continue Thine through all the ages of eternity; ever holding myself in an attentive posture to observe, with zeal and joy, to the immediate execution of it. To Thy direction also I resign myself, and all that I am and have, to be disposed of by Thee in such a manner as Thou in Thine infinite wisdom shall judge most subservient to the purposes of Thy glory. To Thee I leave the management of all events, and say without reserve, 'Not my will, but Thine, be done.'"[3]

III. The Interpretation of Believers' Baptism

"Go therefore and make disciples of all the nations, baptizing them in the name of the Father and of the Son and of the Holy Spirit, *teaching them to observe all things that I have commanded you*" (Matt. 28:19-20, NKJV). The disciples learned quite a lot while they were with the Master, but there was a great deal they did not know until after he had ascended to heaven and the Holy Spirit had come down to interpret the deeper meaning of this wonderful ordinance of believers' baptism (such as Rom. 6). Look at:

A. *Its Mention in the New Testament*

There are some doctrines for which we contend earnestly, yet they are mentioned only meagerly in the New Testament. But baptism is enjoined in the gospels, exemplified in the Acts, and explained in the Epistles:

1. ENJOINED IN THE GOSPELS

The Great Commission (see Matt. 28:19; Mark 16).
Even though the latter is a disputed passage, it is supported by such great expositors as G. Campbell Morgan and F. F. Bruce.

2. EXEMPLIFIED IN THE ACTS

The Day of Pentecost (2:41)
The Baptism of the Eunuch (8:36-38)
The Baptism of Saul of Tarsus (9:18)
The Baptism of Cornelius (10:47-48)
The Baptism of Lydia (16:15)
The Baptism of the Philippian jailer (16:33)
The Baptism of the Twelve at Ephesus (19:5)

3. EXPLAINED IN THE EPISTLES

(See Rom. 6.) This is the greatest chapter on baptism in the New Testament. The teaching is simple, yet profound; simple, because baptism is intended to show us what God has done in Christ in identifying us with his death, burial, and resurrection; profound, because it is one of the great theological passages in Scripture on our union with Christ.

B. *Its Method in the New Testament*

The word *baptism* is a transliteration from the Greek *baptizō* meaning "to make whelmed" (i.e., fully wet) or "to dip." It was used by the Greeks in the dyeing of a garment where immersion, submersion, and emergence are inferred. Anglican Bishop Ryle points out that baptism loses all its significance if we do not see those three acts: death is down—immersion; burial is under—submersion; resurrection is out of—emergence. This is all made clear in Romans 6. The two outstanding examples of the verb *baptizō* are the baptism of our Lord in the river Jordan, not in the temple courts (see Matt. 3:16-17), and the Ethiopian eunuch (see Acts 8:38). Both he and Philip "went down into the water, and . . . came up. . . out of the water"

C. Its Meaning in the New Testament

This can be set out in three very significant thoughts.

1. THE BELIEVER'S OBEDIENCE TO CHRIST

Jesus said, "Go . . . make disciples . . . baptizing them . . . and . . . teaching them to observe all things that I have commanded you" (Matt. 28:19-20, NKJV). There is only one response of a yielded Christian to a command: obedience. Jesus said, "If you love Me, keep My commandments" (John 14:15, NKJV; see also Luke 6:46). When we disobey an express command of our Lord our spiritual growth is stunted, and God will not reveal anything more until we obey. John writes, "If anyone wills to do [God's] will, he shall know concerning the doctrine" (John 7:17, NKJV). And the prophet Samuel declared: "To obey is better than sacrifice, And to heed than the fat of rams" (1 Sam. 15:22, NKJV). There is no substitute for obedience. "Defective obedience is total disobedience" (Dr. William Fitch). The Bible says "whoever shall keep the whole law, and yet stumble in one point, he is guilty of all" (James 2:10, NKJV).

Illustration
A well-known preacher had a brother who was a famous

physician. One day a woman, wishing to speak with the minister but not being sure if the man she was about to address was the preacher or the physician, asked, "Are you the doctor who preaches, or the one who practices?" The words were a goad to the man of God, stirring his conscience. Ever afterward he endeavored not only to hear the Word of God and speak it, but also to do it.[4]

2. The Believer's Oneness with Christ

Baptism symbolizes the believer's oneness with Christ in death, burial, and resurrection. In baptism, the believer shows outwardly that he was crucified, judicially, with Christ 2000 years ago; therefore, he is dead to sin and self. Experientially, the Holy Spirit makes that real to him (see Rom. 8:13).

The believer is also buried with Christ. What is dead must be buried, put out of sight. And if sin and self have been buried, then the believer has no right to visit the cemetery and dig up those bones, representing the flesh, and allow them to paralyze his spiritual walk (see Rom. 6:1-23).

Then there is the believer's oneness with Christ in resurrection. The only grounds on which the Holy Spirit releases the resurrection life of Jesus, in and through a child of God, is when he has accepted, by faith, his place in death and burial (see Rom. 6:11; Col. 3:1-3).

3. The Believer's Offering for Christ

This ordinance is a beautiful figure of a life yielded to another. The person baptized hands himself over to the one who baptizes. This symbolizes the offering of ourselves to Christ. It must be a complete sacrifice (see Rom. 6:13; 12:1), an act of obedience, a public demonstration of our total dedication to Christ without reserve—spirit, soul, and body.

Illustration
In the "horse and buggy" days, a man and his wife were driving along a narrow and dangerous road. The woman became

extremely nervous, and in her fright she grabbed one of the reins. As calmly as possible the husband responded by offering her the other strap, "Oh, no!" she cried, "I don't want them both! I could never manage that animal alone!" "Well, then," he said gently, "you must make your choice. It's either you or me. We can't both drive the same horse." The frightened soul quickly surrendered full control of the wagon to her husband. Everything was once again in good hands, and they journeyed on safely. Similarly, we must turn the "reins" of our life over to Christ and let him take full control.[5]

Conclusion

We have seen what is meant by believers' baptism in terms of its mention, method, and meaning. What hinders *you* to be baptized? Will you go all the way with Jesus?

Trust and obey,/for there's no other way/To be happy in Jesus,/But to trust and obey.
John H. Sammis

9

Church Membership

Romans 12:1-13

"We, being many, are one body in Christ, and individually members of one another" (Rom. 12:5, NKJV).

Introduction

We often use the opening verses of this chapter to challenge *individual* believers to a life of surrender. But to be fair to the context, we must observe that Paul is addressing the saints at Rome both personally and corporately. Here Paul is dealing with:

I. The Basis for Church Membership

"I beseech you therefore brethren, by the mercies of God, that you present your bodies a living sacrifice, holy, acceptable to God, which is your reasonable service. And do not be conformed to this world, but be transformed by the renewing of your mind, that you may prove what is that good and acceptable and perfect will of God" (Rom. 12:1-2, NKJV).

Paul assumes that his readers had experienced the justifying and sanctifying mercies of God; this is the basis of his appeal. But in order to enjoy the harmony and ministry of a local church there are certain fundamental requirements that must be obeyed:

A. *The Dedication of Our Bodies to God*

"I beseech you therefore, brethren, by the mercies of God, that you present your bodies a living sacrifice, holy, acceptable to God, which is your reasonable service" (Rom. 12:1, NKJV). This is not something naive or nebulous. Paul beseeches the saints at Rome—and Christians throughout the centuries—to be totally, worthily, and sensibly dedicated. His appeal calls for:

B. *The Transformation of Our Souls by God*

"And do not be conformed to this world, but be transformed by the renewing of your mind" (Rom. 12:2, NKJV). The Bible reminds us that "as [a man] thinks in his heart, so is he" (Prov. 23:7, NKJV). God starts with the mind in order to affect the life. There is a twofold thrust in his appeal: first, the refusal of worldliness—"do not be conformed to this world," and then the renewal of holiness—"be transformed by the renewing of your mind" (Rom. 12:2, NKJV).

C. *The Satisfaction of Our Spirits in God*

"That you may prove what is that good and acceptable and perfect will of God" (Rom. 12:2, NKJV). When there is the true dedication of our bodies to God, and the transformation of our souls by God, there follows the satisfaction of our spirits in God. There is no more satisfying place on earth than the center of God's "good and acceptable and perfect will" (Rom. 12:2, NKJV). The will of God is good because it is profitable, it is acceptable because it is pleasurable, and it is perfect because it is purposeful.

Find a group of Christians who know this dedication, transformation, and satisfaction in their lives and you will find a basis for oneness.

II. The Beauty of Our Oneness

"For I say, through the grace given to me, to everyone who is among you, not to think of himself more highly than he ought to think, but to think soberly, as God has dealt to each one a measure of faith . . . distributing to the needs of the saints, given to hospitality" (Rom. 12:3,13, NKJV). These eleven verses are full of truth concerning the beauty of our membership, stewardship, and fellowship in Christ.

A. *The Beauty of Our Membership*

"For I say through the grace given to me, to everyone who is among you, not to think of himself more highly than he ought to think, but to think soberly, as God has dealt to each one a measure of faith . . . [for] we, being many, are one body in Christ, and individually members of one another" (Rom. 12:3, 5, NKJV). Paul teaches here that if we are to know the true significance of our membership in the local church we must recognize two important things:

1. OUR INDIVIDUAL MODESTY

"Everyone . . . is . . . not to think of himself more highly than he ought to think, but to think soberly, as God has dealt to each one a measure of faith" (Rom. 12:3, NKJV). Here he warns against self-exaltation—thinking of ourselves more highly than "we ought to think." He also warns against self-depreciation (implied in thinking "soberly"). Instead, we are to seek self-realization, "as God has dealt to each one a measure of faith" (Rom. 12:3, NKJV). There is a redeemed and released self that the Holy Spirit wants to use for the glory of God. This is Christian modesty. Once we recognize that God does not make duplicates, but only originals, then we shall realize the purpose for which he has saved and separated us for his service and glory.

Illustration
The three smallest bones in the human body—the malleus, incus, and the stapes—are located in the middle ear. Only

when they are in proper functioning order is hearing possible.

A surgeon performed an operation (a stapedectomy) on the third smallest of these bones for a man who had not heard anything in 26 years. The patient was under partial anesthesia, and as the surgeon was about to join the bones, he said, "Howie, keep talking as I join the bones and keep your eyes on me." The instant the surgeon joined those bones, the man's eyes got big as saucers. "W-s-what's that? Who's talking? Why, that's me! That's my voice I hear!" Tears streamed down the man's face, and a nurse wiped them away with some gauze.

In the body of Christ, size does not determine the significance of the members. A Christian may belittle himself because he's not an "arm," but he may be as a "stapes" for clearly transmitting communications. Why? Because he is an essential part of the body.[1]

2. OUR INTERPERSONAL UNITY

"For as we have many members in one body, but all the members do not have the same function, so we, being many, are one body in Christ, and individually members of one another" (Rom. 12:4-5, NKJV). As individuals, we are part of a whole. In Jesus Christ, the church is an indivisible unity (see v. 4, NKJV). Even though there are human divisions and factions, God sees us as one. Therefore, there is nothing more serious than rending the seamless robe of Christ.

But more than this, in Jesus Christ we are an indispensable unity—"we, being many, are one body in Christ, and individually members of one another" (v. 5, NKJV). We need each other. The eye can't say to the nose, "I have no need of you." The ear can't say to the mouth, "I have no need of you." The hand can't say to the foot, "I have no need of you" (see 1 Cor. 12:12-31). All are indispensable to one another, and therefore interdependent.

Illustration

Specialists have wondered why Canadian geese always fly in a "V" formation, so their engineers did a study on the subject.

They discovered that the flapping of each goose's wings provided an upward lift for the goose that followed. When all the geese were flying in perfect formation, the whole flock had a 71 percent greater flying range than if each bird flew alone. Each was dependent on the other to reach its destination. Likewise, the church needs to learn that it's at least 71 percent easier to live the Christian life by "flying with the flock" than it is to fly alone.

B. *The Beauty of Our Stewardship (see Rom. 12:6-8)*

In these verses Paul details seven different forms of stewardship which operate within the local church (the very number suggests perfect harmony). No believer with a Christlike estimate of himself and others can set one gift over against another, and so spoil the relationships of the church by jealousy or pride. Paul distinctly says, "Having . . . gifts differing according to the grace given to us, let us use them" (v. 6, NKJV). This means that every believer has a gift, yet no Christian has all the gifts. Consider these seven aspects of stewardship:

1. THE STEWARDSHIP OF PREACHING

"If prophecy, let us prophesy in proportion to our faith" (Rom. 12:6, NKJV). This is the gift of inspired preaching. It is forthtelling rather than foretelling. Paul defines prophecy in 1 Corinthians 14:3 where he says: "He who prophesies speaks edification and exhortation and comfort to men." Such a ministry builds up, stirs up, and cheers up the church.

2. THE STEWARDSHIP OF SERVING

"Or ministry, let us use it in our ministering" (Rom. 12:7, NKJV). This is business and administrative service in the life of the church, though not always limited to mundane and material matters (see Acts 6:1, 4). Both the distribution of money, food, and the preaching of the Word were performed by Spirit-filled deacons.

3. THE STEWARDSHIP OF TEACHING

"He who teaches, in teaching" (Rom. 12:7, NKJV). This is the gift of exposition and interpretation. Priscilla and Aquila possessed this gift; for example, they detected a lack of teaching in the preaching of Apollos. Taking him aside, they "explained to him the way of God more accurately" (Acts 18:26, NKJV).

4. THE STEWARDSHIP OF HELPING

"He who exhorts, in exhortation" (Rom. 12:8, NKJV). This word literally means "consolation," "encouragement," and even "challenge." Exhortation can be used two ways: it can spur people or woo them. Basically, it is a ministry of helping to apply what has already been taught, though it is distinct from the gift of teaching.

5. THE STEWARDSHIP OF GIVING

"He who gives, with liberality" (Rom. 12:8, NKJV). This is the gift of liberality and stewardship in money. There is a sense in which all believers possess this gift to a greater or lesser degree. The ministry of sharing should be exercised with singleness of heart and cheerfulness of spirit "for God loves a cheerful giver" (2 Cor. 9:7, NKJV).

6. THE STEWARDSHIP OF LEADING

"He who leads, with diligence" (Rom. 12:8, NKJV). This gift of leadership can be applied to organizers, superintendents, or directors of Christian work. In the New Testament, it applies to family life (see 1 Thes. 5:12; 1 Tim. 3:4), and also describes the office of the elder (see 1 Tim. 5:17). Such leadership must be exercised with diligence.

7. THE STEWARDSHIP OF CARING

"he who shows mercy, with cheerfulness" (Rom. 12:8, NKJV). This is the gift of pastoral visitation. It includes the care of the sick, the poor, the afflicted, and the sorrowing, and is to be carried out with cheerfulness (or hilarity). It requires a sense of humor born of Holy Spirit joy. This verse could be paraphrased as follows: "If you come to sympathize and sorrow, bring God's sunlight in your face."

Illustration

A Smite

It needs so little sympathy to cheer a weary way,/Sometimes a little kindness lights up a dreary day;/A very simple, friendly word may hope and strength impart,/Or just an understanding smile revive some fainting heart;/And, like a sudden sun-lit ray, lighting a darkened room,/A sunny spirit may beguile the deepest depths of gloom.

C. The Beauty of Our Fellowship (see Rom. 12:9-13, NKJV)

The key verse is verse 9: "Let love be without hypocrisy." A hypocrite originally meant "the stage player" who acted his part but was not real. So the apostle exhorts, "Don't play at church, but be real in your fellowship of love." Paul then outlines the characteristics of love.

1. A LOVE THAT IS PURE

"Abhor what is evil. Cling to what is good" (Rom. 12:9, NKJV). Dr. Graham Scroggie once said, "True love is not present where there is not a moral recoil from evil." True love should bind us to that which is good, and there is a sense in which evil will be abhorred in exact proportion to one's adherence to that which is good.

2. A LOVE THAT IS PERSONAL

"Be kindly affectionate to one another with brotherly love, in honor giving preference to one another" (Rom. 12:10, NKJV; see also 1 John 3:14). True love seeks out individuals and loves them personally. It is a love that gives recognition and honor to all Christians, without respect of persons.

3. A Love That Is Passionate

"Not lagging in diligence, fervent in spirit, serving the Lord" (Rom. 12:11, NKJV). These three exhortations are closely connected. The Christian must be zealous in all he seeks to do for the glory of God and the good of man. The whole thought in this verse is that of a passionate love for the Lord Jesus in every aspect of Christian service.

4. A Love That Is Positive

"Rejoicing in hope" (Rom. 12:12, NKJV). Whatever the circumstances of life, love is always radiantly optimistic. Storms may come and go, but the anchor of hope remains sure and steadfast because it is grounded in God's love. Hallelujah for a love that is positive!

5. A Love That Is Patient

"Patient in tribulation" (Rom. 12:12, NKJV). Whatever the frustrations or persecutions, the believer is to *endure* —a needed quality in Christian life and service. We live in such days of busyness, hurry, and pressure that we have lost the art of being patient.

Illustration
When J. Hudson Taylor was asked what he considered to be the three greatest qualities for a missionary, he replied: "The first is patience, the second is patience, and the third is patience."

6. A Love That Is Prayerful

"Continuing steadfastly in prayer" (Rom. 12:12, NKJV). This exhortation refers to the Christian's activity and attitude of prayer. Such prayerfulness keeps all other expressions of love in a state of health. The effect of such prayerfulness in the life of the church is beyond computation. It is only when people come together in prayer that the fellowship of love is strengthened and deepened.

7. A LOVE THAT IS PRACTICAL

"Distributing to the needs of the saints, given to hospitality" (Rom. 12:13, NKJV). This is love in action, not just in word. John writes in his epistle: "Whoever has this world's goods, and sees his brother in need, and shuts up his heart from him, how does the love of God abide in him?" (1 John 3:17, NKJV). True love communicates to the necessity of the saints in practical benevolence; it provides hospitality. The word "given" to hospitality is the same as that which is translated "to pursue," or "to follow after" (see Phil. 3:6, 12, 14). Paul personifies love as it pursues lonely souls in a loveless world in order that they might be given the hospitality of Christian fellowship. The same thought occurs in Hebrews 13:1-2—"Let brotherly love continue. Do not forget to entertain strangers, for by so doing some have unwittingly entertained angels" (NKJV).

Illustration

"Old Bill" was hired to sweep streets in a small town in the hills. He was a friendly old fellow, and Miss Gidding who lived in the corner house got into the habit all that summer of taking him a glass of lemonade and a slice of cake. He thanked her shyly and that was all. One evening there was a knock at the back door of Miss Gidding's house. Bill was there with a sack of peaches in one arm and a handful of corn in the other. He seemed embarrassed as he said, "I brought you these, Ma'am, for your kindness." "Oh, you shouldn't have," she replied, "it was nothing." "Maybe it wasn't much, Ma'am," he answered, "but it was more than anyone else did."

How can we know the love of God in our lives? Paul gives the secret. He says in Romans 5:5 (NKJV), "The love of God has been poured out in our hearts by the Holy Spirit who was given to us." To know the release of this love we must remove the limitations that prevent the flow of the Spirit in our lives (ignorance, prejudice, unbelief). Then we must renew the obligations that promote the flow of the Spirit in our lives. This involves obedience (see Acts 5:32) and faith (see Luke 11:13).

Conclusion

We see, then, what we mean by church membership. The basis is clear. There must be dedication, transformation, and satisfaction in our lives. The beauty of that oneness must be expressed, by the Holy Spirit's power, through membership, stewardship, and fellowship. Only then will we know what it is to dwell together in unity (see Ps.133:1).

10

Consecrated Living

Romans 12:1-2

"Present your bodies a living sacrifice, holy, acceptable to God, which is your reasonable service" (Rom. 12:1, NKJV).

Introduction

What God wants today is new men, rather than new methods; surrendered people, rather than just saved people, for it is possible to be saved yet not surrendered. The burden of the apostle Paul in this chapter—and particularly verses 1 and 2—is to show that the purpose of our salvation is that we might be truly surrendered to all the will of God. In the preceding chapters, Paul has been dealing with the salvation and sanctification of the believer's life; in these verses his theme is the surrender of the believer's life. Notice:

I. The Divine Obligation to Surrender

"I beseech you therefore, brethren, by the mercies of God, that you present your bodies a living sacrifice, holy, acceptable to God, which is your reasonable service" (Rom. 12:1, NKJV).

The apostle shows us that his obligation is occasioned by:

A. *The Revelation of Divine Love*

"I beseech you therefore . . . by the mercies of God" (Rom. 12:1, NKJV). Mercy is love in action extended to an inferior. When an inferior looks up to a superior, he recognizes that the superior is showing mercy when he expresses love. Notice that it is "mercies" in the plural. In the previous chapter the apostle has unveiled the matchless mercy of God as seen in Christ. Who can remain unmoved by the grace that has appeared to sinful men: justifying, sanctifying, and glorifying them? Paul has described how the sinner, condemned before God, is helpless and meritless; and how God, in the Lord Jesus Christ, comes in grace and mercy, setting the sinner at liberty, and giving him justification, sanctification, and glorification (see Rom. 3:24; 5:8; 6:23; 8:1, 29-30, 38-39).

Illustration

Richard Armstrong, in *Make Your Life Worthwhile,* reports the story about a man in Wales who sought to win the affection of a certain lady for forty-two years before she finally said "Yes." The couple, both seventy-four, recently became "Mr. and Mrs." For more than forty years, the persistent, but rather shy man, slipped a weekly love letter under his neighbor's door. But she continually refused to speak and mend the spat that had parted them many years before. After writing 2,184 love letters without ever getting a spoken or written answer, the single-hearted old man eventually summoned up enough courage to present himself in person. He knocked on the door of the reluctant lady's house and asked for her hand. To his delight and surprise, she accepted. Imagine God's dilemma. Time and time again He has tried to get His message of love through to His human creation with little response. Finally, when there was no other way, He wrapped up His message and came in person. What a revelation of God's love to you and me!

B. The Expectation of Divine Love

"I beseech you therefore, brethren, by the mercies of God, that you present your bodies a living sacrifice, holy, acceptable to God, which is your reasonable service" (Rom. 12:1, NKJV). The apostle John puts it a little differently when he says, "We love Him because He first loved us" (1 John 4:19, NKJV).

True gratitude requires expression. Who can reason out the mercies of God without a deep sense of obligation to respond to these mercies? In other words, the logic of love "demands my soul, my life, my all." None of us can think of all that Christ gave at Calvary without a deep desire to say, "Lord Jesus, you have done all this for me; from now onward I will live only for you." Any person who has been saved but has never surrendered his life to Christ is one who has never given serious consideration to the love of God, as revealed in the Lord Jesus.

Illustration

An aged countryman visited London for the first time. In a great art gallery, he looked at different paintings. He was especially impressed with a picture of Christ dying on the cross. As he gazed fixedly on it, a deeper love for the Savior flooded his heart. With great feeling, he exclaimed, "Bless Him! I love Him! I love Him!" Those standing nearby heard him. They saw tears glistening on his careworn face as he stood completely oblivious of the presence of others. Four of them came close to him and said, "We, too, love Him, brother." Though strangers to each other, they were drawn together in love and adoration for the Savior.[1]

II. The Divine Order of Surrender

"Present your bodies a living sacrifice, holy, acceptable to God" (Rom. 12:1, NKJV). The apostle insists that the act, as well as the attitude, of surrender must be totally offered, and then worthily offered.

A. *Totally Offered*

"Present your bodies" (Rom. 12:1, NKJV). That word *present* means "yield," and suggests the handing over of a gift. It was a term used in the temple. It is the voluntary response of the believer to God's love, grace, and mercy.

Notice what we are to present: our bodies (v. 1, NKJV). The body here stands for the complete man, including soul and spirit. It symbolizes the giving over of everything. The body is that which God must have, if he is to express his perfect will through us to the world. He wants our brains, eyes, ears, tongue, hands, and feet as the vehicle for the divine expression.

What we do with our bodies now will determine our reward or loss in the coming day of judgment. Believers will stand before the judgment seat of Christ "that each one may receive the things done in the body, according to what he has done, whether good or bad" (2 Cor. 5:10, NKJV). Thank God, we are not going to be judged on the sin question; that was dealt with at Calvary, but we shall be judged for service we have rendered in the body down here on earth. So until we surrender our bodies, God can never consecrate us to his service.

It is tremendously important to realize that God never consecrates part of the life, only the whole. When the high priest was consecrated, the anointing oil went from his head to his feet. It was all or nothing. So until you are prepared to surrender spirit, soul, and body upon God's altar, he cannot consecrate you. You may be saved, but you are not surrendered, or consecrated.

In the Old Testament, God had very specific instructions concerning the offering of animal sacrifices. When the priest slew them, he had to lay the pieces of their flesh on the altar with deliberateness and thoughtfulness.

Illustration

Florence Nightingale at thirty wrote in her diary, "I am thirty years of age, the age at which Christ began His mission. Now no more childish things, no more vain things. Now, Lord, let me think only of Thy will." Years later, near the end of her illustrious, heroic life she was asked for her life's secret, and she replied, "Well, I can only give one explanation; that is, I have kept nothing back from God."[2]

B. *Worthily Offered*

"A living sacrifice, holy, acceptable to God" (Rom. 12:1, NKJV). This is a sacrificial phrase and carries the thought of a burnt offering, i.e., an offering wholly consumed. Notice how God insists that our offering should be brought. It should be:

1. A LIVING SACRIFICE (ROM. 12:1)

Three ideas are implicit in that word *living*. To be "a living sacrifice," it has to be *intelligently alive*. The offerer and the sacrifice are one and the same person, which is a complete contrast to the animal sacrifices of the Old Testament (they did not know what was happening). You and I must know what we are doing as we present our offering. What is more, our offering must be *spiritually alive*. An unconverted person can never offer anything to God; he can only receive from God. That is why our emphasis is always that a person who is "dead in trespasses and sins" (Eph. 2:1, NKJV) must acknowledge his sinnership and pray:

> Just as I am, without one plea,/But that Thy blood was shed for me,/And that Thou bidd'st me come to Thee,/O Lamb of God, I come!
> Charlotte Elliot

Only when a person is truly converted does he qualify to bring something to God; he must be indwelt by the life-giving Spirit.

Furthermore, God insists that our offering must be *continually alive*. When the Old Testament priest slew the animal on the north side of the altar, and placed it upon the altar, he knew it must be kept there until it was wholly consumed. So often with a big sacrifice there was the tendency for it to slip off the altar. God foresaw that and instructed Moses and Aaron that they should use fleshhooks (see Exod. 27:3), which were part of the furniture of the tabernacle, to bring the sacrifice back to the center of the flame.

Here is a message for you and me. When we yield our spirit, soul, and body to God, there is the tendency, again and again, to slip from the place of surrender. When that happens we need to use those fleshhooks of determination and discipline to bring us back to the center of the flame, and we will have to do that until Jesus comes or calls.

Illustration

I remember talking to a young lady who said, "Mr. Olford, this business of consecration does not work. Many a time I have stood up and yielded my life to the Lord; but a few weeks later I was back where I started." "You have never really yielded your life to the Lord," I said. "New Testament surrender means that when you put your sacrifice on the altar it is not for a day, or a month, or a year, but forever. Tell me, what are you doing off the altar?"

2. A HOLY SACRIFICE

"Present your bodies a . . . sacrifice, holy" (Rom. 12:1, NKJV). We cannot offer to the Lord "that which costs [us] nothing" (2 Sam. 24:24, NKJV). In Malachi 1:7-8 we read that the people made the altar of the Lord contemptible, and offered the blind for sacrifice. In God's eyes it was evil and defiled. When God asks for a holy sacrifice, he means a sacrifice that has been *initially* cleansed by the precious blood of Christ and then *continually* cleansed by the daily application of the Word of God to our lives.

3. A PLEASING SACRIFICE

"Present your bodies a . . . sacrifice . . . acceptable to God" (Rom. 12:1, NKJV). To the apostle, the word "acceptable" would be associated with what is known as the ascending offering. Whether seen or unseen to the public eye, the sacrifice had to be pleasing.

Similarly, the believer must please God in private and public life. How true this was of the Lord Jesus! As a boy, he said, "I must be about My Father's business" (Luke 2:49, NKJV). And when he stood on the banks of Jordan, at the age of thirty, and was baptized, a voice was heard from heaven, saying "This is My beloved Son, in whom I am well pleased" (Matt. 3:17, NKJV). There are many Christians who look like saints in public, but act like demons in private. We must please God at all times, if our surrender is to be real and sincere.

III. The Divine Object in Surrender

"Do not be conformed to this world, but be transformed by the renewing of your mind, that you may prove what is that good and acceptable and perfect will of God" (Rom. 12:2, NKJV). The object of the believer's surrender is twofold:

A. The Transformation of the Believer's Character

"Do not be conformed to this world, but be transformed by the renewing of your mind" (Rom. 12:2, NKJV). As the believer maintains an attitude of surrender, a daily change takes place in the life, which is here described both negatively and positively.

Negatively, it means nonconformity to the world (see 12:2). To be conformed means to be like, or to take the shape of. The surrendered believer is no longer conformed to the policies, fashions, and practices of the world about him; there is a distinctiveness and difference of lifestyle that sets him apart from the natural and carnal man. So many Christians are like chameleons that change their color according to their surroundings: you cannot tell the difference between them and the unconverted. That is one of the biggest stumbling blocks to the witness of the Christian church.

Positively, it is to be transformed in character. God's redemptive purpose for each one of us is to be like his Son.

This is the reason why he has chosen and called us.

Illustration

On a wall near the main entrance to the Alamo in San Antonio, Texas, is a portrait with the following inscription: "James Butler Bonham—no picture of him exists. This portrait is of his nephew, Major James Bonham, deceased, who greatly resembled his uncle. It is placed here by the family that people may know the appearance of the man who died for freedom." No literal portrait of Jesus exists either. But the likeness of the Son who makes us free can be seen in the lives of his true followers.[3]

Conformity to Christ takes place when the believer is yielded, fulfilling the divine order of surrender day by day. So we are changed "from glory to glory, just as by the Spirit of the Lord" (2 Cor. 3:18, NKJV). One of the greatest thrills for a pastor is to see almost a facial, external change coming over a person—an index to the inner change of character. That is why the hymn is so true.

What a wonderful change in my life has been wrought
Since Jesus came into my heart![4]

B. The Regulation of the Believer's Conduct

"That you may prove what is that good and acceptable and perfect will of God" (Rom. 12:2, NKJV). There is no greater joy on earth or in heaven than the realization of the will of God, and you can never be in the center of his will until you are a yielded Christian. God's will is *good;* that is, it is beneficial in its effect upon us. Therefore, we need never fear the consequences of obeying God. God's will is *acceptable,* or pleasing. It is never irksome or grievous (see 1 John 5:3). God's will is *perfect;* that is, flawless and mature. In his Sermon on the Mount, Jesus said, "you shall be perfect, just as your Father in heaven is perfect" (Matt. 5:48, NKJV). The only way to be perfect in condition—and one day in consummation—is to be a yielded Christian.

Conclusion

We have seen that if a life is truly surrendered, it is to be a living, holy, and acceptable sacrifice, evidenced not only in the transformation of character, but the regulation of conduct. May we know in experience the divine obligation to surrender, the divine order of surrender, and the divine object in surrender, and so be able to say:

> Savior, Thy dying love Thou gavest me,/Nor should I ought withhold, Dear Lord, from Thee:/In love my soul would bow,/My heart fulfill its vow,/Some offering bring Thee now,/Something for Thee.
> Sylvanus D. Phelps

Can you change that last line and say, "My ALL for Thee"? Remember, he consecrates only the whole.

11

Systematic Giving

2 Corinthians 9:5-11;
1 Corinthians 16:1-2

"Enriched in everything for all liberality, which causes
thanksgiving through us to God" (2 Cor. 9:11, NKJV).

Introduction

Can a Christian give sacrificially and save money? The answer
will be given in the unfolding of our message, but suffice it to
say that this subject is of the utmost importance to all
Christians.

Have you ever stopped to consider how many hours you
spend, outside of sleeping and eating, in the business of making money? What we do with it, then, our approach and attitude to it, is a top priority in our thinking and living.

Of course, there can be a false motive in earning money.
There is the vice that grips people's minds and hearts, so that
they burn with a passion to get rich. The apostle Paul warns
young Timothy very solemnly of this when he says, "The love
of money is a root of all . . . evil" (1 Tim. 6:10). It can be

demonstrated that practically every kind of evil can spring from the lure and lust of getting rich.

What we are concerned about now, however, is the ministry of giving. We shall think of it in three aspects:

I. The Motive in Giving

"Enriched in everything for all liberality" (2 Cor. 9:11, NKJV). The supreme motive is not "What shall I gain?" but "What shall I give?" It is not one of satisfying myself, but rather of pleasing and honoring God.

A. *Pleasing God*

"But do not forget to do good and to share, for with such sacrifices God is well pleased" (Heb. 13:16, NKJV). If someone were to ask you, "What is the greatest ambition of your life, now that you are a Christian?" what would you say? After some thought, you would possibly reply, "My greatest ambition is to please God. I love God, I love the Lord Jesus and his Word, and I want to please him." Well, here is one way in which you can please him.

Illustration

Dr. Paul White of *Jungle Doctor* fame tells of two African lepers who were desperately eager to help the missionaries. Their hands were badly disfigured with leprosy. For several weeks they worked in the sawpit, sawing logs into boards for the extension of the bush hospital. When they were given their wages, the doctor noticed them dividing their money into two piles of silver. They explained that half was for the Lord. "But that's too much. God only asks for a tenth." "But Bwana," one of them replied quickly, "we love Him far more than that!" Here were two men who desired to please God.

B. *Honoring God*

"Honor the LORD with your possessions, and with the firstfruits of all your increase" (Prov. 3:9, NKJV). That is good Old

Testament language. Remember also the word from the Old Testament which God spoke to the people: "Those who honor Me I will honor" (1 Sam. 2:30, NKJV). When we come to the New Testament, we read such verses as: "It is more blessed to give than to receive" (Acts 20:35, NKJV). Next to pleasing God is honoring him with our substance. Failure to do this dishonors God.

Illustration

Mr. W. R. Spight was a wholesale grocer in Decatur, Alabama. A friend who knew him said that he gave $500 to the Lord every Sunday of the year while he lived. The Lord has said, "Them that honor me I will honor" (1 Sam. 2:30). Only eternity will reveal the vast amount of good accomplished by his giving. What better use of money than honoring the Lord![1]

II. The Method of Giving

"'Bring all the tithes into the storehouse, That there may be food in My house, And try Me now in this,' Says the LORD of hosts, 'If I will not open for you the windows of heaven And pour out for you such blessing That there will not be room enough to receive it'" (Mal. 3:10, NKJV). The method in giving concerns four sections of our income: (1) tithes; (2) offerings; (3) savings; and (4) expenses.

A. Tithes

"Bring all the tithes into the storehouse" (Mal. 3:10, NKJV). God demands our tithes. The tithe is one-tenth of our [gross] income. Today we think in terms of money, but in olden times it was always in terms of substance.

The tithe was spoken of long before the giving of the Law. Abraham tithed, Melchizedek tithed, Jacob tithed. God introduced this principle of tithing into the life of man right from the beginning, just as he introduced the law of rest, the Sabbath, to Adam. In the same way, the giving of the tenth was that which God built into the very moral structure of his universe. The principle of tithing goes right through Scripture, and there is nothing in the New Testament that abrogates or rescinds it. As a matter of fact, the law of grace underlines it, for grace does not make void the law: it enables us to keep the law, by the very power of the indwelling Christ. If the Jew, under law, gave a tithe, can we, under grace, give any less?

One of the key passages in Scripture concerning tithing is found in Malachi 3:10, as we have seen already. Just before that God had said to the nation, "You have robbed Me!" (Mal. 3:8, NKJV), and then he explains how they had robbed him: "In tithes and offerings" (Mal. 3:8, NKJV). Now the "storehouse," in olden times, was the temple at Jerusalem. Since Jerusalem was the city of the king, and the temple was at the heart of it, all gifts had to be brought to the one place. And sometimes cattle had to be sold for that which was cash, in order to bring it into the storehouse of God.

Paul teaches this conclusively in that first verse of 1 Corinthians 16, where he talks about laying aside that portion, which God has blessed us with, and bringing it to God. Our first responsibility, as Christian people, is to bring our tithe to the place of our "Jerusalem," our "temple"—the local church.

A tithe is something that God demands. Any Christian who withholds it is, in fact, robbing him. Our money belongs to God, even before we offer it. One of the secrets of blessing is not only the yieldedness of the life, but the givingness of the life.

Illustration
The greatest surprise of Mary's life was receiving a dollar on her fourth birthday. She carried the bill about the house and was seen sitting on the stairs admiring it. "What are you going to do with your dollar?" her mother asked. "Take it to your teacher?" Mary shook her head. "No," she said, "I'm going to give it to God. He'll be as surprised as I am to get something besides pennies."

B. Offerings

"Enriched in everything for all liberality" (2 Cor. 9:11, NKJV). If

God demands our tithes, he deserves our offerings. An offering is that which is given voluntarily, over and above the tithe. That is clear from any careful study of that word "offering" throughout the Old Testament Scriptures, and particularly that passage in Malachi (3:8). It usually represents something that is extra; maybe the result of a bonus, or an increase in salary, or some unexpected windfall. Or it may be in response to some blessing God has lavished on you and you want to give him an extra thankoffering, a love offering.

That is absolutely consistent with New Testament teaching, for when Paul asked the Corinthian believers for money for the deprived saints in Jerusalem, he was asking them for the extra tithe to cover the needs there (1 Cor. 16:3).

Illustration

Pastor Howard Conaster of the 4,000 member Beverly Hills Baptist Church in Dallas once preached a series of sermons on the types of offerings in Scripture. At one midweek prayer meeting he announced that a freewill offering would be received. Normally, collections are not a part of the church's prayer meeting. Conaster told his audience of 950 that the church didn't really need the money. "We are already $100,000 over our budget for this year," he said. "But you need to be blessed; you need to experience the grace of giving." After the offering was received the pastor directed the deacons to return to the congregation with the baskets, which contained more than $1,000. "It's God's money," he explained. "If you need money and have asked God to help you get it, take what you need." Only a few did, but for them the collection in reverse was a godsend, observed reporter Helen Parmley of the *Dallas Morning News*. One parishioner told of a clean but poorly dressed youth who took a couple of bills from the basket as it passed, then lifted his head and said softly, "Praise the Lord."[2]

C. Savings

God defends our savings. Drawing an illustration from nature, the apostle Paul says in 2 Corinthians 12:14: "The children ought not to lay up for the parents, but the parents for the children" (NKJV). Every one of us has a moral obligation in relation to finance; we should save to meet our commitments. The husband who does not save for his wife, in case anything happens to him; the parents who do not save for their children; the children who do not help their widowed mother or some other dependent, when they have the ability to do so, are all breaking a very clear injunction of Scripture. First Timothy 5:8 says: "If anyone does not provide for his own, and especially for those of his household, he has denied the faith and is worse than an unbeliever" (NKJV). The teaching is clear: we must save in order to cover our dependents. Each one of us must think this through for ourselves. True, some wonderful stories are told of men who have given everything to missions, and through lack of foresight and careful understanding of the Word of God, have left their wives or children without adequate provision with tragic consequences. This kind of thing does not match up with the plain, practical teaching of the Bible. We must care for our dependents.

D. Expenses

God directs our expenses. We must live within our means in order to cover all liabilities. The Word of God says, "Repay no one evil for evil. Have regard for good things in the sight of all men"; and again: "Render therefore to all their due: taxes to whom taxes are due . . . Owe no one anything" (Rom. 12:17; 13:7-8, NKJV). If we are living a yielded Christian life, then our expenses should be directed by God. We should be living on a level at which we can meet all our expenses. We should never undertake any project that legitimately cannot be underwritten. It does not mean that you necessarily have to pay your bills on the spot, or that you cannot borrow on the bank; it refers rather to business transactions which you know you cannot justifiably and honestly cover.

Since every power is ordained of God, we should "Render

. . . to all their due" (Rom. 13:7, NKJV). This means paying our income tax or custom fees.

To meet our obligations it may be necessary to tighten our belts, or to seek help if we are having problems arranging our financial affairs, so that our testimony as citizens, and as Christians, is above reproach.

III. The Miracle in Giving

"That you, always . . . have an abundance for every good work" (2 Cor. 9:8, NKJV). God is no man's debtor. As we give in the right spirit, he blesses, and that in a twofold way:

A. *Materially*

"God is able to make all grace abound toward you, that you, always having all sufficiency in all things, have an abundance for every good work . . . enriched in everything for all liberality, which causes thanks giving through us to God" (2 Cor. 9:8, 11, NKJV). While God blesses materially, he does not necessarily make us millionaires. There are some men and women whom God selects, because of their business skills, and uses them to produce the money for the work of the church. Even though everyone is not chosen to prosper, God will see to it that we have enough to meet our needs—if we fulfill our commitments to him. Paul had "learned in whatever state [he was], to be content." He knew "how to be abased, and . . . how to abound" (Phil. 4:11-12, NKJV). That is the supreme secret of it all. When a man has been completely delivered from the spirit of materialism, it's just as easy to be a king as to be a slave. Why? Because his contentment is in Jesus Christ.

Illustration

The history of Christian giving demonstrates that there is none so poor that he cannot give. A woman with no money was too old to work. She began to pray, "Teach me to obtain. Give me someone to send out and support as a missionary." Before her death, she was supporting ninety-three missionaries!

When William Colgate left home as a boy of sixteen, the only trade he knew was soap and candlemaking. One day he met the captain of a canal boat who gave him this piece of advice: "Someone will soon be the leading soapmaker in New York. It can be you as well as anyone . . . . Be a good man, give your heart to Christ. Give the Lord all that belongs to Him of every dollar you earn. Make an honest soap. Give a full pound, and you will be a prosperous and rich man." On arrival in the city, he joined a church, and sought to "seek first the kingdom of God and His righteousness" (Matt. 6:33, NKJV). As his business prospered, he gave ten cents of every dollar to the Lord, then two-tenths, rising to five-tenths. Later when his children were educated, he gave all his income, amounting to millions, to the Lord.

B. Spiritually

"Do not be deceived, God is not mocked; for whatever a man sows, that he will also reap. For he who sows to his flesh will of the flesh reap corruption, but he who sows to the Spirit will of the Spirit reap everlasting life" (Gal. 6:7-8, NKJV). We quote these verses for all manner of things. We say that if you sow a sinful life you reap a wasteful life. We speak about an individual sowing his wild oats, but primarily these words refer to giving. The Bible says, "Let him who is taught the word share in all good things with him who teaches" (Gal. 6:6, NKJV). In other words, the ministers of God should be well supported. Here is one of the crying sins of our time.

Whether or not the Christian who gives to God is prospered materially, he is always prospered spiritually. We have no problem about yielding our lives to God. We have little doubt as to our church responsibilities, but so often there is a lack of teaching on this important subject of giving.

Conclusion

Remember the motive in giving. You give not to get, but because you want to please and honor God. As to the method, remember the tithe is God's. He demands it, he deserves the offering, he defends the savings, he directs the expenses. Then the miracle will happen. God will prosper you sufficiently for you to be content. He may even make you the steward of great wealth. Certainly he will bless you spiritually. Next time you sing that beautiful consecration hymn, may it be more than just words:

Take my silver and my gold,/Not a mite would I withhold . . .
Frances R. Havergal

12

Dedicated Serving

Exodus 21:1-6; Romans 12:9-11

"Not slothful in business; fervent in spirit; serving the Lord"
(12:11, KJV).

Introduction

Dedicated service touches every department of our lives. Service for Jesus Christ is as much an attitude of life as it is an activity of life. Whether it be so-called full-time service, a regular secular job, or caring for the home, all should be done to the glory of God with equal efficiency and fervency. Scripture makes no distinction between so-called "full-time" service and secular work; the distinction is purely an artificial one. A housewife doing her task in the home—bringing up the children, peeling the potatoes, polishing the brass, or making the beds—serves the Lord just as much as a preacher in the pulpit, or the missionary on the foreign field, if she does her job in the power of the Holy Spirit. There are three aspects of dedicated service to which I want to draw your attention:

I. Determined Service

"Not slothful in business" (12:11, KJV). Paul is calling for diligence and determination in whatever the Christian is called to do, whether he be a chimney sweep or whether he be a lecturer; whether he be a preacher or a missionary. Study the various translations, and you will see that the idea of business, as such, is not necessarily in this text. A better rendering is, "Never let your zeal flag." In other words, service for the Lord Jesus Christ is not so much what you do but how you do it. Paul gives few hints in his writings as to what the Christian should do by way of service, outside of witnessing, the winning of precious souls, and the preaching of the Gospel. All of life is an arena in which we witness by life and by lip, but it's how we do what we do that is all-important. This is a call to:

A. Enthusiastic Determination

"Not slothful in business" (12:11, KJV). The purpose of our redemption, according to Titus 2:14, is that we might be a purified people, a special people, "zealous for good works." If you read the passage and see the whole sweep of truth, you will see that salvation and service are simultaneous in their impact upon us. The moment a man is saved he serves. Salvation and service happen together. When Saul of Tarsus was converted on the Damascus road, the first question he asked was, "Lord, what do You want me to do?" (Acts 9:6, NKJV). And when our Lord called his disciples, he said, "Follow Me, and I will make you fishers of men" (Matt. 4:19, NKJV). The "come" of salvation and the "call" of service were married together in the Master's one sentence.

It is sad to see how many people who call themselves Christians are lacking in this zeal; they have never interpreted their salvation as a total commitment to Jesus Christ, in terms of service. Given a job to do, they go about it as though it were boring and uninteresting, whereas it should be the most thrilling and fascinating thing in all the world. No Christian should face his job without asking himself, "Has God called me to do this work? Is this a vocation? Is this the purpose of God for my life?" If it is, then it's not just a job, it's a ministry, and the monotonous is transformed into the momentous. Every day becomes a glorious adventure with the Lord Jesus Christ.

Whatever our Master did, he did it enthusiastically and fervently, whether serving as a carpenter or carrying through his redemptive task on the way to Calvary. Indeed, he preached with such fervor, he worked so untiringly, that the disciples, on one occasion marveled at the passion with which he worked for God. Turning to them he asked, [have you never read] "The zeal of thine house hath eaten me up" (John 2:17, KJV; see Ps. 69:9). It is the same word that Paul uses in Titus 2— "zealous for good works." In winning us to himself, he desires that we might have the same zeal in our service for God.

So often in Christian circles we find three kinds of people: the workers, the shirkers, and the jerkers. The *workers* are people who always have their sleeves rolled up to do a real job for God. They're at the task, whether it's snowing or the sun is shining; whether the work is easy or difficult. You can depend on them to be faithful all the time. The *shirkers* are always conspicuous by their absence when there is any hard work to be done. The *jerkers* are people who are full of enthusiasm when something special is going on, but afterward they are as flat as pancakes! Enthusiasm is a God-given quality in the Holy Spirit and is characteristic of all those whose attitude to life is one of commitment.

B. Enduring Determination

"Not slothful in business" (12:11, KJV). My dad had a motto that he drilled into the lives of his three boys: "Determination, not desire, controls our destiny." Some people have a desire to do things, but it gets them nowhere; they need determination to see them through.

We find the Master was characterized by this enduring determination. At the outset of his ministry; yes, even as a boy, he had a sense of vocation and calling. When his mother,

Mary, remonstrated with him concerning his absence from them for three days, Jesus said, "Did you not know that I *must* be about My Father's business?" (Luke 2:49, NKJV). *There* was determination. Later on, he declared, "I *must* work the works of Him who sent Me while it is day; the night is coming when no one can work" (John 9:4, NKJV). When his disciples reasoned with him, and Peter would have prevented his going to the cross, he set his face determinately to go to Jerusalem (see Luke 9:53). Is there a "must" in your life? That is the acid test of true service.

Illustration

A twenty-three-year-old youth saw this advertisement in a Boston newspaper: "Wanted, young man as an understudy to a financial statistician. P. O. Box 1720." He answered the ad but received no reply. He wrote again—no reply. A third time—no reply. He decided to go to the post office and ask the name of the holder of Box 1720. Refusal was given; it was against the rules. Early one morning the young man rose early, took the first train to Boston, went to the post office and stood sentinel near Box 1720. After a long wait, a man appeared, opened the box, and took out the mail. The young man trailed him to his destination, which was the office of a stock brokerage firm. The young man entered and asked for the manager. When an interview was granted, he explained how he had applied for the position several times without receiving a response, and he went on to tell of the problem he encountered at the post office. "But how did you find out that I was the advertiser?" queried the manager. "I stood in the lobby of the post office for several hours watching Box 1720," answered the young man. "When a man came in and took the mail from the box, I followed him here." The manager said, "Young man, you are just the kind of persistent fellow I want. You are employed!"[1]

II. Dynamic Service

"Fervent in spirit" (Rom. 12:11, NKJV). The word *fervent* means "boiling" or "seething." The whole idea behind the word is that we are to allow the Holy Spirit to keep us passionate and dynamic in our service all the time. Fervency is to be expressed in the realm of:

A. *The Believer's Spirit*

"Fervent in spirit" (Rom. 12:11, NKJV).The Christian temperament is compared to water boiling and bubbling over a flame; and we must always be boiling hot for God. In Revelation 3:15-16 the Lord says to the Laodicean church: "I know your works, that you are neither cold nor hot. I could wish you were cold or hot. So then, because you are lukewarm, and neither cold nor hot, I will spew you out of My mouth." He wished they were either frigid in hostility and opposition, or fervent in their love and service. This is a solemn word, and explains what we see in Christendom today. We all know of people who were once committed Christians and fervent in the work of the Lord, but they allowed their glow for Jesus Christ to cool, by neglect of communion with him and Christian fellowship and service. Such lukewarm Christians are anemic and nauseating to our Lord.

Illustration
Dr. J. H. Jowett, a famous preacher of a former generation, once confessed that his supreme difficulty during his years of training for the ministry was that of keeping his own spiritual life in warmth and vigor. Instead of being hot, on fire, we may become lukewarm or cold—spiritually slack, lazy, and undisciplined.[2]

While attending a university in London, Mahatma Gandhi became convinced that the Christian religion was the one true, supernatural religion in the world. Upon graduation, and still seeking evidence that would make him a committed Christian, Gandhi accepted employment in East Africa, living for seven months in the home of a family who were members of an evangelical Christian church. Here he felt would be the place to find the evidence he sought. But as the months passed he saw the casualness of their attitude toward the cause of God, heard them complain when they were called upon to make sacrifices for the kingdom of God, and sensed their general religious apathy. Gandhi's interest turned to disappointment. "No, it is not the one true supernatural religion I had hoped to find," he said to himself. "A good religion, yes—but just one more of the many religions in the world."[3]

B. The Believer's Speech

In Acts 18:25 we read of Apollos who was "fervent in spirit [and] spoke." No wonder he moved people! It is a sure sign of lukewarmness when lips are seldom opened in prayer, praise, or testimony; but when the youngest convert speaks from the heart in prayer or in testimony, however simple the language, folk will listen. Too often the outsider is put off by the person who speaks "professionally" without any sense of fervency. What the world is looking for today are people who speak with sincerity, earnestness, and fervency. It's not so much what they say as the spirit in which they say it.

Illustration

Aunt Sophie, a converted scrub woman, used to say that she was "called to scrub and preach." Wherever she went, she would tell others of Jesus, the Savior. Someone made fun of her by saying that she was seen talking about Christ to a wooden Indian, standing in front of a cigar store. When Sophie heard this, she replied, "Perhaps I did. My eyesight is not good. But talking about Christ to a wooden Indian is not so bad as being *a wooden Christian and never talking to anybody about the Lord Jesus!*" How many souls have you brought to the Lord Jesus? Are you busy telling others about the Savior?[4]

III. Devoted Service

"Serving the Lord" (Rom. 12:11, NKJV). The word *serving* conveys the idea of "bondservice" or "bondslave." The apostle

Paul was fond of calling himself a "bondslave." Scholars believe that the apostle took this word from the passage in Exodus 21.

When a Hebrew servant had served his master for six years, he was allowed to go free in the seventh year; but if he had come to love his master and would not leave him, a sacred ceremony was performed. He would be brought before the judges to make his decision publicly known. Then he was led to the doorpost of his master's house, and his ear lobe was bored with an awl, as an indication that he was committed to his master forever.

Our Lord considered himself a bondslave. Not only were his ears "opened" (Ps. 40:6), but he allowed his hands and feet to be nailed to a cross, because he delighted to do God's will. The bored ear of the bondslave indicated devotedness in:

A. Lowly Service

"He shall serve" (Exod. 21:2, NKJV). A slave did anything his master required of him, however lowly the service. The test of true devotedness is doing the little things. Most of us seize the opportunity to do something great and impressive, but the Lord Jesus takes cognizance of the most lowly things we do for him.

The most condescending act our Lord ever performed—outside of the cross—was when he kneeled as a slave to wash the disciples' feet. This made such an impression on Peter that years later he wrote in his epistle, "Gird up the loins of your mind, be sober" (1 Peter 1:13, NKJV); or more literally, "Gird up the loins of your mind with the towel of humility." Washing feet was a slave's job; it was lowly service. So the first characteristic of a true servant is willingness to do anything.

Illustration

One day someone asked "Sophie, the scrub woman" a question as she was scrubbing the steps of a large New York City building. "Sophie, I understand you are a child of God—a child of the King. Therefore, don't you think it is beneath your level to be scrubbing these dirty steps?" Undaunted, she replied, "There's no humiliation whatever. You see, I'm not washing these steps for Mr. Brown, my boss. I'm scrubbing them for Jesus Christ, my Savior!"[5]

B. Loving Service

"I love my master" (Exod. 21:5, NKJV). Nothing inspires service like love. Once you love a person you will do anything for them. If you fall in love with Jesus Christ you never have to be prodded into service; you can't help but serve. When we get to that place, devoted service is as natural as breathing. We do it for sheer love of Jesus.

Illustration

The story is told of how St. Anthony prayed and read his Bible for hours every day, and in time became a good man. But one day the Lord told him that there was one man better than he: Conrad, the cobbler of Jerusalem. Anthony went to visit the cobbler to learn the secret of his goodness. Conrad remonstrated as to his goodness, but said: "If you wish to know what I do, I don't mind telling you I mend shoes, and I do every pair as if I were mending them for Jesus.

C. Loyal Service

"I will not go out free" (Exod. 21:5, NKJV). Many people start a job with enthusiasm, but they never see it through; their loyalty breaks down. The Lord Jesus never forces us to give our lives to him, but he expects us to do it voluntarily because we love him. Out of that love is born a loyalty.

Loyalty and teamwork in the service of the church is a wonderful thing. The church is essentially a team, and a team is built on loyalty to one another. Loyalty is fundamental to our Christian faith and service. Pray that you will always be loyal to Jesus Christ—come what may—loyal to your church, loyal to your pastor, loyal to your fellow members.

Illustration

A tourist recalls the impression made on him as he studied Poynter's great picture, "Faithful unto Death," which hung in the Walker Art Gallery in Liverpool. There stood the Roman guard on duty while the palace was falling into ruins during the destruction of Herculaneum. The dead were lying in the background, others were falling to the pavement amid the red hot eruptions of Vesuvius. Everyone who could was fleeing for his life. The Roman guard might have made his escape, but there he stood like a marble statue, preferring to remain at his post, faithful unto death. Said the tourist, "The picture has haunted me ever since. Not simply the man standing at his post of duty, but the expression of faithfulness that showed in his countenance. I have thought of it a hundred times, and I have felt its influence as I have felt that of a living person."

D. Lasting Service

"He shall serve Him forever" (Exod. 21:6, NKJV). At the end of his life our Savior could say, "I have finished the work which You have given Me to do" (John 17:4). And when Paul wrote his final letter to Timothy he said, "I have finished my course, I have kept the faith" (2 Tim. 4:7, KJV).

Conclusion

You can never be devoted without being dynamic, and you will never be dynamic without being determined. Are you prepared to be a bondservant of Jesus Christ? He accepted this contract. Dare you refuse?

13

Covenant of Membership

1 Corinthians 14:36-40

"Let all things be done decently and in order"
(1 Cor. 14:40, NKJV).

Introduction

Our God is a God of order. It does not matter what passage of
Scripture is turned to; whether in relation to his activities
within the individual Christian or the corporate body of
Christ, he is always a God of order. He is "not the author of
confusion but of peace" (1 Cor. 14:33, NKJV).

Everyone who comes into the fellowship of an evangelical
church should seriously consider the terms of membership,
and then accept those terms of reference as a covenant
between God and himself. It is a sad indictment on the church
of Jesus Christ today that people can drift in and out of membership without anybody knowing about it; that would have
never happened in New Testament times. The church of Jesus
Christ, locally centered, is a family, and if an individual joins a
church, whether by conversion, letter, or experience, then

that person is part of the church family, and he or she can't move away without the church being painfully conscious of his or her absence.

Paul puts it all in the figure of a body in 1 Corinthians 12:26 where he says, "If one member suffers, all the members suffer with it." God has made us that way.

There is such a thing as the sympathetic system within the church of God. When someone is going through trial and tribulation, the church should seek to lift the burden and suffering of God's people. We are commanded to "Bear one another's burdens" (Gal. 6:2, NKJV), and, therefore, we must know the terms of our oneness and operation in Christ. These are clearly set forth in the Covenant of Membership before us. We start off, of course, with the basic fact:

> Realizing my guilt before God, I CONFESS MY SINS to him, and received the Lord Jesus Christ, who bore my sins on the cross, as my personal Savior (see Rom. 3:19, 23; 5:8; John 1:12).

These statements concern our sinnership—the fact that Jesus died for us, and the fact that he can be received by faith into the heart and life. No one has the right to be in a local church without having experienced a conviction of sin, a conversion of life, and a confession of faith. John 1:12 says, "As many as received Him, to them He gave the right to become children of God, even to those who believe in His name." If I have truly received the Lord Jesus Christ into my heart and life I have a right to be in the family of God, and, therefore, in the fellowship of God. Contrary to some teaching abroad today, my right to be in the church of Jesus Christ is not the measure of *light* I have, but the measure of *life* I have. My right to be at the Lord's table, my right to be in the local fellowship, is the fact that I share the same resurrection life of Jesus Christ that you share. My children have a right to sit at my table and eat my food, not because they know as much as Father does, but because they share my life; they are my children.

> I ACKNOWLEDGE the Lord Jesus Christ as Lord of all my life and seek to confess him as such before others by the testimony both of life and lip (see Rom. 10:9; 2 Cor. 5:14-15).

Some religious leaders speak of the church as the final authority. The evangelical church, on the other hand, talks of Christ mediating and ministering authority through the Spirit, by the Word. To challenge the authority and sovereignty of Jesus Christ in a local church is to bring confusion into the assembly of God's people. Jesus said, "Every . . . house divided against itself will not stand" (Matt. 12:25). A church can only live in revival blessing when there is the total recognition of the Lordship of Jesus Christ. We talk about the Lord's table that we recognize. We talk about the Lord's death that we celebrate. We talk about the Lord's body that we discern. We talk about the Lord's day that we observe. So his sovereignty is absolutely essential in a church where holiness and harmony are going to be enjoyed.

> I TRUST in the power of the Holy Spirit, who lives in my heart, to keep me, guide me, and lead me in the way of purity and holiness (see John 14:26; 16:13; Rom. 8:2-4; Gal. 5:22-25).

The more we study the Bible and pray, the more we realize that the supreme purpose of revelation and redemption is the holiness of God's people, both individually and corporately.

Think for a moment. Why did God give us this Bible? Not that we might know all that God is like; for, ultimately, we do not have a complete revelation of him in the Bible. It isn't to have a full story of the life of Jesus Christ, for the revelation we have of him is quite fragmentary. We know nothing, for instance, of the first thirty years of his life, except for one brief glimpse at the age of twelve. Practically all that is said about the Lord Jesus Christ is related to those final few weeks before he died. The Bible isn't a final statement on cosmology, anthropology, history, or poetry. Why then has it been given to us? Second Timothy 3:16-17 gives us the answer: "All Scripture is given by inspiration of God, and is profitable for doctrine, for reproof, for correction, for instruction in righteousness, that the man of God may be complete, thoroughly equipped for every good work."

The revelation of God in the Bible is to make us like Jesus, to make us perfect, to make us holy (see 1 Thes. 4:7). You ask, "Why did Jesus die?" "Why did he rise from the dead?" "Why has he become a mighty Savior?" Titus 2:11-14 (NKJV) tells us: "For the grace of God that brings salvation has appeared to all men, teaching us that, denying ungodliness and worldly lusts, we should live soberly, righteously, and godly in the present age, looking for the blessed hope and glorious appearing of our great God and Savior Jesus Christ, who gave Himself for us, that He might redeem us from every lawless deed and purify for Himself his own special people, zealous for good works." So whether it's revelation or redemption, the purpose is the same: to make us holy men and women. The whole sweep of Scripture is to bring individuals to the place of holy living. No wonder that saintly man of God, Robert Murray McCheyne (who died at the age of thirty), made this statement: "The ambition of my life is to be as holy as a saved sinner can be."

Many people think that the local church is a social club, a place to meet for dances or bazaars, but the Bible makes it clear that the reason we belong to a local church is that by the study of God's Word, by prayer, by the filling of the Holy Spirit, we might be guarded and guided in the way of holiness, fellowship, and service.

> I ACCEPT the Bible as the inspired Word of God, and my final authority in all matters of faith and practice (see 2 Tim. 3:16; 2 Peter 1:20-21).

We believe that the Scriptures were originally inspired of God and preserved throughout the ages as the infallible rule of faith and practice. It is of first importance that we believe that; otherwise we become the victims of human judgment.

It is not what humans have to say, but what God has to say that matters. If we make the Bible the absolute standard of faith and practice we can never go wrong. The person who argues "Yes, but that was sufficient for apostolic times; we have gotten beyond that" immediately undermines the position we stand for, namely, that the Scriptures are sufficient for all matters of faith and practice. Everything we need to know is included in this wonderful book. So constitutional requirements for pastors, elders, deacons, deaconesses, and members, as well as all matters of church polity and government, must conform strictly to what the Bible has to say. Should we be unclear on any matter, then let's table it and study the Scriptures together until we are clear. But let the answer come from the Word of God, for God has only promised to bless what we do, "according to the pattern . . . shown . . . on the mountain" (Exod. 25:9, 40, NKJV).

> I RECOGNIZE my responsibility by tithes and offerings to extend the kingdom of the Lord Jesus Christ both at home and abroad (see Mal. 3:8-10; 1 Cor. 16:2; 2 Cor. 9:7).

The Bible teaches clearly that pastor and people are responsible for tithes and offerings (see Mal. 3:8-10)—a tithe being a tenth of my income; the offerings being over and above the tithe. Whatever God lays on our hearts to give should be done out of sheer love and devotion to him. Every church should be self-supporting. The seal of God's blessing on a local church is its ability to carry its entire financial load. Anything less than that should be examined and corrected. If people give in accordance with the terms of this covenant they will never lack. J. Hudson Taylor put it perfectly when he said, "God's work, done in God's way, will never lack God's supply."

> I RECOGNIZE my responsibility to pray regularly for the work of this church, for its pastors, officers, and members, that the witness of all concerned may be to the glory of God and to the salvation of souls (see Eph. 6:18-19; 1 Thess. 5:17, 25).

At our weekly prayer meetings, in our own quiet times, and at our family altars with our children, we should pray for the pastors, the officers, the members, and the work of the church. This is part of our total responsibility.

At my former church (Duke Street Baptist Church, Richmond, Surrey, England) the names of all the members were printed in a prayer calendar called "Prayer Requests." The names were listed alphabetically under each day of the month (31 days in a month). On the first day of the month each member would start to pray for the group in which his name occurred. The second day would be the next letter, and so on. This meant that every day everybody in the church was prayed for at least once, and those who used that prayer list morning and evening were prayed for twice. People who were serious about prayer couldn't go on praying for Mrs. Brown month after month without finding out who Mrs. Brown was! After awhile people were meeting and talking together. (Incidentally, all the addresses were given out so that members could visit each other. As a result, the fellowship became a closely knit one.)

> I RECOGNIZE my responsibility to be regular in my attendance at the services of the church, and at the Lord's table (see Acts 2:42; Heb. 10:25; 1 Cor. 11:26).

No one should join a local church and then fail to support that church by regular attendance at all official services—official services being Sunday morning, Sunday evening, Wednesday prayer meeting, and every church business meeting. Over and above that would be extra meetings, such as the missionary conference, or other similar gatherings. Attendance should not be simply to please the pastor, or to impress fellow members, but to obey and honor the Lord. Our responsibility in this regard is absolute, not relative.

In my church in England, there was a dear man who regarded attendance at all services such a covenant with his Lord that he would send a letter of apology whenever he was unable to attend. It was sent either to the secretary of the church or to the pastor, and read something like this: "Dear Pastor," or "Dear Mr. Edwards, I just want to tell you that I shall not be at the prayer meeting next week. I have a commitment that has been booked for many months. I shall be very sorry to miss the blessing, but I will be with you in spirit."

Oh, for that kind of spirit today in an hour when folk shrug their shoulders and say, "So what! Who is going to involve me in such a commitment as to attend church services regularly?" Yet it has nothing to do with the pastor, or a church, but with the Lord.

> I HAVE BEEN BAPTIZED by immersion, in obedience to my Lord's command, thus signifying my union with Christ in his death, burial, and resurrection (see Matt. 28:19-20; Rom. 6:4).

In the early church, there was no such person as an unbaptized believer. All who were able to be baptized were baptized. There was only one exception, and that was the thief on the cross. We are right and in accord with Scripture when we insist that before people come into membership they should show their oneness with Jesus, oneness with his people, oneness with the Word, by obeying the simple rite of baptism, and entering into the blessing. Jesus said, "If you know these things, blessed are you if you do them" (John 13:17, NKJV).

At this point in the instruction, potential members should be asked to indicate that they have read the Articles of Faith as contained in the by-laws, and that they are in perfect agreement with them. In the presence of the Board of Elders, the candidates must then sign their names to the Covenant, implying the ready assent of their hearts to each of the clauses, and acknowledging their dependency on the Lord to fulfill its terms. They are also encouraged to review the Covenant of Membership from time to time and reaffirm the pledge they have made to the Lord.

We have seen, then, what we mean by the Covenant of Membership—guidelines based on Scripture so that individuals seeking to align themselves with a local church might not come in confused, perplexed, or bewildered, but rather "decently and in order" (1 Cor. 14:40, NKJV). God, enable us to remember these terms, that we might be loyal, loving, and living members of the local church.

Covenant of Membership

Realizing my guilt before God, I have confessed my sins to him, and received the Lord Jesus Christ, who bore my sins on the cross, as my personal Savior (see Rom. 3:19, 23; 5:8; John 1:12).

I ACKNOWLEDGE the Lord Jesus Christ as Lord of all my life, and seek to confess him as such before others by the testimony both of life and lip (see Rom. 10:9; 2 Cor. 5:14-15).

I TRUST in the power of the Holy Spirit, who lives in my heart, to keep me, guide me, and lead me in the way of purity and holiness (see John 14:26; 16:13; Rom. 8:2-4; Gal. 5:22-25).

I ACCEPT the Bible as the inspired Word of God, and my final authority in all matters of faith and practice (see 2 Tim. 3:16; 2 Peter 1:20-21).

I RECOGNIZE my responsibility by tithes and offerings to extend the kingdom of the Lord Jesus Christ both at home and abroad (see Mal. 3:8-10; 1 Cor. 16:2; 2 Cor. 9:7).

I RECOGNIZE my responsibility to pray regularly for the work of this church, for its pastors, officers, and members, that the witness of all concerned may be to the glory of God and to the salvation of souls (see Eph. 6:18-19; 1 Thess. 5:17, 25).

I RECOGNIZE my responsibility to be regular in my attendance at the services of the church, and at the Lord's table (see Acts 2:42; Heb. 10:25; 1 Cor. 11:26).

I HAVE BEEN BAPTIZED by immersion, in obedience to my Lord's command, thus signifying my union with Christ in his death, burial, and resurrection (see Matt. 28:19-20; Rom. 6:4).

I HAVE READ the Articles of Faith as contained in the by-laws and am in complete agreement therewith (see 1 Tim. 6:12; 2 Tim. 4:7; Jude 3).

Recognizing my inability in my own strength to adhere to

the terms of any covenant, yet believing that my Lord will enable me to fulfill the terms of this Covenant, I hereby attach my signature below, implying the ready assent of my heart to each of the above clauses (see Phil, 4:13).

Signature

Date

Witness (Pastor)

Articles of Faith

We believe in one God, eternally existent as God the Father, God the Son, and God the Holy Spirit.

We believe that the Bible, composed of the Old and New Testaments, is God's inspired and infallible Word, and is the supreme standard and final authority for all conduct, faith, and doctrine.

We believe in the deity of the Lord Jesus Christ, in his virgin birth, in his sinless life, in his miracles, in his vicarious and atoning death, in his bodily resurrection, in his ascension to the right hand of the Father, and in his premillenial, personal return in power and glory.

We believe that man was created in the image of God, but by willful transgression became sinful and is justly under the condemnation and wrath of Almighty God.

We believe that the only salvation from this guilt and condemnation is through faith in the righteousness and atonement of the Lord Jesus Christ, and that this salvation is the free gift of God's love and grace.

We believe in the personality of the Holy Spirit and that his ministry is to reveal Christ to men, to convict of sin, to regenerate repentant sinners, and by his presence and power, to sanctify the lives of the redeemed.

We believe that the Lord Jesus Christ instituted the ordinances of baptism and communion; that baptism is only to be administered upon profession of faith in Christ, by immersion, thereby declaring our faith in a crucified, buried, and risen Savior; that communion is only for believers, is to be preceded by faithful self-examination, and is in remembrance of the Lord's death until he comes.

We believe that a New Testament church is a body of believers, baptized by immersion, associated for worship, service, and the spread of the Gospel of the grace of God to all the world.

We believe that there will be a resurrection of the just and the unjust; the just, having been redeemed by the shed blood of the Lord Jesus Christ, to be with him throughout eternity in glory; the unjust, having died impenitent and unreconciled to God, to eternal condemnation in hell.

ENDNOTES

Chapter 1

1. *Sunday School Times,* quoted in Walter B. Knight, *Knight's Master Book of New Illustrations* (Grand Rapids: Eerdmans, 1956), p. 638, adapted.

2. A. Naismith, *1,200 Notes, Quotes, and Anecdotes* (Hammersmith: Pickering & Inglis, 1963), p. 55.

3. Walter B. Knight, *Knight's Master Book of New Illustrations,* p. 139.

4. *New Illustrator,* quoted in Walter B. Knight, *3,000 Illustrations for Christian Service* (Grand Rapids: Eerdmans, 1952), p. 431, adapted.

5. *The King's Business,* ibid., p. 427, adapted.

Chapter 2

1. Naismith, p. 197.

2. T. T. Shields, *The Gospel Witness.*

3. Henry G. Weston.

4. *Gospel Herald,* quoted in Knight, *3,000 Illustrations for Christian Service,* p. 296, adapted.

Chapter 3

1. V. Raymond Edman, "The Discipline of Discipleship" in *The Disciplines of Life* (Wheaton, Ill.: Scripture Press, 1948), pp. 12-13.

2. Dietrich Bonhoeffer, *Life Together* (New York: Harper and Brothers, 1954), p. 8.

3. See Leon Morris, *The Gospel According to St. Luke,* Tyndale New Testament Commentaries (Grand Rapids: Eerdmans, 1960), p. 180.

4. H. G. Bosch, *Our Daily Bread* (Grand Rapids: Radio Bible Class, n.d.).

5. David Brown, *Commentary on the Old and New Testaments,* vol. 5 (Chicago: Moody Press, 1945), p. 56.

Chapter 4

1. Albert Mygatt, quoted in Paul Lee Tan, *Encyclopedia of 7,700 Illustrations* (Garland, TX.: Bible Communications, 1979), p. 541.
2. James C. Hefley, ibid., 757.
3. John Wesley, quoted in *Christian History,* vol. II, no. 1.

Chapter 5

1. *Gospel Herald,* quoted in Knight, *3,000 illustrations for Christian Service,* pp. 516-17.
2. A. J. Gordon, quoted in Knight, *Knight's Master Book of New Illustrations* , pp. 288-89.

Chapter 6

1. *Our Daily Bread* (Grand Rapids: Radio Bible Class, n.d.), adapted.

Chapter 7

1. Jesse B. Deloe, *Sweeter Than Honey* (BMH, 1979), p. 151,
2. H. G. Bosch, *Our Daily Bread* (Grand Rapids: Radio Bible Class, Sept. 20, 1972).
3. Amos R. Wells, *Pulpit Helps* (Chattanooga, Tenn.: AMG International).

Chapter 8

1. John Stott, *Baptism and Fullness: The Work of the Holy Spirit Today* (Downers Grove, Ill.,: InterVarsity Press, 1976), p. 16.
2. *Leadership* (Fall 1985), p. 76.
3. Fetters, Paul R. *Drastic Discipleship* (Grand Rapids, Michigan: Baker Book House, 1963), adapted.
4. *Choice Gleanings* (Grand Rapids: Gospel Folio Press, Dec. 6, 1978).

5. R. W. DeHaan, *Our Daily Bread* (Grand Rapids: Radio Bible Class), adapted.

Chapter 9

1. Howard G. Hendricks, *Say It With Love* (Wheaton, Ill.: Victor Books, 1972), p. 49, adapted.

Chapter 10

1. Tan, p. 763, adapted.
2. Paul S. Roes, ibid., 271.
3. *Leadership* (Fall 1983), p. 87.
4. Copyright 1914 by Charles H. Gabriel. © renewed 1942 by The Rodeheaver Company. All rights reserved. Used by permission.

Chapter 11

1. *Now,* quoted in Knight, *Knight's Master Book of New Illustrations* , p. 244, adapted.
2. *Christianity Today,* quoted in Tan, p. 1353.

Chapter 12

1. *Sunshine Magazine,* quoted in Tan, p. 1672.
2. Derek J. Prime, "Aglow With the Spirit," *Christian Irishman* (Belfast, North Ireland, June, 1985), p. 8.
3. Tan, pp. 765-66.
4. *Gospel Herald,* quoted in Knight, *Knight's Master Book of New Illustrations* p. 649.
5. ibid., 746.

FOR FURTHER READING

Barclay, William. *Daily Study Bible (1 Corinthians)*. Rev. ed. Philadelphia: Westminster Press, 1975-1976.

_____. *Daily Study Bible (Matthew)*. Rev. ed. Philadelphia: Westminster Press, 1975-1976.

_____. *Daily Study Bible (Romans)*. Rev. ed. Philadelphia: Westminster Press, 1975-1976.

Barnhouse, Donald Grey. *Exposition of Bible Doctrines: Taking the Epistle to the Romans as a Point of Departure*. 10 vols. Grand Rapids: Wm. B. Eerdmans Publishing Co., 1952-1963.

Bonhoeffer, Dietrich. *The Cost of Discipleship*. New York: Macmillan Publishing Co., Inc., 1963.

Brisoce, D. Stuart. *The Communicator's Commentary (Romans)*. Vol. 6. Waco, Texas: Word, Inc., 1982.

Bruce, F.F. *The Letter of Paul to the Romans*. Rev. ed. Tyndale New Testament Commentaries. Grand Rapids: Wm. B. Eerdmans Publishing Co., 1985.

Bush, George. *Notes on Exodus*. 2 vols. in 1. Minneapolis: Klock and Klock Publishing Co., 1976.

Craigie, P.C. *New International Commentary on the Old Testament*. Grand Rapids: Wm. B. Eerdmans Publishing Co., 1976.

Edwards, Thomas Charles. *A Commentary on the First Epistle to the Corinthians*. 2nd ed. London: Hodder and Stoughton, 1885.

Getz, Gene A. *A Biblical Theology of Material Possessions*. Chicago: Moody Press, 1990.

Godet, F. *Commentary on First Corinthians*. Grand Rapids: Kregel Publications, 1977.

Haldane, Robert. *Exposition of the Epistles to the Romans*. Evansville, Ind.: The Sovereign Grace Book Club, 1958.

Haks, Billie, Jr., and William A. Shell, eds. *Discipleship*. Grand Rapids: Zondervan Publishing House, 1981.

Henrichsen, Walter A. *Disciples Are Made—Not Born*. Wheaton, Ill.: Victor Books, 1974.

Hobbs, Herschel. *The Epistles to the Corinthians.* Grand Rapids: Baker Book House, 1960.

Hodge, Charles. *An Exposition of the Second Epistle to the Corinthians.* Grand Rapids: Baker Book House, 1980.

Ironside, H.A. *First Epistle to the Corinthians.* (Thirteenth Printing) Neptune, N.J.: Loizeaux Brothers, Inc. (1978)

_____. *Lectures on the Epistle to the Romans.* Neptune, N.J.: Loizeaux Brothers, Inc., 1962.

Johnson, Alan F. *The Freedom Letter.* 2 vols. Chicago: Moody Press, 1985.

Law, Henry. *Christ Is All: The Gospel of the Pentateuch.* 4 vols. 1867. Vols. 1 (The Gospel in Genesis) and 2 (The Gospel in Exodus). Reprint. London: Banner of Truth Trust, 1967.

Lloyd-Jones, D. Martyn. *Romans: An Exposition.* Grand Rapids: Zondervan Publishing House, 1971.

Luther, Martin. *Commentary on the Epistle of Romans.* Grand Rapids: Zondervan Publishing House, 1960.

Mackintosh, Charles Henry. *Genesis to Deuteronomy: Notes on the Pentateuch.* 6 vols. 1880-1882. Reprint ed. 1 vol. Neptune, N.J.: Loizeaux Brothers, Inc., 1972.

Meyer, F.B. *The Christ-Life for the Self-Life.* Chicago: Moody Press, n.d.

_____. *Devotional Commentary (Exodus).* London: Marshall, Morgan & Scott, 1952.

Morgan, G. Campbell. *The Corinthian Letters of Paul: An Exposition of I and II Corinthians.* Westwood, N.J.: Fleming H. Revell, 1946.

_____. *Discipleship.* London: Allenson & Co. Ltd., 1934

_____. *The Gospel According to Matthew.* New York: Fleming H. Revell Co., 1929.

Morris, Leon. *The First Epistle of Paul to the Corinthians.* Tyndale New Testament Commentaries. Grand Rapids: Wm. B. Eerdmans Publishing Co., 1958.

Moule, Handley C.G. *The Epistle of St. Paul to the Romans.* Minneapolis: Klock and Klock Christian Publishers, 1982.

Moule, Handley. *The Second Epistle to the Corinthians: A*

Translation, Paraphrase, and Exposition. Ed. A.W. Handley Moule. London: Pickering & Inglis, 1962.

Murphy, James Gracey. *A Critical and Exegetical Commentary on the Book of Exodus.* Minneapolis: Klock and Klock Christian Publishers, 1980.

Newell, William R. *Romans Verse by Verse.* Chicago: Moody Press, 1938.

Olford, Stephen F. *The Grace of Giving.* Rev. ed. Memphis: Encounter Ministries, Inc., 1990.

Ortiz, Juan Carlos. *Disciple.* Carol Stream, Ill.: Creation House, 1975.

Phillips, John. *Exploring Romans.* Chicago: Moody Press, 1969.

Rendall, T.S. *Discipleship in Depth: What It Means to Be Christ's Disciple in the Space Age.* Three Hills, Alberta, Canada: Prairie Press, 1981.

Schultz, Samuel J. *The Old Testament Speaks.* New York: Harper Brothers, 1960.

Spurgeon, C.H. *The Gospel of the Kingdom.* Grand Rapids: Zondervan Publishing House, 1962.

Stifler, James M. *The Epistle to the Romans.* Chicago: Moody Press, 1960.

Sugden, Christopher. *Radical Discipleship.* London: Marshall, Morgan & Scott, 1981.

Tasker, R.V.G. *The Gospel According to St. Matthew.* Tyndale New Testament Commentaries. Grand Rapids: Wm. B. Eerdmans Publishing Co., 1961.

Thomas, W. H. Griffith. *St. Paul's Epistle to the Romans.* A Devotional Commentary. Grand Rapids: Wm. B. Eerdmans Publishing Co., 1946.

Verwer, George. *No Turning Back.* Wheaton, Ill.: Tyndale House Publishers, Inc., 1983.

Vine, W.E. *I Corinthians.* Grand Rapids: Zondervan Publishing House, 1961.

Walvoord, John F. *Matthew: Thy Kingdom Come.* Chicago: Moody Press, 1974.

Watson, David. *Called and Committed: World-Changing Discipleship.* Wheaton, Ill.: Harold Shaw Publishers, 1982.

_____. *Discipleship*. Copyright 1981 by Shalom Trust. London: Hodder and Stoughton, Ltd.,1983.

Wiersbe, Warren W. *Be Right (Romans)*. Wheaton, Ill.: Scripture Press, 1977.